Next-Generation Internet: Creating Advanced Networks and Services

Joel Mambretti
Andrew Schmidt

Wiley Computer Publishing

John Wiley & Sons, Inc.

NEW YORK · CHICHESTER · WEINHEIM · BRISBANE · SINGAPORE · TORONTO

For Andrew's parents
and
For Catherine

Publisher: Robert Ipsen
Editor: Marjorie Spencer
Assistant Editor: Margaret Hendrey
Managing Editor: Micheline Frederick
Electronic Products, Associate Editor: Mike Sosa
Composition: Benchmark Productions Inc., Boston

Library of Congress Cataloging-in-Publication Data:

Mambretti, Joel, 1948–
    Next generation Internet : creating advanced networks and services / Joel Mambretti, Andrew Schmidt.
        p. cm.
    "Wiley computer publishing."
    Includes bibliographical references and index.
        ISBN 0–471–32762–X (pbk. : alk. paper)
        1. Internet (Computer network) — Technological innovations. I. Schmidt, Andrew.
II. Title. III. Title: Internet two.
    TK5105.875.I57M362 1999
        004.67'8--dc21   99–30832
                                                                             CIP

Printed in the United States of America.
10 9 8 7 6 5 4 3 2 1

CONTENTS

The world is experiencing a dynamic, continually evolving communications revolution, driven in large part by the explosive growth of the Internet and the development of new and exceptionally innovative Internet technologies, and other related technologies. The Internet is beginning to transform all major sectors of the national economy—communications, e-commerce, financial services, manufacturing, health care, transportation, and so on. Every day, news stories report how Internet technologies are changing basic business models. New types of businesses and industries are being created, while traditional ones are evolving or being eliminated.

These trends are only the beginning of a great new age of digital communications that is being driven by innovative technical advances. The capabilities of the Internet as a powerful communications medium are continually being enhanced as various components are improved. Remarkable new applications based on Internet technologies are emerging and additional opportunities for such applications are constantly being discovered. Meanwhile, the underlying technologies continue to evolve as part of a movement toward what has been referred to as a "new" Internet or a next-generation Internet.

The term "next-generation" Internet is somewhat metaphoric and therefore requires explanation. At its core, this "next" Internet is almost identical to the traditional Internet, driven by powerful and flexible IP technologies. The next-generation Internet resembles a rapid evolution of the broader suite of Internet technologies more than it resembles a new set of core technologies. In this respect, the next-generation Internet is not "new" but rather another phase in a continuing series of advances.

This book was developed to present one perspective on the next-generation Internet by describing some of the basic concepts that are part of its ongoing development. It also provides contextual background to the creation of the next-generation Internet, as well as some of the general policies, projects, activities, architecture, and technologies that continue to drive it forward.

ACKNOWLEDGMENTS

The Internet has been developed through a spirit of cooperative partnership, among many projects, organizations, and individuals. Much of the information in this book was acquired through the experience of working in cooperation for many years with numerous exceptional technologists on countless research and development projects, experiments, forums, demonstrations, conferences, operational systems, policy reports, and strategic plans. We would like to express our appreciation to all of those with whom we have had the good fortune to share these experiences. Special thanks to Mort Rahimi and Gordon Reichard for their enthusiastic support of a wide range of regional, national, and international advanced networking projects.

We would like to express particular appreciation to those with whom we have worked on the following projects: Metropolitan Research and Education Network (MREN), especially Linda Winkler (Technical Director of MREN and senior network engineer extraordinare), and Larry Amiot (a chief instigator), Tim Kuhfuss, Phil Demar, Mark Kaletka, Ahmed Kassem, Tony Rimovsky, Gary Corbett, Randy Butler, Rich Carlson, Charlie Catlett, Tad Pinkerton, Eric Aupperle, Jeff Ogden, Bill Decker, Sharon Hogan, Lew Greenberg, Gary Augustine, John Steele, Tom Barron, Carolyn Parnell, Sue Hares, Don Riley, Mike McRobbie, Chris Peebles, Mark Luker, George Badger, Jim Davis, Jose Marie Griffiths, Doug Pearson, Kevin Peterson, Mike Noth, Joe Douglas, George Covert, Larry Rapagnani, Jeffrey Kipnis, Bob Vonderohe; Computational Science and related projects: Robert Rosner, Don York, Rick Stevens, Andrea Malagoli, Ian Foster, Larry Smarr, and many communities of high energy physicists, Advanced Photon Source experimentalists, imaging scientists, geophysicists, computational chemists and biologists; National Science Foundation (NSF) George Strawn, Javad Borumond, Steve Goldstein; Science and Technology Transit Access Point (STAR TAP) Tom DeFanti, Maxine Brown, Paul Zawada, Bill St. Arnaud, Kilnam Chon, Kazunori Konishi, Kees Neggers, Manjeet Singh, John Jamison; MCIvBNS: the entire network engineering team; International Center for Advanced Internet Research, Northwestern University (iCAIR), Irving Wladawsky-Berger, John Patrick, Lee Caldwell, Brian Carpenter, Robert Poston, Jim Chen, Micah Beck, Marcel Kinard, Ralph Demuth, Ian Duff, Marina Libmann, Geoff Gass, Mike James, David Martin, Ross Aiken, Martin Kienzle, Wil Belnap, Gary Singer, Rich Wall, Matt Ganis, Steve Wolff, Bob Aiken, David Carr, Tim Ward; UCAID, Doug Van Houweling, Guy Almes, Terry Rogers, Ted Hanss, Ben Teitelbaum, and Paul Love.

CHAPTER 1

Creating the Next Internet: A New Model for Communications Services and Technologies

National Policy, Information, and Economics

The Internet is one of the most rapidly developing and important technologies in history. Industry leaders, politicians, policy makers, and economists have long recognized the positive impact of information technology, particularly the Internet, on national economies. A primary reason for its significance is that modern economies are based on the need to effectively manage extremely large amounts of information. The Internet is driving a communications revolution that is motivated by these economic, and wider societal, needs to create, process, disseminate, and integrate vast quantities of different types of digital information efficiently. In an era that has been termed the "information age," strong national economies increasingly are built on productive information flows, access to information repositories, and effective processing of information with computer-based knowledge tools. The information age requires sophisticated techniques for transforming oceans of information into knowledge and understanding.

Because of its power and flexibility as a communications medium, the Internet is rapidly becoming the foundation technology for many of society's most important functions—not only for communications, but also for commerce, industry, education, health care, government services, agriculture, transportation, and entertainment. The Internet is transforming virtually all major economic sectors. In addition, dramatic new applications based on Internet technologies are being created, and these applications in turn are giving rise to completely new industries—and to the elimination of some existing industries.

To begin to set the background context of the Internet revolution, it is important to note that the world is experiencing a profound revolution in all communications. The concept of convergence in the communications industry envisions all types of information—voice, data, video, and other media types—supported by the same infrastructure. The real benefit of convergence, however, is not merely the goal of a shared infrastructure. Convergence will enable integration among these traditionally separate communications modalities to permit the development of powerful new types of communications services. This goal is beginning to be realized through preliminary deployment of innovative new digital communication systems. This communication revolution is driven by many new dynamics: traditional communications services providers must respond to changing government policies, new and evolving markets, new technologies, and radically different financial and economic models, which require new business models and organizational structures.

A new model for providing communications technologies and services has begun to emerge and has already created thousands of new companies. New approaches to communications sharply distinguish the traditional from the emerging next-generation Internet with regard to requirements, design, development, technologies, implementation, management, and continual improvement. These developments mark the initial stages of a period in which previously unimaginable applications will be developed and deployed over global networks, requiring network services which are not provided by the first-generation Internet. They mark the initial stages of a great new age in digital communications.

The Traditional Model of Communications Services

The traditional models for communications services have increasingly become removed from the requirements of their customers. The traditional model for these services provides for separate and different environments for each major service supported, including voice, video, data, and specialized services, such as wireless digital messaging. Different communications modalities have been difficult or impossible to integrate. Not only are these communications environments discrete, but so are their business models, economic fundamentals, and service models.

The majority of existing traditional communications services and systems are based on legacy technologies, many of which employ closed, proprietary architectures. Developers of traditional communication systems and providers of services based on these systems have presumed slow rates of development for new service requirements and for technical change and implementation. They have developed complex systems based on economic and underlying financial models that assume long service and technology life cycles, sometimes measured in decades. Services in the traditional communications industries and their underlying financial models are implemented with a significant degree of complex administrative overhead.

To some extent, this situation arises because the policy environment for communications services has been restrictive to the industries that provide them. Communications systems have been regarded by policymakers as scarce, expensive resources that have to be rationed carefully, as well as highly regulated—and to some degree micro-managed by extensive rules and regulations, complex and arcane laws that were developed decades ago for situations that no longer exist, and administratively intensive bureaucracies.

A New Model for Communications—The Internet

A new model for communications is evolving that provides for common, ubiquitous network-services and infrastructure supporting integrated digital voice, video, data, specialized services, innovative new services (including new forms of interactive multimedia), and sophisticated applications—all with a high degree of interoperability.

Although when measured within normal time cycles the Internet is a relatively recent technological development, in terms of its own measure of time ("Internet time") it is already entering its third technology cycle—the Internet has its own very fast clock. The Internet has become one of the most important technologies driving much of the digital communications revolution. Particularly important to the creation of this new world of digital communications are the Internet protocols, Internet Protocol (IP) in general and the TCP/IP protocol suite, as a common basis for communications. These protocols continue to evolve.

Although this design and development work is being undertaken by many organizations and individuals, much of it is being addressed by the research communities that were responsible for the first generation Internet. Researchers have long recognized and appreciated the power of the Internet. During the 1980s, the Internet thrived in research labs, universities, and government agencies. Beginning in the early 1990s, a wider community discovered the Internet and turned it into one of the most rapidly adopted technologies in history. The Internet expanded in many directions, for example, as measured by volume of traffic, by the number of individual users, by the number of networks and computers connected, by the degree of access, by the locations to which it expanded, and by the numbers of applications available and their sophistication.

Within corporations in the 1990s, Internet-based digital communication systems began evolving from an initial role as a backroom operations utility to a central position as a strategic resource. Some industries are beginning to recognize that their survival depends on appropriately deploying Internet-based technology. The Internet is increasingly being regarded as an especially critical value-added communications resource, not just for businesses but for almost all organizations that require interactive communications with their stakeholders—customers, employees, suppliers, partners, and others. Not only commercial enterprises, but government services and nonprofits are being transformed by the Internet. The new communications model is serving as the impetus for new enterprise models and new ways of delivering services.

Service providers within the new environment now tend to assume that customer requirements, technologies, and services will change rapidly—in Internet time. Few service providers complacently accept the status quo as the model for their five-year business plans. The new providers are developing economic and financial models that assume short services and technology life cycles, with continual upgrades and minimal administrative overhead.

A key element of the new model for communications is open standards and wide participation in decision-making and direction-setting. From its inception, the Internet has used nonproprietary architecture, based on open standards and common protocols for software and hardware, to ensure interoperability. The Internet is governed by cooperative partnerships rather than closed bureaucracies. It is widely believed that the Internet should be a prolific resource accessible by everyone. Also, it is generally recognized that access would have to be restricted if costs are artificially inflated by needless administrative regulation and bureaucracy. One policy imperative of the emerging, new communications model is to ensure that the Internet is recognized as radically different from more familiar, traditional communications technologies, such as telephony and broadcast television; therefore, it should not be considered within the same policy context. In particular, the Internet should not be considered a scarce resource that should be rationed. Without artificial restraints the new, emerging, communications systems and services will be abundant, inexpensive, and ubiquitous.

Creating a New Internet

Even as the first generation of the Internet continues its phenomenal growth, a second, or "next-generation," Internet is well underway and a third is being planned and will be in limited deployment by the end of 1999. Some in the Internet development community are already envisioning the design of a fourth-generation Internet. To a large degree, these efforts are evolutionary stages within a fundamental continuum, but it is nonetheless useful to begin to consider the requirements and design of the next-generation Internet. In any case, the cycle continues—at an accelerating pace.

During the late 1980s and early 1990s, the first-generation Internet emerged from research labs and universities—it was just beginning to become popular and was beginning to attract wide media attention. However, it grew rapidly from its initial deployment among the research community in the early 1980s. The expansion, from 1983 (when there were approximately 200 computers on the network) to 1993 (when there were 1.3 million computers connected by the Internet) was only the beginning of a phenomenon of exponential growth. In 1983 there were a handful of networks, but now there are more than 50,000, comprising the "core of the Internet."

By 1993, Internet traffic was doubling every 10 months, the Internet linked 15,000 networks worldwide, and Advanced Network Services (ANS) completed its fifth major upgrade to the backbone infrastructure, including the addition of support for full-duplex DS-3 (45 Megabits per second) and the doubling of switching capacity of the backbone routers. By the mid-1990s the first-generation Internet became a successful commercial and consumer technology—a widely-used "commodity Internet."

Much of the early expansion of the Internet was driven by its initial users, that is, research labs and by major universities. The majority of growth in the first generation Internet, however, was driven by the increasing commercial use. This commercial growth created numerous opportunities and gave rise to various challenges, especially the stress on various technical components that resulted from rapid expansion and high volumes of traffic.

The Rise of the Commercial Internet[1]

In the 1990s, commercial Internet Service Providers (ISPs) formally emerged from intermediate-level networks that were sponsored by the National Science Foundation (NSF). Prior to 1994, NSFnet was the major backbone network interconnecting IP regional networks. This arrangement was helpful because it fostered growth of the network and provided stability; however, because the network was funded by government, its uses were limited by the NSF's Internet use policy restrictions, referred to as "Acceptable Use Policy (AUP)." For example, intercompany communication was prohibited because (appropriately) the NSF cannot subsidize commercial activities. The commercial Internet eliminated these restrictions.

A number of the earliest commercial Internet Service Providers were those that had been nonprofit providers of network services based at first on protocols other than IP. Beginning in 1989, some of the nonprofit organizations, which were originally formed to provide local network services, combined to create larger organizations serving larger regions. For example, CSNET and BITNET merged that year to form a single commercial firm, the Corporation for Research and Education Networking (CREN). (CSNET, BITNET, and CREN were originally not IP networks, www.cren.net/cren/cren-hist-fut.html.) In 1987, an interesting trend started with the commercial introduction of UUCP and Usenet available through UUNET (Salus 1995). The first relays between commercial electronic mail carriers and the Internet were created via MCI Mail through the Corporation for National Research Initiatives (CNRI) and via CompuServe through Ohio State University (Hafner 1996).

Internet technologies were rapidly commercialized during the early 1990s, especially after the appearance of Web technology in December 1993. From 1988 to the present, the number of host computers with direct connection to TCP/IP has doubled every year. This commercialization led to the rise of Internet software and equipment providers, Internet Service Providers (ISPs—more than 7,000 had been established worldwide at the beginning of 1999), corporate Internets, intranets, extranets, specialized Internets, portals, search sites, and much more, including businesses that are exclusively dedicated to conducting commerce over the Internet. Commercialization as well as new innovation continues to drive the evolution of the Internet, a trend that will continue for the foreseeable future. ISPs and Internet-based businesses, which range in size from small entrepreneurial firms to divisions of large, multinational telecommunications firms, are rapidly expanding, offering new services, and are providing opportunities for new business models.

Formal recognition that the Internet was becoming a widely used resource (rather than a specialized tool for scientists and researchers) came in 1991, when the Commercial Internet Exchange (CIX) was established as a trade association for Internet carriers, with offices in Washington, D.C. (www.cix.org). Although the overall role of the CIX has remained fairly modest, its establishment along with that of a number of such Internet organizations and associations was an indication of the rapid spread of the Internet from government-funded organizations into the commercial sector.

Driver Tools and Applications

The Internet has always been a testbed for new tools and applications. An early driver of the expansion of the Internet was the development of new software tools for manipulating and linking practical information (as opposed to providing access to specialized databases). In 1988, Archie, written by Peter Deutsch, Alan Emtage, and Bill Heelan at McGill University, was made available on the Internet. Archie was one of the first mainstream Internet tools that allowed users to scan lists of information with a single, easy-to-compose query. It proved to be a groundbreaking interface to Internet information.

From Archie-related concepts came several data-access tools, including Campus Wide Information System (CWIS), HYTELNET, and WAIS. In 1991, Mark McCahill and others from the University of Minnesota developed Gopher, a CWIS that organized data on the Internet into hierarchical menus that users could then scroll through. This capability provided a method of pointing to information and also dramatically increased the ability of Internet users to search through the rapidly growing number of online archives.

A seminal event in information-retrieval on the Internet, however, occurred in the late 1980s and early 1990s at CERN (the European Laboratory for Particle Physics) where Timothy Berners-Lee was involved in data-depository research. Berners-Lee developed the Hypertext Transfer Protocol (HTTP) and the Hypertext Markup Language (HTML), which led directly to the development of the World Wide Web, in 1993 at the National Center for Supercomputing Applications (NCSA) in Champaign-Urbana, Illinois, when a group of young programmers were assigned to a project to create an information browser for the Web. This project was conceptualized initially for accessing linked information, images, and data across the Internet; it was particularly intended to be flexible and extensible. In December 1993, the resulting browser, Mosaic, was distributed without charge over the Internet, and within a few months it was being used by more than a million individuals. A short time thereafter it was being used by several millions worldwide, giving rise to the WWW phenomenon and propelling the Internet forward with additional energy.

The Challenge of Rapid Growth

The more popular the Internet became as a commodity consumer and business service and the more celebrated in the press as an exciting new technology, the more problematic it became for the scientific community that depended on it. Research experiments had to compete for the same resources that were used by business and consumers. The research communities that motivated the Internet's creation and development throughout the 1980s became increasingly dissatisfied and more vocal about its inadequacies. By the late 1980s, specialists within the research community that had created the first generation Internet began to express concerns about its limitations. They also became concerned that the infrastructure was becoming over-subscribed by hundreds of thousands of new users and that capacity was not developing fast enough to keep pace with demand.

The research communities and others with aggressive network applications found that performance on their data communications links was rapidly deteriorating. What was once a shared network for research was now being used by the general population, whose numbers and aggregate usage contended for the same resources as the scientists. The additional traffic on Internet links interfered with scientific experimentation and prevented valuable investigations. This meant that researchers, such as those with high-energy physics research applications, were using a network that was designed on a principle of "best effort" service for all users. For example, scientific applications modeling global warming competed on an equal "best effort" basis with banking transactions and consumers checking sports scores.

Even more problematic for this community were the conclusions of requirements analysis and strategic planning studies for advanced networking showing that some of the major scientific projects planned for the mid-90s could not be accomplished if the existing situation continued. Through these studies, as well as through direct experience and technical analysis, the research community became convinced that the Internet was not advancing rapidly enough to meet its emerging and projected future requirements for high-performance organizational networking, intranetworking, and internetworking.

In the early 1990s, a number of discussions took place in the research and education communities (especially the most advanced scientific research communities), about the nature of this problem. Various solutions were proposed to address it. Proposed solutions included increasing capacity, enhancing existing technology, creating new technology, creating separate research networks, and blending these solutions in various combinations. Many outside the research community argued that advanced scientific experimentation and general Internet usage could coexist on the same infrastructure. Given an appropriate Internet technology, it was generally believed, the needs of each community could be satisfied with the same communications system. Experience proved otherwise: the commodity Internet did not provide the right technology for such multipurpose use. For example, extremely large-scale file transfers from scientific databases contended often unsuccessfully for bandwidth with numerous other applications.

For the research community and for some of those providing network services to them, the need for a new Internet was clear. This new Internet would not be a totally separate network, but one that would be sophisticated enough to satisfy multiple communities of users with different requirements within the same basic infrastructure.

National Research and Education Network (NREN)

In the early 1990s, some initial policy steps were taken to address these problems and to move toward the goal of creating an advanced Internet. Several specialized national conferences addressed various policy and technical issues related to this topic.

In 1990 an initiative was begun to explore the potential for designing and building a National Research and Education Network (NREN), which was to be a national network for use principally by the research and education community to develop advanced applications and networking technologies. This initiative was first presented for funding in 1991 as part of the federal government's High Performance Computing Program.

The 1991 High Performance Computing Act contained provisions to fund research on advanced networking and to authorize the NREN's establishment. The specific constituencies that required NREN included some of the same researchers whose aggressive applications drove the original development of the Internet. NREN's design anticipated an 18-node backbone network based on MCI fiber optic circuits, linking more than 20 state and regional networks, serving hundreds of individual institutions. In promoting the NREN, the initiative was compared to the development of the interstate highway system in the 1950s, giving rise to the term "Information Superhighway." Although the NREN was never actually implemented as originally envisioned, its concepts became the core of related initiatives.

National Information Infrastructure (NII)

In 1993 a proposal was presented in a variety of national forums to create a National Information Infrastructure (NII), to build on the High Performance Computing Act. The NII initiative proposed federal funding to create capabilities for advanced network-based applications and advanced network technologies, especially for health care, libraries, and universities. Later this initiative was expanded to include a wide range of additional elements, such as communications deregulation, corporate development of infrastructure, universal service, secure transmissions, digital intellectual property rights, and more.

The enlarged scope of the NII agenda as well as related issues prevented a consensus vision of the various aspects of the initiative from emerging. There were many misperceptions about the goals and services implied by the NII initiative and it was not clear to many who were discussing these issues how the NII related to communications industry investments in broadband infrastructure and other advanced infrastructure initiatives.

Some participants in these discussions, as well as external observers, did not believe that initiatives like NREN and NII were needed. They argued that carrier investments and the growth of the Internet through commercial providers demonstrated that needs were already being met. Some believed that the NII already existed in the form of broadband offerings by carriers, which were used by corporations and the growing commercial Internet.

The original NII proposals soon became topics of intense debate and led to a long series of policy discussions related to governance, commercial carriers, deregulation of the communications industry, government policy priorities, and other issues.

Meanwhile, the Internet resources available to researchers with requirements for advanced networking capability continued to deteriorate. In a number of universities and research labs, however, a variety of innovative efforts began to take shape and to address these issues. These projects were the beginnings of an effort to create a second-generation Internet, motivated in large part by the development of advanced scientific applications. Another motivation was a series of issues related to requirements for scalability.

Internet Services

The new model for digital communications will be based on the Internet. Yet, the current Internet cannot meet many of today's expectations, much less future expectations. Despite the success of the first-generation Internet, its limitations are readily apparent as increasing demands for its services stress its technologies at every level, especially those components affected by scalability. The need for an advanced Internet is obvious from its current restrictions, (for example, the common experience of the "World-Wide-Wait" when using a browser). It is difficult to base a crucial service on a system that is unpredictable, occasionally unreliable, and often insecure. For general users, the Internet experience is still too complex, problematic, and expensive. It seems to be based on fragile technologies, which break in mysterious ways and which require advanced specialists to fix.

Many consumers would like more from the Internet than common application services such as e-mail. They would like to see the Internet approach the ease of use of a common electronic appliance—even though the Internet is expected to do much more than those simple devices. Most users already expect the Internet to accomplish powerful tasks, quickly and easily. A key goal envisioned for the advanced Internet is to have it provide any type of information, anywhere, anytime. The new Internet revolution is based on the concept of a convergence of computation and communications—which cannot be fully implemented with the limited technology of the first-generation Internet. The complexities of the technology must be pushed away from the users into processes that are hidden from view. This approach makes technologies easier for users, although more difficult for the technologists who design and develop these systems.

The common Internet does not support advanced applications. It is still primarily a text and image medium; digital video remains low-quality and problematic, even though it is not an overly aggressive application in terms of its technical requirements.

The traditional Internet has minimal dependable implementations of capabilities for supporting delay-sensitive media services and has limited options for some highly specialized and customized services. These types of capabilities are crucial components for a next-generation Internet. The next generation Internet will support digital video data, that is, digital video as a common data type—full motion, full screen, full color video, with at least CD quality audio.

The Revolution within the Revolution: Next-Generation Internet Services

Until now, the majority of public discussions about the Internet have been about the first-generation Internet. However, within the larger revolution in digital communications, another revolution is occurring, that is, the transformation of the first-generation Internet into the second-generation Internet. Against the backdrop of the widespread publicity over the first-generation Internet, the second-generation Internet has barely been visible. Yet, the second-generation Internet, not the first, will lead the digital communications revolution that will fundamentally change all sectors of society. The advanced Internet will provide all users with the ability to choose among a wide range of new services and capabilities (discussed in Chapter 3 and throughout the book).

In part, the gap between expectations for the Internet and its reality is common for technologies early in a development cycle, and, despite its rapid adaptation, the Internet is still a fairly young technology. Its second major technology cycle did not begin until the mid-1990s, and it is not yet widely accessible.

The New Global, Ubiquitous Internet

The new Internet will provide access to a wide world of products and services—general consumer items, specialized training, financial services, government-agency information, health care, and entertainment. E-business solutions will become more sophisticated and more directly accessible by customers. The new Internet will be pervasive. It will interlink vast arrays of inexpensive, easy-to-use, new devices: mobile phones and pagers; hand-held information assistants; desktop and laptop computers; television-top boxes and "smart TVs" with embedded computer processors; specialized processors in vehicles and in consumer electronics, especially appliances and toys, smart cards, and gadgets that attach to these devices and allow for specialized information processing; and much more.

The new Internet will link IP devices to national and international distributed-computing infrastructures, supporting specialized, interactive environments (including collaborative virtual spaces) and ready access to distributed digital-resource centers—repositories of large amounts of organized data, images, digital video, and other digital information. These powerful resources will be much more accessible, widely distributed, and easier to use. Finally, it will also provide support for direct access to specialized facilities and to advanced applications and devices not yet invented.

The idea of easy Internet access to ubiquitous information and functional services that anyone can obtain from virtually anywhere around the globe remains primarily conceptual. Even though this vision is not yet a reality, steps are being taken to move toward it through the design and development of a second-generation Internet, and toward early deployment of its technologies. In order to attain the goals envisioned for future digital communications, a dramatically new digital-communications infrastructure is needed—a persistent, high-performance, reliable, high-capacity set of network services that can be rapidly scaled and readily managed.

Best Effort versus Differentiated Services

When the second-generation Internet becomes more widely implemented, its distinction from the first-generation Internet will be obvious—because its key feature will be differentiation. The current Internet model is based on a lowest-common-denominator, best-effort IP service. Applications contend for the same shared resources. Currently, few applications are network-aware, much less aware of specific network services and resources that may be available. Policy tools for managing use of network resources are primitive—where they exist at all. Few capabilities exist for common applications to be mapped to specific qualities of service over predetermined, designated routes. Scalability is not completely dealt with by network layers, and dealing with scalability usually is accomplished by adding bandwidth. Yet, additional bandwidth alone does not resolve the issue of end-to-end performance.

The next-generation Internet model is based on a concept of differentiated IP services with access to a wide range of dependable media services and options for specialized and highly customized services. Applications not only will be network-aware, they will signal their requirements to the network to reserve specific network services and other resources. The network will be aware of the services and resources available and will provision them within a defined policy context.

Provision will be made for policy development, implementation, and management for allocation of network services and resources among different organizations, groups, and individual network users. Applications will be linked to specific qualities of service and classes of services at specific levels and mapped to designated routes in accordance with predetermined policies. Scalability will be addressed at all network layers. High performance will be based on more than bandwidth. Network security will be enhanced for facilities, services, and information.

The Internet as a Global Resource

Another crucially important difference between the first- and second-generation Internet will be an enhanced partnership within the international community. The Internet is a global resource, and, as it expands throughout the world, it becomes more valuable for everyone who uses it. The next-generation Internet will be global. Two important programs are currently directed at promoting the development of international partnerships: the Global Information Infrastructure (GII) program, described briefly in this chapter, and the National Science Foundation-funded Science, Technology, and Research Transit Access Point (STAR TAP), described in Chapter 4.

Global Internet Project

An Internet industry policy forum, the Global Internet Project was recently established by a number of information technology and communications companies to provide a technology and public policy framework to address issues related to the rapid growth of the Internet. The Global Internet Project addresses issues within a policy architecture with six levels:

1. *Infrastructure.* The challenge of meeting the demand for reliable and scalable access to the Internet.

2. *Governance.* Addressing the questions of who or what owns or controls the Internet and when such mechanisms are necessary.

3. *Security.* The policies, procedures, and protocols necessary to ensure the security of electronic communications on the Internet.

4. *Privacy.* Protecting the confidentiality of information stored digitally.

5. *Content.* Empowering Web users to maximize their time online by viewing only the content they want to see.

6. *Commerce.* Ensuring that electronic transactions on the Internet develop in a manner conducive to the emergence of a global economy.

Conclusion: National Policy and Digital Communications

The importance of the ongoing revolution in advanced digital communications is now formally recognized by national policies and at the highest government levels in countries worldwide. It has been noted by policy leaders that modest investments in research and development in computing, communications, and related information technologies have already sparked remarkable advances in science, technology, and major sectors of the economy. Policy makers have realized that a robust national digital communications infrastructure is crucial to a strong national economy and is vital to global market competitiveness. One-third of the total growth in U.S. production from 1992 to 1998 was generated by information technology corporations, many driven by products and services related to the Internet (PITAC 1999). Also, the pace of this growth is accelerating.

In addition, an advanced, high-performance Internet is crucial for almost all national research in any knowledge discipline; the Internet provides a means of access to large amounts of distributed data, to remote instrumentation, and to collaborative environments.

Such an enhanced Internet also promotes standards development and energizes the technology transfer from research labs to productive use in the public sector, where it provides a foundation technology for new advanced applications and allows for important Internet services to be accessible to the general population. Technology transfer promotes better work processes, better educational experiences, and enhanced health care—in general, a better quality of life.

The U.S. government's emphasis on national information-technology research was recently articulated by the National Coordination Office for Computing, Information, and Communications, the "President's Information Technology Advisory Committee Report to the President" (February 1999), also known as the "PITAC Report." Its Executive Summary states the following:

> Information Technology (IT) will be one of the key factors driving progress in the 21st century—it will transform the way we live, learn, and play. Advances in computing and communications technology will create a new infrastructure for business, scientific research and social interaction. This expanding infrastructure will provide us with new tools for communicating throughout the world, and for

acquiring knowledge and insight from information. Information technology will help us to understand how we affect the natural environment, and [how] best to protect it. It will provide a vehicle for economic growth. Information technology can make the workplace more rewarding, improve the quality of health care, and make government more responsive to its citizens. Vigorous information technology research and development (R&D) is essential for achieving America's 21st century aspirations.

Note: Government program recommendations based on the PITAC report are available at www.ccic.gov, such as "Information Technology for the Twenty-First Century." Further information is available on national policy and programs in advanced information technology through yearly "Blue Books," such as the *FY 2000 Blue Book on High Performance Computing and Communications: Information Technology Frontiers for a New Millennium* (May 1999), at the same Web site.

End Note

[1]Portions of this section ("The Rise of the Commercial Internet") and the next one ("Driver Tools and Applications") are based on a treatment in *Internet Architectures*, by Dan Minoli and Andrew Schmidt (1999, John Wiley & Sons).

References

Comer, Douglas. 1995. *Internetworking with TCP/IP: Principles, Protocols, and Architecture*. 3d ed. Upper Saddle River, NJ: Prentice-Hall.

The Corporation for Research and Education Networking. [Available May 1999]. www.cren.net/cren/cren-hist-fut.html

Hafner, Katie and M. Lyon. 1996. *Where Wizards Stay Up Late*. New York: Touchstone. This book presents a general history of the early days of the Internet, the participants in its development, and the process of technical evolution.

The Internet Society. *A Brief History of the Internet and Related Networks*. [Available May 1999]. www.isoc.org/guest/zakon/Internet/History/Brief_History_of_the_Internet

Minoli, Dan and A. Schmidt. 1999. *Internet Architectures*. New York: John Wiley & Sons.

President's Information Technology Advisory Committee (PITAC). 1998. "Report to the President: Executive Summary." Chairpersons: Bill Joy and Ken Kennedy. National Coordination Office for Computing, Information, and Communications: Arlington, VA. (February 1999) p.1 of 5. [Available May 1999]. www.ccic.gov

Salus, Peter H. 1995. *Casting the Net: From ARPANET to Internet and Beyond.* Reading, MA: Addison-Wesley Publishing Company.

URLs

Commercial Internet eXchange: www.cix.org

Computer Systems Policy Project: www.cspp.org

Global Information Infrastructure Project: www.gii.org

Global Internet Project: www.gip.org

CHAPTER 2

First-Generation Internet: The Development of Internet 1.0

Introduction

The development of the next-generation Internet should be viewed in part from the perspective of the development of the first-generation Internet.[1] The Internet has been variously described as a new communications medium, as a set of infrastructure technologies, as the physical manifestation of particular protocols, as a particular type of integrated system, as a cooperative engineering project, and as an ongoing experiment.

Internet versus Open Systems Interconnection Reference Model (OSI)

Although an exact definition may remain elusive, the Internet is clearly a digital communications system; therefore, it is sometimes useful to discuss some of its architectural components in terms of the layers defined by the standard reference model for such systems, the Open Systems Interconnection Reference Model (OSI or OSIRM), even though Internet technology does not actually conform to that model.

The Open Systems Interconnection Reference Model (OSI) was developed long after the origination of the Internet in an attempt to create a standard suite of digital communications protocols. When it was being developed, some standards developers considered it a rival to the Internet model. Internet developers were highly skeptical of this concept. Although OSI was not a success as a standard, it does provide for a useful general reference model that describes a seven-layer architecture: (1) Physical, (2) Data Link, (3) Network, (4) Transport, (5) Session, (6) Presentation, and (7) Application. For convenience, some of the discussion that follows refers to these layers, especially Layers 2 through 4.

Packet Switching

One of the most fundamental revolutions in communications is the migration away from traditional telephony, based on circuit switched, to the packet-based Internet. In the late 1960s, most data-communications systems were closed and proprietary, and general communications traveled over circuits. The advantages of packet technology were recognized as early as the late 1960s, but increasingly through the 1970s, and 1980s, and not exclusively in the context of the Internet.

Traditional telephony systems allocate bandwidth in fixed increments, across the entire length of the network, for the duration of an average conversation. The allocation is typically 64 kilobits per second (Kbps) in both directions, a resource that is allocated whether it is necessary or not. For example, if someone places a call between Chicago and Tampa, the telephony carrier(s) will create an end-to-end circuit of 64 Kbps dedicated to this single session. This type of communication is sometimes called time division multiplexing (TDM).

Packet switching, on the other hand, transmits data into the network only when actual data must be communicated. Packet switching places the user data into variable-size packets that have a source and destination address. Because each packet is a stand-alone entity, like a piece of postal mail, all packets can share a common infrastructure without dedicating bandwidth to any particular user-to-user communication session.

Early Developments in Packet Switching

Several individuals played key roles in the development of packet switching. Some of the most important were Leonard Kleinrock at UCLA, Paul Baran of The Rand Corporation, and Donald Watts Davies of the National Physical Laboratory in the United Kingdom. Each independently conceived the principle of packet-switching. In 1957, Kleinrock began researching data networks and, from this research, developed the underlying principles of packet switching. In 1961, Kleinrock published a paper that analyzed the problems of network data flow and related issues (Salus 1995).

Kleinrock's work was complemented when, in 1959, Paul Baran joined Rand and began his study of packet switching. Communication networks of the day were chained point-to-point systems, with each point on the network dependent on the link before it. Consequently, damage to one point in the network affected the entire network. Baran began studying how to maintain functional communication networks when parts of the systems are damaged; he also redesigned communications infrastructure to ensure that the remaining viable components continued to function as a cohesive entity when some of the parts were disabled. To achieve this goal, he used digital computer technology because digital data could be reproduced accurately and signals could be moved from switch to switch with less degradation than the existing method of analog transmission. He also proposed building the infrastructure using a distributed network instead of the existing centralized networks, which had vulnerable central switching points.

Baran further proposed breaking messages into smaller parts, called "message blocks," and designed a scheme in which each was sent out using a variety of potentially different routes and reassembled at the destination. An analogue of this method is a process of shipping a house by first disassembling it into its component parts (message blocks) and placing each piece into a separate truck. Each truck needs to get to its destination taking the fastest possible route, which is determined by considering various conditions, such as traffic, weather, and road conditions. All of these conditions could differ depending on when each truck left the point of origin. Because assembly occurred only after all the pieces had arrived at the address (destination host), order of arrival would be unimportant. Metaphorically, this example describes how packet switching on the Internet works. This approach was radically different from traditional communications, which employs circuit switching.

At the time Paul Baran joined Rand, communications network lines were reserved for a single call and held open for the time period the line was being used, regardless of the number and duration of pauses in conversation. As mentioned, because data being transmitted over the line was released in short bursts followed by pauses, much of the bandwidth was "wasted." Baran proposed allocating bandwidth to permit resource sharing among different messages. Each message block would be dynamically routed in the network by switching nodes capable of directing the message block to the fastest route depending on the conditions of the nodes, the distances, and delays (Hafner 1996).

Baran also proposed that large messages that had to be moved across the network, for example, video clips, first be subdivided into smaller pieces. Each piece is placed in a completely self-contained package and transmitted. Before transmitting, some error correction/detection information is placed in the packet so that the receiver can be certain that the message arrived correctly. A video clip is segmented into some number of packets, so that each can take a different path across the network (unlikely but possible). Once the packets have arrived at the receiver, they can be reassembled to the original video clip. The receiver can choose to wait until the entire set of packets has arrived or start reassembly as soon as it has two concurrent packets.

In 1965, another researcher, Donald Watts Davies, formally proposed the idea of packet switching. His ideas of packet switching and message blocks were similar to Baran's because they both used digital computer technology, switches, identical packet size and data-transmission rate, but differed fundamentally in motivation because his packet-switching concept was not designed with a need for redundancy and decentralization. In addition, Davies considered the problems of using disparate computer languages, hardware, and software and began to consider the use of an intermediary device that would translate, assemble, and disassemble digital messages for other machines. In 1968, Davies's ideas were implemented with the first packet-switching network being set up at the National Physical Laboratory in England by his team.

Packet switching provided a new approach to a wide range of key communications issues. These concepts were key to the development of Internet technologies, but that development also included close consideration of specific application requirements.

The Origins: Seeking Solutions to Real Problems

The Internet was not devised to revolutionize the world of communications—a result that may be ascribed to unintended consequences. The Internet was developed to resolve several basic communications problems. The Internet had its origin in an urgent need to provide real, practical solutions to problems of incompatibility among numerous, diverse systems. The first Internet evolved from requirements for resource sharing, especially sharing expensive computer systems. It was also developed to meet the need for a type of data-communications system that allowed for interconnections among computers at many locations from multiple vendors. Later, additional protocols were developed to address application requirements, principally file transfer (moving data from one computer to another, that is, via the File Transfer Protocol or FTP), e-mail (collaboration and general communications), and access through remote log-on (Telnet).

The architectural approach taken to develop the first-generation Internet was based on a concept of levels or layers of capability, each with its own function and features and supporting services, processes, interfaces, and protocols. The lower layers are standard and therefore common, allowing the upper layers to be more differentiated. This approach was crucial to its success.

Several New Protocols

In 1969, the Advanced Research Projects Agency (ARPA, a Department of Defense [DoD] organization, which became DARPA in 1971) established a project to investigate common methods, technologies, and techniques that would reliably provide a means of linking many different types of computers, operating systems, and specialized data-communications systems. Reliability was a key goal: For example, the network had to survive cuts at any given link. Reliability was to be ensured by creating redundant paths so that traffic could be routed around any infrastructure failure. Interoperability was also important because of the diversity of systems that had to communicate through the network. This type of approach is closely related to the concept of open systems, that is, technologies that have publicly announced specifications that can be widely implemented.

Internet Protocol Creation

Although it was a project formulated at the Defense Advanced Research Projects Agency, the ARPANET was intended to connect research facilities so researchers could share computer resources and to facilitate communication among research facilities.

ARPA was formed, in part, in 1957 because U.S. President Eisenhower wanted to establish a research and development agency. It was designed, though, to be a temporary agency, to function only until the National Aeronautics and Space Administration (NASA) could be approved. After NASA's creation in 1958, ARPA's director, Roy Johnson, defined its mission as a sponsor of basic research, and it focused on military research and development. In 1962, the third director, Jack Ruina, hired Joseph C. R. Licklider to head Command and Control Research. Licklider sought contracts with academically based computer facilities and advanced research to replace batch processing with time sharing. This new focus on supporting research and development of advanced technology was reflected in the renaming of his division as the Information and Processing Techniques Office (IPTO).

IPTO evolved under the directorships of Licklider (1962–1965) and his successor, Robert Taylor (1966–1969). In addition to supporting research in time-sharing technology, Licklider also supported research in computer graphics and computer languages, and he was the first person to envision a network of interconnecting computers where people could access data from any other site. Taylor was responsible for implementing the idea of interconnecting computers to form the nascent Internet. Before this project, computers connected to a mainframe computer and shared memory and resources with other attached computers. There was no way to interconnect the mainframes so that people could use resources other than those found on the mainframe to which they were directly attached. Taylor's contribution involved creating the network so that resources could be shared among all attached mainframes.

While still at ARPA, Taylor received approval to fund an experiment—creating a testbed that would interconnect computers found at separate locations. This testbed essentially would create interactive computer communication. Larry Roberts became the program manager in 1966; prior to joining ARPA, he had created an early wide-area computer network experiment (point-to-point) with Thomas Marill. Roberts joined ARPA to develop his ideas of computer networks and ARPANET. In 1967, he presented his ideas at the same conference at which Davies was advancing his concept of packet switching.

ARPANET

As a part of this research project, ARPA began to design and build a reliable packet-switching network based on point-to-point serial links—ARPANET, a national testbed for innovative networking concepts.

In order for ARPANET, or any packet-switching network, to work, computers with different operating systems needed to understand each other. This objective required basic standardization of not only the packet format but also of what the data inside the packet should look like, that is, a standardized network had to be developed.

In 1967, the notion of building a prototype network was discussed, which would be comprised of Interface Message Processors (IMP), as conceived by Wes Clark. These IMPs provided the foundation for the world's first packet-switching router—and they were approximately the size of household refrigerators. The IMPs would be connected to leased telephone lines, and thereby they would become the core packet-switching nodes. The IMPs would be used to interconnect each of the host computers to the network. This technique would standardize the network by having each IMP communicate with the other IMPs. Additional protocols had to be developed, however, in order for communication to take place between the hosts.

In 1968, the contract for developing the IMPs was awarded to Bolt, Beranek and Newman (BBN), then a small company based in Cambridge, Massachusetts. BBN designed the IMPs and established the protocols allowing IMPs to communicate with each other. The protocols that permitted communication between an IMP and its host, the local area network, were left to each of the host site's computer scientists. Kleinrock and his team at UCLA were responsible for the network measurement system, and Roberts designed the network topology (Hafner 1996). Figure 2.1 shows the distribution of IMPs in the ARPANET.

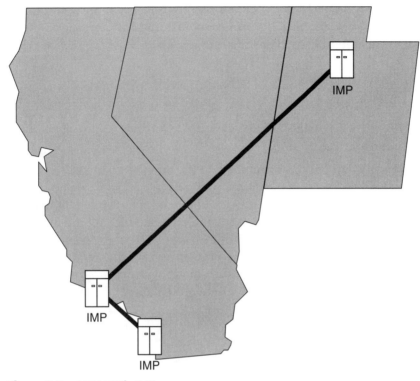

Figure 2.1 ARPANET's IMPs.

ARPANET began operating in 1969, thereby making that year the one during which the Internet "began." (The project, as noted, actually started in 1968, based on ideas that had been presented earlier.) In 1969, the Network Working Group (NWG) was formed to ensure the stability of the communication protocols. This group was composed of graduate students from the first four host sites on the ARPANET. Initially, the NWG focused on developing the host protocol design, called host-to-host protocols. These protocols allowed a host computer to communicate with another host computer, in addition to the host-to-IMP interface.

The first IMP was installed at Kleinrock's Network Measurement Center at UCLA in September 1969; over the course of three months, the other three nodes were installed, at SRI UC Santa Barbara, and the University of Utah. The latter two nodes incorporated visualization projects: UCSB investigated methods for display of mathematical functions using storage displays to deal with the problem of refresh over the net, and Robert Taylor and Ivan Sutherland at Utah investigated methods of 3-D representations over the net. Once the four sites were interconnected, the IMPs could exchange packets; thereby, ARPANET was born, enabling researchers to access remote computers, share information by file transfer, and perform remote printing.

Establishing ARPANET with these first four hosts was a significant accomplishment because the IMPs connected to both host computers and other IMPs and accomplished the following:

- Received data
- Checked for errors
- Retransmitted data if errors occurred
- Routed the packets
- Verified that packets terminated at the intended address

The IMPs used hop-by-hop acknowledgments and retransmissions to ensure that distinct messages were correct, then reassembled all the packets into the message. Because the host computers could be from different manufacturers, software was designed (called a *device driver*) to facilitate host computer-IMP communication. A device driver is a software utility program that acts as the interface between the host's operating system (central control software) and the networking hardware. (See Figure 2.2.)

ARPANET Succeeds

As noted, at that time, packet switching, that is, sending information in pieces as discrete packages, was still a novel idea. The potential of this successful experiment was recognized. Packets could carry content (data or payload) and header information with destination information that allowed them indepen-

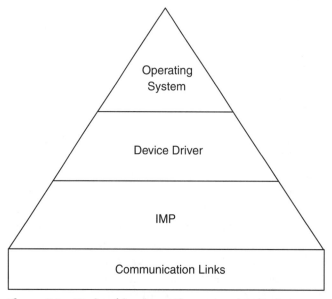

Figure 2.2 Device driver/operating system interaction.

dently to be transmitted around the network without requiring specific end-to-end connections. Also, the experiment was successful because it demonstrated that packet-switched networks could maintain a high degree of reliability.

The first ARPANET implementation interconnected various government sites, commercial research labs, and universities with 56 Kbps (kilobits per second, 1000 bits) dedicated leased lines. By 1971, 23 hosts and 15 IMP nodes had been established including those at BBN, MIT, Rand, SDC, Harvard, Lincoln Lab, Stanford, University of Illinois, Case Western Reserve University (CWRU), Carnegie Melon University (CMU), and NASA/Ames. Also during that year, AlohaNet (www.alohanet.com) was created at the University of Hawaii. It used radio links between computers spread out across four islands to broadcast data back and forth.

In 1972, the network had grown to 37 nodes. In addition, a demonstration at the *International Conference on Computer Communications* (ICCC) successfully show-cased ARPANET to the public (Hafner 1996). Also, during this same year, the *Internetworking Working Group* (INWG) was formed to establish protocols; its first chairman was Vinton Cerf at Stanford.

Shortly thereafter, Abhay Bhushan designed the first electronic mail, or e-mail, program capable of running on the network; although other programs did exist and could run between computers, they had not been implemented on the open network. Additionally, Ray Tomlinson at BBN wrote basic send and read software for e-mail messages. Roberts further developed Tomlinson's programs by giving them abilities taken for granted today, such as list, selectively read, file, forward, and respond to messages. As its popularity increased, changes were implemented to improve compatibility among disparate e-mail programs.

In July 1975, ARPANET had become so useful to a growing level of military-related network traffic that it became a production network, run by the Defense Communications Agency (DCA). This event led to the formation of other networks because ARPANET's guidelines had restricted access to its network. New projects, however, were initiated to continue improving ARPANET. For example, other DARPA research projects investigated wireless networks, especially using satellites and radios for transport.

Because the overall vision of the Internet was to have many independent networks interconnected, researchers had also been developing other networks such as packet satellite and ground-based packet radio networks. Essentially, this approach would create an open-architecture network in which each network could be designed differently, both architecturally and technologically, but could interface to all others.

In 1977, Internet communication was successfully demonstrated to the Defense Department with a simulation of communication during a mobile battlefield situation using a continental network. A continental network (mobile Packet Radio network and ARPANET) sent a message across an intercontinental satellite (SATNET) network to Europe, back to USC Information Sciences Institute in America (via SATNET and ARPANET).

Development of the Transmission Control Protocol (TCP)

From the earliest days of the ARPANET project, efforts began to interconnect various types of networks under a common framework of protocols.

In 1970 ARPANET hosts started to communicate using what was called the *Network Control Protocol* (NCP). This event was a key step in the history of the Internet because it helped formulate the idea of multiple *interworking* protocols cooperating to provide reliable, end-to-end communication. NCP is a protocol describing host-to-host communication, and it goes beyond the packet format to describe the format of data within the packet.

Attachment of the first four hosts completed the initial phase of the network project, and by the summer of 1970 the following nodes were added: BBN, MIT, Rand, System Development Corporation, and Harvard.

The NCP protocol did have a fundamental flaw in that it was able to transmit only a single packet at a time. NCP sends a packet and then waits for an acknowledgment before sending another. In modern terminology this would be called a *window of 1*. Waiting for an acknowledgment before sending more information can reduce performance, and this problem was fixed as protocol research continued.

When Robert Kahn arrived at ARPA in 1972, he proposed the idea of an *open-architecture network*. Essentially, this concept implied setting standards so that each component had a clearly defined role and several different vendors' products would seamlessly interwork, allowing compatibility among the networks. Because the components would be standardized, networks could communicate regardless of the type or manufacturer of the host computer.

A common interoperability protocol was required to link heterogeneous systems. In 1973, Vint Cerf and Robert Kahn proposed the first draft of *Transmission Control Protocol* (TCP), which was intended to improve network reliability by placing the responsibility for that reliability on the source and destination hosts. Later, they and Jon Postel decided to separate out the part of the protocol that defined methods for guaranteed delivery (for example, ensuring ordered byte streams and reliable transfer through mechanisms, such as retransmission, which remained part of TCP) from that which defined addressing and forwarding, which in turn became the Internet Protocol, or IP. Danny Cohen, one of Postel's colleagues at ISI, also was part of the initial formulation of the concept of separating TCP into TCP/IP. In 1978, Cerf, Postel, and Cohen presented the core concept at an ISI meeting after the three had held a preliminary hallway discussion.

Although hardly noticed at the time, the development of the TCP/IP protocol for connectionless communications over multiple interconnected networks was one of the most important events in the history of communications. This very powerful protocol combination now is a core part of the general infrastructure on which the Internet relies and from which numerous new applications are being created.

TCP is a transport layer protocol (later, under the OSI Reference Model, related to Layer 4) that provides for dependable end-to-end connectivity. TCP usually connects hosts through specific ports related to specific services. These ports ("protocol ports") are abstractions, identified with small positive integers, that indicate a specific destination within a host computer. TCP packets are sent as data encapsulated within IP packets. Most Internet services such as FTP and Telnet use TCP for transport. Other, generally-specialized, system services use related protocols such as the User Datagram Protocol (UDP, which is primarily used for the Network File System (NFS) described later in this chapter) and the Internet Control Measure Protocol (ICMP). (See Figure 2.3.)

TCP guarantees reliable delivery by segmenting and reassembling datagrams, detecting errors, and retransmitting datagrams that do not arrive at their destination. TCP is a protocol that specifies the format of data within a packet. TCP takes a larger message and segments it into smaller units that can be placed into packets. TCP also performs two critical functions:

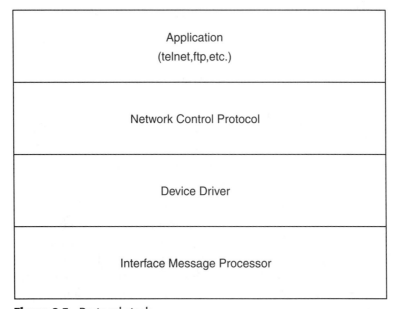

Figure 2.3 Protocol stack.

Flow control. TCP provides what is called "positive acknowledgment"; that means, when a packet reaches the receiver, a message is sent back to the source signifying that the packet arrived successfully. If the source does not receive an acknowledgment, it assumes that the loss was due to network congestion. The source can then reduce its transmission rate and monitor for a series of successful acknowledgments. The source increases its transmission rate until it begins to see missing acknowledgments, at which point the cycle of reduced transmission rate repeats.

Error detection. TCP has the ability to detect errors because the protocol keeps track of sequence numbers of packets as they cross the network. If there is a gap in the sequence numbering, then the missing data will not be acknowledged and will subsequently be retransmitted. In addition, TCP calculates a checksum over the packets, which means that if any of the bits within the packet were corrupted during transmission, the receiver will discard the packet; subsequently the sender will not receive an acknowledgment and will retransmit the packet.

During the mid-1970s the TCP specification evolved, and one of the major iterations of the TCP suite came out in 1978. TCP marked a paradigm shift for the IMPs because it migrated the responsibility of data formatting away from the network and made it the responsibility of the host transmitting the data. This development was a fundamental change in the way in which gateway computers communicated with other networks, interpreted and routed packets by reading the address, leaving the receiving hosts to read the contents of the packet, and then assembling them. TCP provides for a key component of the principle of end-to-end service. Like other protocols, TCP continues to evolve.

IP

As noted, in 1978, Cerf, Postel, and Cohen at ISI proposed the idea of a separate *Internet Protocol*, or IP. Essentially, the IP datagrams would contain addressing, and they could be given to routers that would then forward the individual packets. This design created yet another layer in the protocol stack; however, it provided critical segregation between data addressing and error/congestion detection. IP provided all the information needed by the interconnecting routers to perform their basic packet switch role.

IP is a protocol (later, under the OSI model, related to Layer 3) designed to provide a means of ensuring that packets will arrive at their intended destination, even with connectionless communications. IP employs a 32-bit address identifier that has three major components: (1) significant bits that provide the address classification (addresses are divided into three basic classes, A, B, and C, which relate to types of networks), (2) the local network identification, and (3) the host identifier. IP also provides information that allows for packet fragmentation and reassembly. (Classless Inter-Domain Routing, CIDR, is discussed in a later chapter.)

The current version of IP is version 4, or IPv4. In addition to source and destination addresses and information related to assembling and disassembling packets, IPv4 packet headers carry other fielded information, including the IP version number, the length of the packet header, the length of the complete packet, a time-to-live (TTL) designation to prevent looping (by decrementing a number—at 0 the packet is discarded and the host sender notified), a header checksum field for transmission error checking, a designation of the higher-layer protocol with which the packet is associated, and a type of service (ToS) bit. The ToS bit is rarely used, but it was intended to allow for specifying among different types of services related to such parameters as delay and jitter.

Proliferation of the TCP/IP Protocol Suite

When the Defense Communications Agency (DCA) began managing the operations of ARPANET in 1975, the Transmission Control Protocol/Internet Protocol (TCP/IP) protocols began to stabilize. This layering of protocols through the TCP/IP set of protocols (termed the TCP/IP protocol suite), proved to be a particularly useful approach to internetworking. The Defense Data Network was created in 1982 as the core interconnect facility for the various existing Internets and, in 1983, specified TCP/IP as the interconnection protocol. Then MILNET was established based on TCP/IP. When TCP/IP became a military standard in 1983, its use grew dramatically. The acceptance of TCP/IP as the standard of a major agency led to a rapid proliferation of TCP/IP across many other organizations, including universities and commercial firms, which began implementing networks based on the TCP/IP set of protocols.

The integration of TCP/IP and the Unix operating system was one of the most significant events that drove the Internet. DARPA funded projects that added TCP/IP to the University of California at Berkeley's Standard Distribution of Unix (BSD Unix, also known as Berkeley Software Distribution). Researchers at the university had been producing and distributing a public-domain version of the Unix operating system. This circumstance was critical because it moved the documented standard into functioning software that was freely distributed. Because BSD Unix was the operating system of choice for virtually all university computer science departments and research labs, TCP/IP became widely available. Also, applications were distributed that utilized these protocols, including Unix tools for I/O, such as sockets. More importantly, TCP/IP came into a domain of innovative programmers who continually adapted and improved implementations and related applications. During the early 1980s, local area networks proliferated, as a means to enhance communications and to share resources. A key factor in the proliferation of LANs was the development of the Ethernet protocol (discussed in a later section). By 1983, the TCP/IP protocol suite was in fairly wide use, and its growth rapidly continued throughout the 1980s and 1990s.

Corporations such as Sun Microsystems started using the software in their commercial workstation products, and the TCP/IP protocol reached a new level of general acceptance as the de facto standard for university data communications.

Growth and Further Protocol Development

In the 1980s, network growth occurred at multiple levels; because of the TCP/IP protocol suite these networks could communicate with each other. In 1981, the 3Com Corporation came out with UNET, a Unix TCP/IP product running on Ethernet. Prior to the split of the ARPANET, BBN opened Telenet, which was the first public packet data service. The Defense Data Network (DDN) in 1982 became the coordinator of the various networks that were the emerging Internet.

The early 1980s were a time for regional growth via the creation of networks, such as CSNET, that connected computer research facilities and computer science departments to allow non-ARPANET users to use dial-up connections to send and receive electronic mail. BITNET (Because It's Time Network), connecting IBM systems, also came into being as a cooperative effort to provide electronic mail and Listserv access. These and other networks were collectively referred to as the Internet. Internet with a capital "I" referred to the federally subsidized network, and internet with a lowercase "i" referred to any network using TCP/IP protocols. Local area networks, LANs, many of which utilized Ethernet, became popular on university campuses because the new protocols allowed communication within the campus network, as well as communication among other LANs connected to the Internet.

Simple Mail Transfer Protocol (SMTP)

The substantial growth of e-mail eventually changed so that messages that originally rode on File Transfer Protocol were sent by a separate mechanism. In 1982, Simple Mail Transfer Protocol (Comer 1995) and the e-mail format were created. In the Internet, every computer needs a unique IP address. The routers use this address to direct packets to the computer as they traverse the Internet. When the network was small, computer scientists who were using it could easily remember the IP addresses. To make the association easier, some computers were given names, and then the IP address-to-name mappings were kept in a file, called the host table. For example, sun.com mapped to 192.9.49.33.

Listserv capabilities also became popular. A Listserv is a means for distributing information via electronic mail. A group of users that want to conduct a discussion can have their e-mail addresses subscribed to a *list server* (Listserv). The Listserv then has a special e-mail address for the group, and when it receives an e-mail addressed to that address it forwards a copy to the entire list.

This system of placing a new entry in the host table when a university added a new computer was sufficient when the network was small; however, it clearly does not scale globally. To solve the problem of exchanging information about IP address-to-host name mappings globally, a protocol called the Domain Name System (DNS) was created.

Domain Name System (DNS)

In the mid-1980s, the Domain Name System (DNS) was created as a management tool for addresses of host computers and other devices on a network, including other networks. DNS provides a convenient means of keeping track of network-attached components through a distributed database that holds the IP addresses and aliases of those components. DNS provides for mapping from textual host device names to IP addresses. Rather than require a given host to maintain a file that would have to be continually updated, this mechanism allows for a distributed system, usually with a backup or two, to resolve acquiring address names of desired targets.

DNS also provides support for mapping between the destinations of mail messages and IP addresses. The DNS structure is hierarchical, specifying one of several top-level domains (.com, for commercial organization; .edu, educational entities; .gov, government agencies and departments; .net, networks; .org, nonprofits; .mil, military; and .int for some types of international organizations). Domains have designated name-servers that resolve specific IP host addresses.

The DNS is essentially a hierarchy of computers maintaining a database of host name-to-IP address mappings. The system can be queried to resolve, that is report, what the IP address would be for a specified name, thus rendering host tables obsolete. In 1986 consensus was achieved to adopt the DNS for general use.

Internet Corporation for Assigned Names and Numbers (ICANN)

Recently, a new entity was established to guide Internet identification number assignments. Until then, the official registration of the identifiers was accomplished through a government-funded function entitled the Internet Assigned Numbers Authority (IANA), managed until 1998 by Jonathan B. Postel, in conjunction with the Internet Registry (IR), which controlled the use of unique identifiers and managed the Domain Name System (DNS) root database, which populated other core DNS servers at various locations on the Internet. More recently, the Internet Corporation for Assigned Names and Numbers (ICANN), a private nonprofit corporation, was established to begin to migrate this function in the private sector.

User Datagram Protocol (UDP)

By standardizing on a single transport and addressing protocol suite, TCP/IP, the network could branch anywhere; however, sending multimedia, such as audio/video, over the network was problematic due to errors in the transmission of packets. As previously noted, TCP was designed to ensure reliability and forced retransmission of lost packets, creating significant delays. TCP's process of reassembling all packets as a collection required significant buffering, which caused problems maintaining the continuation of voice streams without a break. Voice transmission requires a continuous stream.

To correct this problem the *User Datagram Protocol* (UDP) was designed. UDP provides some of the same functions as TCP; however, it leaves to the application the decision about whether lost data should be retransmitted. Unlike TCP, UDP does not provide for data transport guarantees, for example, by using retransmissions. In the case of streaming audio or video lost data never is retransmitted because once the data is gone it would no longer make sense to play it at the receiver. UDP ignores the criterion of reliability, thus improving transmission of multimedia over the network. As noted, however, its primary use is for NFS.

Simple Network Management Protocol (SNMP)

In the early days of the Internet, network management was conducted with fairly primitive, but generally useful, tools. Over time, a much wider range of tools began to develop around TCP/IP. Additional tools were added such as: Packet Internet Groper (ping, which uses ICMP), which allowed for checking on the status of devices (sending an echo request and receiving a reply from a host); and, for checking network performance through timing round-trip messaging (Round Trip Time, RTT, can be a convenient general measure of network status), the Simple Gateway Monitoring Protocol (SGMP), which later became the Simple Network Management Protocol (SNMP); and others.

The Simple Network Management Protocol (SNMP) allows for fetching and storing data values related to network status information. SNMP employs the User Datagram Protocol (UDP) for transport. SNMP allows for the creation of traps that can be used to send messages if a particular event occurs, for example, loss of a network interface.

Remote Procedure Calls (RPC)

Remote Procedure Calls (RPC, which provides support for Network File System, NFS) provides for another set of useful tools that allow for a program to send informational requests to computers on a network and have variables and other information returned. RPC can be used to distribute components of a program to various computers on a network. RPC can be used as a basis for simple utilities or as part of a fairly large scale distributed computing environment.

Ethernet

In the early days of the Internet, numerous research organizations implemented LANs that utilized TCP/IP. Many of these LANs use Ethernet, a broadcast technology developed at the Palo Alto Research Center (PARC), which was established by Xerox Corp. in 1970. In 1973, Robert Metcalfe, a PARC researcher, originally devised Ethernet as a substantially faster means of linking computers to printers over networks. In 1970, while still a graduate student at Harvard, he had used queuing theory to address the problem of message failure while transmitting to improve the performance of AlohaNet. Then, while at PARC in 1973, he designed a simple network of computers communicating with each other in close proximity linked by cables with a significant reduction in message failure, and thereby utilizing a large portion of potential capacity. Metcalfe called this technology *Ethernet*; it was essentially a network without switches or routers. Ethernet was a broadcast media like air or a party-line telephone in which any time a computer transmitted a message it could be heard by all of the other computers on that Ethernet.

In 1974, the first Ethernet protocol was proposed. Ethernet was fairly standardized by 1978, although the 2.0 10 Mbps version was not fully specified until 1982. Today, this protocol interconnects the majority of LAN-attached computers in the world.

Ethernet is prolific, open, inexpensive, easy to implement, and it works particularly well with TCP/IP. These factors led to thousands of LAN implementations across the country based on a "TCP/IP over Ethernet" specification. The two sets of protocols work well together at the lower layers of the network stack. Ethernet functions as a data link protocol at Layer 1, for example, providing for physical specifications, and at Layer 2. At Layer 2, packets are received from Layer 3 and prepared for transit over specific media, such as physical media with standard characteristics or wireless media.

Ethernet has a 48-bit address mechanism that it allows to intercommunicate with devices on a network through network interface cards (NICs). Because IP addresses are different from Ethernet addresses, a mechanism was needed to provide for mapping between them. The Address Resolution Protocol

(ARP), which is part of the TCP/IP protocol suite, was developed to allow for this type of mapping between the two types of addresses. Given an IP address, ARP can determine the physical address of a specific node. Later revisions of ARP extended it beyond Ethernet. ARP uses a table (also known as an ARP cache) to accomplish this translation. When the address is not found in the ARP cache, a broadcast message, called the *ARP request*, is sent over the network. If one of the devices on the network recognizes its own IP address in the request, it sends an *ARP reply* to the requesting entity. The reply contains the physical hardware address of the destination. This newly received address is then placed in the ARP cache of the requesting device. All subsequent requests to this destination IP address are then directly translated to a physical address.

Ethernet continues to be improved through developments that enhance throughput, such as Fast Ethernet (100 Mbps), Gigabit Ethernet (1 Gbps), and tagging schemes to indicate priority. The basic standard for tagging Ethernet frames for priority is the IEEE 802.1p standard, which utilizes a field specified by the IEEE 802.1Q standard. This method explicitly indicates designated priorities within a frame. This mechanism allows applications to be network-aware, in that nodes can mark packets for specific types of treatment by the network.

Routers and Border Gateway Protocol (BGP)

In general, on a small local area network based on TCP/IP over Ethernet, it is inconsequential if all packets are broadcast everywhere. It was obvious, though, that this technique was inefficient if used on a larger scale, and various solutions were proposed for making packet distribution more efficient over wide area networks. A network-connected device was required that would contain information about the network at large, especially the interconnections that linked various networks. Given that information, the device (a router or gateway) could optimally send packets to their destinations.

In the mid-1980s, real routers were more of a concept than a reality outside of research labs. One early version was created based on a minicomputer. Such a system depends on the exchange of location information among thousands of autonomous networks. The protocol developed to accomplish this was the Exterior Gateway Protocol (EGP). A similar, closely related protocol, the Border Gateway Protocol (BGP), became widely used after it was implemented as part of an NSF backbone network project.

Routers were a major enhancement to the Internet. Hosts generally have designated permanent IP addresses. (A more recent development, the Dynamic Host Configuration Protocol (DHCP), allows for temporary address allocations.) Routers allow local traffic to stay local and provide for efficient forwarding of packets to nonlocal destinations. Packets with a nonlocal destination are sent to the local router with which they are associated. The router checks the IP destination address of the packet against its routing table to determine the location of the destination and forwards it.

For local destinations, routers use ARP to map IP addresses to local media access control (MAC) addresses. Routers can also transmit a request for an unknown MAC address. For nonlocal destination addresses, the router forwards the packet to the next-hop router with that router's MAC address substituted for the one from the original router. Dynamic updates for routing-table information are provided by the Router Information Protocol (RIP) and the Open Shortest Path First (OSPF) protocol, both examples of IGPs (Internet Gateway Protocols). (These topics are discussed in later chapters.)

The Internet in the Mid-1980s

In 1982 a decision was made that all systems on the ARPANET would convert from NCP to TCP/IP, and by 1983 the ARPANET had transitioned to TCP/IP. When the ARPANET started using TCP/IP exclusively on January 1, 1983, the next major phase of the Internet began.

In 1983, the Defense Communications Agency split ARPANET into two separate networks, the MILNET for sites that shared nonclassified military information and the ARPANET for the research community. MILNET would later be integrated with the Defense Data Network. During that year, the CSNET/ARPANET *gateway* was put into place. A gateway is like an IP router, only more sophisticated, because it allows communication between two dissimilar networks or networking protocols.

Significant growth in Internet products occurred in 1985 when a major emphasis was placed on replacing time-sharing computers with LANs connected to the Internet. In addition, desktop workstations were being shipped in record numbers, running the Unix operating system and networking software.

A National Backbone Network: NSFNET

In the mid-1980s, through a series of programs the National Science Foundation (NSF) began designing and building a national network to interconnect researchers, especially at academic institutions and national research centers. In 1985 and 1986, the NSF established five national supercomputing centers. To assist researchers in accessing these supercomputers over networks, the NSF established a program to link these centers—the Pittsburgh Supercomputing Center (PSC), the National Center for Supercomputing Applications (NCSA), Cornell, the San Diego Supercomputing Center (SDSC) and the

John Van Neumann Center (JVNC), and the National Center for Atmospheric Research (NCAR) in Colorado through a 56 Kbps dedicated-line backbone network. The TCP/IP protocol suite was adapted for this network at inception. In 1985, the "interim" backbone was deployed.

The NSF was also instrumental in funding regional Internets and the research that was directed at improving such networks. They funded a program that assisted researchers in creating regional research networks that established connections among universities and research labs in wide geographic regions. For example, CICNet was formed to interlink the "Big Ten" universities as well as a number of others (MERIT, BarrNet, NorthwestNet, SDSCnet, WestNet, Midnet, Sesquinet, SURAnet, JVNCnet, PrepNet, NYSERnet, etc.). The result was a huge increase in the number of connections, especially from the universities. The NSFnet had become the first multipurpose, national IP backbone.

Each organization had proprietary control over its regional connections to the backbone and was responsible for building out its regional distribution. The regional networks built star-like topologies that first provided hubs back to major universities, and at the second level of aggregation, linked back to the university in the region with the NSFnet backbone link.

The Early International Internet

An international program was established to allow for interconnectivity with the global community. As early as 1973, the first international connections to the ARPANET were established from the University College of London in England and the Royal Radar Establishment in Norway. As the Internet expanded, many countries established transoceanic links. Early participants included Canada, Sweden, France, Denmark, Iceland, Norway, Finland, Netherlands, England, Mexico, Japan, New Zealand, and Australia. Later, in 1989, Reseaux IP Européens (RIPE) formed to permit the operation of the Pan-European IP Network. RIPE played an important role in coordinating plans for government-sponsored research networking in Europe and implemented a system for IP address allocation.

Campus Networks

The NSFnet funding program also encouraged the development of campus data networks to support research. These capabilities were vitally important to many researchers, who required access to external resources such as remote data repositories and computers, especially supercomputers at several national sites. Researchers also required a capability for easily communicating with each other to allow for enhanced exchange of ideas and data.

NSFnet Phase 2: The T1 Upgrade

Projections of network traffic in 1986 indicated that an upgrade of the 56 Kbps backbone would be needed by 1987. Consequently, a solicitation for the development, engineering, and production management of another backbone network, the NSFnet T1 backbone network, was issued in 1986. The NSF national network design was based on a concept of a backbone network of T1 lines (1.544 Mpbs) linking the original six sites and seven hubs to regional networks (primarily academic consortiums interlinking universities), academic institutions, research laboratories, and commercial firms engaged in research.

In 1987, the NSF awarded the contract to Merit, Inc., at the University of Michigan in Ann Arbor, which managed the Michigan state-wide network (MERIT), with two joint study corporate partners, MCI and IBM. MERIT established a network operations center (NOC) for the network in Ann Arbor. IBM provided and configured systems, and MCI contributed fiber links.

In 1988, the NSF announced that it would be the primary federal agency for national digital networking. In July of 1988, the interim backbone was phased out, and the new production backbone was put into production service. The T1 backbone served an additional eight sites beyond the original five super-computing sites, including the University of Michigan, National Center for Atmospheric Research, Princeton, BARRNet at Palo Alto, Wetsuit at Salt Lake City, NorthWestNet Seattle, Rice University at Houston, and Georgia Tech.

By 1989, the T1-based NSFnet backbone had been built, interconnecting a growing number of regional Internets and over 600 individual networks. By the end of 1989, approximately a thousand networks were connected. In 1990, to accommodate ever-increasing volumes of traffic, the backbone network was upgraded to T3, and its ownership as a resource was transferred to a nonprofit corporation, ANS (Advanced Network Services). MERIT, with its subcontractor ANS, continued to perform such services as operating circuits and serving as the Internet routing authority. This service administered the database that provided the core information used by the packet-routing algorithms of the Internet worldwide.

Computer Emergency Response Team (CERT)

In 1988 the Internet was invaded by a worm virus. The virus was called a worm because of the way that it snaked its way from computer to computer across the Internet. It is estimated that it affected from 6,000 to 60,000 hosts and wasted ten of thousands of staff-hours in repairing the damage.

The result of the 1988 worm incident was the creation of the Computer Emergency Response Team (CERT), which then, and now, whenever there have been reported security compromises, sends out bulletins describing the compromised system and the way to fix it. Another outcome was the departure of connectivity to sensitive governmental agencies, like the military. It could be said that the worm was actually beneficial because the extent of the damage was limited to staff over the course of a few days removing the program and the worm; however, the worm focused attention on the increased potential risks of computer crime that the Internet had created.

Internet Standards, Governance, and Ongoing Partnerships

Ever larger populations of Internet users gave rise to issues of scalability. Currently, all component parts of the existing Internet are under stress from high demand, rapid expansion, and its increased importance to all sectors of worldwide national economies. Fortunately, mechanisms are in place that have been effective in responding to these pressures. The Internet consists of a number of basic technical components that undergo continual transformation and renewal, including a set of protocols within a set of core and related technologies—shaped by the inventiveness of a large community of cooperative partners.

The Internet has been successful partly because of its culture. The Internet has always been more than a set of protocols and technologies. Within the Internet community, its governance and policies are the result of a cooperative collaborative effort of thousands of individuals and organizations working in partnership. It is also the result of the activities of various constituency requirements, entities, and cooperative research and development processes and projects undertaken by researchers, technologists, and scientists at universities, government agencies, and commercial firms. The attributes of these cooperative partnerships and their relationships characterize the Internet, give it a distinctive culture of partnership, and have significantly contributed to its success. No single organization could have accomplished the achievements of the Internet development community. Because no single organizational entity owns or governs the Internet, it allows for a community of developers from thousands of organizations to contribute to its advancement. At the center of these activities is the Internet Engineering Task Force (IETF), which also develops some types of Internet governance policies.

Internet Engineering Task Force (IETF)

Although no one entity manages the Internet, there are organizational entities that provide directional guidance for technology standards development, selection, and implementation. They also provide a means of communicating information and organizing the processes that provide for the stability, reliability, and improvement of the Internet, and especially ensure the continual improvement of the TCP/IP protocol suite. The roots of the IETF were established during the early days of the Internet. The policies that governed the early Internet were more technical than general. In 1979, a DARPA research project was formed to guide the development of the TCP/IP Protocol Suite and to iterate protocols into Internet operation, the Internet Configuration Control Board (ICCB). In 1983, it became the Internet Activities Board (IAB). IAB was chartered to provide advice and guidance on research to the Internet community, publish Internet-related documents, and record various identifiers needed for protocol operation. (Currently the IAB is chaired by Brian Carpenter.) The Internet Research Task Force (IRTF) organized and explored advanced concepts in networking.

A major restructuring in 1989 specified the formulation of a more representative Board that was established to guide two separate entities, the Internet Research Task Force (IRTF), with an Internet Research Steering Group, and the IETF, which comprised an Internet Engineering Steering Group and numerous working groups that each focus on specific issues and problems. The IETF is organized as a collection of area subgroups, each with its own director, set of working groups, and projects. The IRTF focuses primarily on longer-term goals, such as research projects. The IETF focuses more on near-term operations and implementation issues, although their work overlaps. In 1992, the Internet Activities Board was renamed the Internet Architecture Board. The IAB addresses issues related to the general evolution of the Internet policies, standards, and technology.

IETF Requests for Comment (RFCs)

Contributions toward the development of Internet standards are made through a process described in a document called "Procedures for Internet Standardization." Technical reports and documentation on proposals for revision of protocols are published as Requests for Comment (RFCs) and Internet Engineering Notes (IEN).

In 1969, Steve Crocker, a graduate student at UCLA, wrote the first minutes of the meetings and distributed it, calling it *Request for Comments* (RFC). The intent was to solicit suggestions and comments from people who could contribute to the development and improvement of the workings of ARPANET. Today, RFCs are among the principal methods used to communicate within the computer networking community and are regularly produced by the IETF.

RFCs can describe experiments, proposals, drafts, and standards. RFCs also designate the status of concepts, such as whether they are elective, recommended, or required. Requests for Comments continue to provide for ongoing, updated information, including development efforts related to protocols. The RFC method for discussion provides a powerful means of moving a process toward an optimal solution. The process is open to anyone with a useful contribution, and online discussions are undertaken as a public forum, not a closed process. Good ideas are accepted; less-than-optimal ideas screened. In a sense the RFC process works similarly to scientific peer review, but with many more participants.

Network Information Center (NIC)

Separately, for many years a nonprofit organization, the Network Information Center (NIC), provided administrative support for general Internet logistics and for information coordination and distribution. The NIC was centered at the Stanford Research Institute (since 1977, SRI, International, formally separated from Stanford in 1970 is a nonprofit scientific research institute). Later, InterNIC in part evolved into a cooperative activity between the U.S. government and Network Solutions, Inc. Originally established by Douglas Englebart, the NIC served as a clearinghouse of standards information from the time of the ARPANET. The process of developing, organizing, and maintaining a repository for domain names is crucial to the worldwide Internet. Dozens of nations have now established NICs.

Federal Initiatives

In the early 1990s, the Federal Networking Council (FNC) functioned as a coordinating body that guided federal agencies developing intranets (primarily for individual organizations), supporting Internet policy development activities, and establishing goals and objectives for development projects. Major agencies included the Defense Advanced Research Projects Agency (DARPA), the National Science Foundation (NSF), the Department of Energy (DOE), the National Aeronautics and Space Administration (NASA), and the Department of Defense (DoD).

Conclusion

The current generation of the Internet will evolve into a second generation only through the same spirit of cooperative development and deployment that characterized the first. This spirit and tradition of cooperative development are more important to this effort than any given individual component.

End Note

[1]Portions of this chapter are based on a treatment in *Internet Architectures*, by Dan Minoli and Andrew Schmidt (1999, John Wiley & Sons).

References

Comer, Douglas. 1995. *Internetworking with TCP/IP: Principles, Protocols, and Architecture*. 3d ed. Upper Saddle River, NJ: Prentice-Hall.

Hafner, Katie and M. Lyon. 1996. *Where Wizards Stay Up Late.* New York: Touchstone.

The Internet Society. *A Brief History of the Internet and Related Networks.* [Available May 1999]. www.isoc.org/guest/zakon/Internet/ History/Brief_History_of_the_Internet

Salus, Peter H. 1995. *Casting the Net: From ARPANET to Internet and Beyond.* Reading, MA: Addison-Wesley Publishing Company.

URLs

AlohaNet: www.alohanet.com

ICANN: www.icann.org

Internet Engineering Task Force: www.ietf.org

Network Solutions, Inc.: www.networksolutions.com

RIPE: www.ripe.net

SRI International: www.sri.com

Next-Generation Internet Requirements, Advanced Internet Driver Applications, and Architectural Framework

Next-Generation Internet Requirements Specifications

As noted in Chapter 1, a new model for digital communications services and infrastructure is needed. A new model is emerging, based on a wide spectrum of requirements and on multiple innovations in information technology. Many new ideas related to advanced networking are being developed within research labs and through activities such as testbed network research, including projects established by commercial firms.

Just as the first Internet was developed in the advanced network and scientific research community, the second one also was originated by this aggressive networking constituency. These communities continue to drive the leading edge of advanced networking because of the requirements of their complex, demanding applications. In the early 1990s, as a response to their continuing problems with insufficient network services, these research communities established a number of projects in an attempt to begin to move toward the resolution of some of the basic issues. Some of these projects were conceptual and architectural, some involved technical research, some related to policy development, and a few were initial implementations of new technical approaches. Many of these projects were attempting to resolve network issues not simply by allocation of additional resources, but by optimizing and integrating multiple different types of resource allocations, including highly distributed computing resources.

An Internet Technology Spiral

These activities were part of a natural technological progression. The National Science Foundation has developed a chart that depicts a "technology spiral"—a technology life cycle (see Figure 3.1). The chart depicts four quadrants linked by a spiral loop. The spiral originates in the lower-left corner, depicting research labs (the origin of innumerable creative innovations). It then loops through the lower-right quadrant, denoting cooperative project partnerships among research labs, which collectively improve the technology models and prototype them. The spiral ascends through the upper-right quadrant, depicting more general, wider partnerships (including commercial partners, which provide both assistance in development and wider deployment), and then through the upper-left quadrant, depicting widespread commercialization. The spiral then descends to the lower-left part of the chart (research), beginning anew a continuing cycle of technology improvement through ongoing innovation and deployment among many cooperative partners.

Many influential innovations that have had an impact on Internet development have been developed by many different types of commercial activities, especially those related to microprocessor development and other informa-

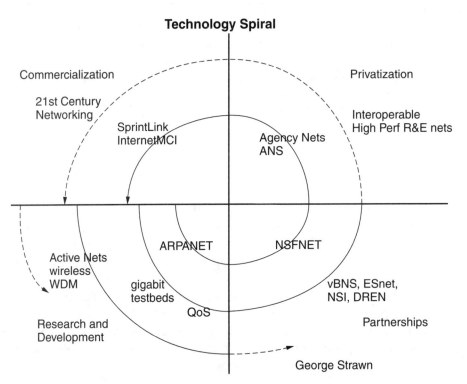

Figure 3.1 Internet technology spiral. (Courtesy of George Strawn, National Science Foundation, based on a concept presented by Juan Campas, 1996.)

tion technology components. However, commercial firms have also provided innovative service development, deployment, and distribution models for information technology.

In the labs where the first Internet was developed, a second-generation Internet was quietly being conceptualized, designed, and implemented in prototype from 1992 to 1995. Research, planning, design, and development efforts related to a new type of Internet started with a few small projects but rapidly accelerated throughout the rest of the decade. During this period, a number of activities set the stage for the next phase of the Internet's evolution. Along with presentations of potential action plans, innovations, demonstration projects, prototype networks and several early implementations of production advanced networks all occurred. These activities accomplished much to develop an enhanced Internet infrastructure and to indicate where additional efforts were required.

Corporation for National Research Initiatives (CNRI) and Testbed Networks

Testbed networks are critical for researching advanced networking concepts, architecture, and technology. In the late 1980s and early 1990s, several testbed networks were established by consortia including government agencies, universities, and commercial companies.

The Corporation for National Research Initiatives (CNRI) in Reston, Virginia, proposed the creation of testbed networks to assist in the development of concepts in next-generation networking, including gigabit networking and a wide range of protocols and emerging networking standards. Testbed advanced applications included weather simulation (for example, thunderstorms), earthquake analysis, and medical applications, such as the real-time distribution of computed tomography (CT) scans, magnetic resonance imaging (MRI), and positron emission tomography (PET).

Funded jointly by the National Science Foundation and the Defense Advanced Research Agency (DARPA), five testbeds were formed, along with a sixth funded by solely DARPA: CASA, BLANCA, VISANET, NECTOR, AURORA, and MAGIC. With AURORA, two related testbeds were established, plaNET, a wide-area testbed that supported a packet transfer mode, and ORBIT, a Gbps fiber LAN ring.

Other separately-funded testbed network initiatives were established later, including ATDnet, BAGNET, NTON, and ARIES. The Collaborative Advanced Internet Research Network (CAIRN) is an important DARPA-funded network that supports a wide range of innovative research. In 1991, T. J. Watson Research Center researchers created Rainbow, a prototype of an all-optical wave division multiplexing (WDM) network.

Next-Generation Digital Communications Requirements and Architecture

The numerous testbed projects in the early nineties investigated multiple, different, technical approaches. Given a large number of potential technical options, there must be some criteria for selection. The core requirements for the new digital communications model are often derived from the requirements of advanced applications. In technical design, as with other types of architecture, form should follow function—the design and implementation of a technical architecture should directly flow from the functional objectives of that architecture. To design an optimal technology architecture, it is important to have an in-depth understanding of the specific set of requirements, especially those defined by the applications that will be supported by that architecture.

Prototyping the Future

An optimal architecture should not only provide blueprints for development that meet current requirements but also anticipate future needs. The architecture should also allow for flexibility, expansion, and enhancement through future technical development. Accomplishing these goals is not necessarily a direct process. The particular challenge and strength of the Internet are the rapid dynamics of its application requirements, technologies, and component economics.

Addressing Internet development issues is similar to attempting to solve a complex equation while the number of its variables, their relationships, and the weights of those values continually change. In addition, when undertaking these design processes, it is almost more important to know where the requirements and technology will be, rather than where they are. All of this information may not even be sufficient to provide for the optimal architecture. The history of information technology development is littered with the remains of promising technologies terminated by the market realities, some of them incorporating amazingly innovative architectural designs, but ultimately proving unsuccessful.

Form and Function: Application Requirements for Next-Generation Internets

The relationship between the applications that drove the technical design of the first-generation Internet and its implementation is fairly straightforward and readily understood. As noted, the first Internet was designed based on requirement specifications for reliable communications among distributed shared resources and, as it evolved, for three core applications: file transfer among computers, communications (e-mail), and remote access. The design also met the need for interconnection interoperability among computers at various locations from different companies.

The design of the second-generation Internet is being developed to meet similar needs—but it also must do more, much more. Certainly, it must address the same set of basic requirements as the first-generation Internet, but on a different scale and with a far greater degree of complexity. For example, the second-generation Internet must provide for reliable interactive communications across diverse systems worldwide. It must also allow for multimedia options, including multimedia e-mail that is integrated with other applications such as IP telephony, digital video, and sophisticated 3-D collaborative environments for global communications. The next-generation Internet must provide not only for common file transfer among computers but for communication of many different types of files—some very large and complex, including multimedia—to and from many different types of devices, ranging from advanced supercomputers to toys, at any location in the world. In other words, the next-generation Internet must do more than accommodate advanced applications: It must anticipate ubiquitous IP devices, including pagers, hand-held personal information organizers, TV-top boxes, home appliances with wireless connectivity, and cars with interactive digital maps.

The next-generation Internet must provide for super high-definition, interactive, digital video; e-commerce, remote digital health care; data-intensive applications (which require direct access to extremely large amounts of data); distributed, high-performance computing; and advanced, specialized computing. It must also provide for efficient information flow to and from digital systems of all types from anywhere to anywhere worldwide.

In addition, the next-generation Internet must provide for differentiation among various services—or for differentiated services.

Continuous Exponential Growth

These are the initial baseline requirements, after which the specifications become more demanding. The next-generation Internet must accommodate exponential growth in users, applications, and use of applications. It must also continue to advance the ongoing technical revolution in digital communications. This last issue leads to a design paradox. Even as application requirements are specified and designs developed, the applications and the technologies that are to be used for implementation are rapidly changing. Advanced networking is truly the proverbial moving target.

Specifying Requirements for Next-Generation Internets

Requirements for the various next generation Internet initiatives are being driven by the needs of new, emerging applications and anticipated, future applications rather than the applications that are generally known today. Given the design paradox noted in the last section, the task of requirements definition is a significant challenge, especially designing today for changing, future requirements. If it is more important when designing technology to know where the requirements and technology will be, rather than where they are, it is also necessary to have a window into the future. Fortunately, such a window exists: The future manifests itself through aggressive applications emerging in research laboratories.

Origin of "Killer Apps" for the Next-Generation Internets

As Larry Smarr, Director of the National Computational Science Alliance has noted, to view the future one should visit a national supercomputing center.

Leading-edge Internet technologies have always been driven by the advanced research community. For example, the future Internet requirements of the high-energy physics community may seem like a particularly distant, rarified activity to today's general Internet user, but it was that community that began developing Web servers at the CERN particle physics lab in the early 1990s.

In 1993, a project established to develop an enhanced viewer for high-energy physics data and related Internet-based information led to the development of Mosaic at the National Center for Supercomputing Applications—the first widely deployed Web browser. A few months after Mosaic was invented, millions of Internet users were employing it worldwide. Only a few months after that, Netscape Communications Corp. (now incorporated into America Online) was established. The history of the Internet consists of such examples, and the current trend is following the same path. A number of these advanced applications are described later in this chapter.

SIGGRAPH 92 Showcase, Supercomputing 92

In 1992, the SIGGRAPH 92 Showcase and Supercomputing 92, and during the following year during Supercomputing 93, demonstrated how collaborative research linking computational science with visualization could produce unique insights that supported the process of scientific discovery. These events proved the importance of a high-performance, computing, networked environment in linking interactive visualization, applications, and collaborations. The broadband wide area networks required to support such advanced applications were difficult and expensive to develop, even in the few places where they were available.

National Computational Science Alliance and National Partnership for Advanced Computing Infrastructure

The National Computational Science Alliance and the National Partnership for Advanced Computing Infrastructure (NPACI) are two programs funded by the National Science Foundation's PACI program. These programs are directed at building the next-generation national and international computational-research infrastructure and applications. Both are centers of scientific research activity that are driving the leading edge of networking. High-performance scientific application programs that utilize advanced networks for remote large-scale parallel-processing provide for interesting, complex problems in network provisioning. The Alliance is centered at the National Center for Supercomputing Applications (NCSA) at the University of Illinois at Urbana-Champaign. NPACI is centered at the University of California-San Diego and the San Diego Supercomputing Center (SDSC).

The National Computational Science Alliance is a partnership of computational scientists, computer scientists, technical professionals, and other academic and corporate researchers who are prototyping the computational and information infrastructure for the next century. The Alliance is developing a National Technology Grid (Grid) that will integrate high-performance computers, advanced visualization environments, remote instruments, and massive databases through high-speed networks, in order to create a powerful environment to solve extremely complex research problems. These problems are formulated within many different knowledge disciplines, including chemical engineering, cosmology, environmental hydrology, molecular biology, nanomaterials, and development of new scientific instrumentation.

Emerging Killer Apps for Advanced Internets

Inevitably with multiple, contending requirements for a system's design, conflicts arise among requirements; and compromises must be made. A number of candidate applications may evolve to become the "killer apps," or meta-drivers, of the next-generation Internet, for example, advanced, interactive, digital video. Although a single killer app for the next-generation Internet may emerge and drive all other design requirements, this scenario is unlikely. Also, even if a single killer app were to be identified and accommodated at any given time, others would inevitably be proposed immediately—technology expectations are always high. The design of the next-generation

Internet must account for the requirements of many different killer apps, as well as tens of thousands of general, pedestrian applications.

Internet Digital Video

A number of advanced research projects involve addressing the challenges of latency-intolerant applications such as digital video, which will eventually become another common data type such as text. The current Internet provides primarily for images and text. The next-generation Internet will provide interactive digital video, not simply delivering TV broadcasts over the Internet (which is simply an extension of the traditional analog model, although this application is possible and perhaps inevitable), but a totally different interactive video experience that will be directly linked to other types of digital data. Rather than provide for a passive experience at a given time and place, the viewer will be able to determine what he or she will see at what time and at what place. The viewer's selection options will be extensive; but perhaps more importantly, the content will have dynamic links to other types of digital information, including text, still images, and separate audio tracks. It will also have links to different types of transaction-processing systems. Because digital video streams are latency intolerant, they require more than bandwidth. They require that network resources be reserved to ensure that the streams are continuous.

E-Commerce

Although e-commerce has been much discussed in the press, the real potential of this application has barely begun to be realized. No other technology has the Internet's potential to link so many customers across the world with so many products and services—and, more importantly, information about those products and services, including ongoing support information. Internally, corporations are being transformed by a revolution based on reengineered processes enabled by network-based applications designed to efficiently support corporate missions. E-commerce will also benefit by differentiated services because one of the benefits of Internet-based commerce is the potential for customization of products and services for specific individual requirements.

Telemedicine, Health Care, and Medical Sciences

Much of the advanced Internet technology development is focused on enhancing health care through new processes for new research methodologies (for example, DNA sequencing and use of genome databases), remote diagnostics, computer-assisted diagnostics, new types of treatments, development of new pharmaceutical products, enhanced administrative and patient care processes, new procedures for health maintenance, and professional skills training.

Advanced medical imaging, in particular, is a fast-growing application area that depends on high-performance networks. Medical researchers are developing numerous advanced, network-based applications utilizing specialized medical software, linked to visualization technology that enables radically new types of health care. Some leading-edge medical-visualization applications provide for projecting 3-D, virtual-reality images, for example, one that renders spiral CT images in 3-D space, allowing for unique insights.

Other heath-care-related areas being transformed through the use of the Internet include basic science, structural biology, biochemistry, and biophysics. Also, a number of projects are being formulated to develop health-care testbed networks that will link hospitals, clinical practices, medical schools, and research centers to allow them to communicate better, to share instrumentation and information securely (such as medical images and data), to administer enhanced types of medical care, and to employ other new, innovative techniques.

One of the most promising areas of research includes network-based computational molecular biology, which is beginning to delve into the core molecular processes that make up the basis of life. Researchers use the Internet to access the Advanced Photon Source (APS) synchrotron, a unique scientific instrument, and its experimental stations at Argonne National Laboratory, where they are engaged in leading-edge research in X-ray and time-resolved crystallography of biological macromolecules. APS X-rays are 10,000 times brighter than those in common use. This research has already led to dramatic new scientific discoveries. Use of remote instrumentation is another type of application that often requires guaranteed network services because of the ongoing fine tuning adjustments required between the user and the instrumentation settings.

E-Government

Many federal, state, and local government services involve Internet information flows to and from citizens. Governments are already devising and implementing Internet-based applications that enhance their services through direct links to their constituencies. The U.S. federal government has already implemented a number of such projects. Many states are planning advanced statewide networks. Large-scale Civic Nets are being planned in a number of cities, not only to enhance interactions with citizens but also to allow for better communications among government agencies.

Architectural Design

Internet-based visualizations are being used for remote, collaborative architectural design and development projects. These Internet-based visualizations are being used to model concepts and to provide the experience of encountering architectural spaces before those spaces are built. The spaces not only allow for optimal designs but also provide better realization of requirements in the architectural blueprints before construction starts. One project in Japan is developing an application for city planning that provides for plans to be experienced in 3-D virtual reality.

Digital Learning and Research Environments

The digital learning environments being designed today for learning in the future are not robotic teachers, but supplemental support environments that enhance classroom learning through compelling educational experiences. These environments also provide capabilities for life-long learning by anyone wishing to continue his or her education. Internet-based digital learning and research environments can provide virtual laboratories, which are detailed virtual spaces allowing for experimentation and exploration by learners.

Digital Libraries

Digital libraries are being designed that will hold vast repositories of not only digital books, images, video and audio but also simulations, animations, and digital objects. For example, advanced Internet-based virtual-reality technology allows for 3-D images of ancient archeological artifacts and for experiencing virtual historical environments, such as re-created ancient cities and specific places such as the Roman Forum.

Digital Museums

Digital museums will not simply be collections of art and historic artifacts, but will provide interactive experiences of past ages and events. For example, advanced Internet-based virtual-reality technology could be used like a time-machine so that travelers could be transported to the past to visit historic sites and interact with historic personages. Because this information is digital, it can be cross-linked across networks by means of an infinite number of cross-connections. For this reason, applications related to digital objects must provide for repositories of not only the objects but also related metadata (data about the data) that can be searched and cross-linked.

Astrophysics, Astronomy, and Space Sciences

Astrophysicists, astronomers, and space scientists have always been at the forefront of advanced networking because of their need to access remote instrumentation, to store and process extremely large datasets, and to visualize that data. For example, the Sloan Digital Sky Survey will collect 40 terabytes of data to create a 3-D map of a large part of the universe. NASA is also involved in many projects that are network-intensive. The NASA Goddard Earth Observing System (GEOS) Data Assimilation System is one of a number that utilizes extremely large amounts of data from satellite observations to generate global weather predictions. Its General Circulation Model (GCM) uses very large amounts of data to compare observations against predicted models.

Geosciences

The geosciences have been using advanced networks from the time National Center for Atmospheric Research (NCAR) was first linked to the 56 Kbps National Science Foundation backbone network. Geosciences researchers now use advanced networks to access remote supercomputers and large amounts of data to support investigations into general atmospheric sciences and global climate modeling. Some of the most advanced and complex current work involves combined oceanographic and atmospheric models, with a high degree of granularity.

Engineering Science

Advanced engineering projects are increasingly employing a wide range of Internet-based techniques for computational processing, modeling, simulation, and visualization. Multidisciplinary centers for imaging sciences are developing core imaging and visualization theories, concepts, and techniques that are allowing for radically new "imaging tools," including specialized systems for specific disciplines: imaging systems for the development of instrumentation prototypes, image reconstruction for medical applications, and molecular processes, such as computational chemistry and computational biology.

Chemistry/Physical Chemistry

Advanced Internet capabilities are substantially enhancing interchange and collaborative research activity among researchers in chemistry and physical chemistry, especially those that are employing applications requiring remote high-performance computing, for example, computational chemistry involving large models. Using advanced networks, these models can be used for basic research and for development, such as for prototyping new substances.

Enhancing Human Perception

Advanced Internet applications that provide for significant enhancements to human perception are among the most complex and challenging. Yet, this area holds a significant potential for different types of human activity. Digital technologies are significantly extending the powers of human perception.

Using technology to extend the senses is a process as ancient as history, but digital technologies allow for powerful new means to amplify the patterns of the physical universe and to model what may not exist, such as mathematical models and simulations of the effects of experimental pharmaceuticals in digital patients. These techniques require accessing enormous amounts of information that cannot be stored locally and must be shared with many people at diverse locations.

Enhancing Vision

People acquire more than 80 percent of information visually, and the visual sense is often the quickest path to information. Throughout history, scientists have broadened their understanding by creating new viewing instruments, such as the microscope and the telescope. The majority of imaging and visualization modalities, generated by instruments from CT scans to telescopes, however, have been invented comparatively recently. Almost all of these modalities are becoming digitized.

Advances in digital information technology have provided powerful new visualization tools. These new tools not only allow viewers to see physical realities (from systems as small as atoms to those as large as the universe) but also allow them to interact dynamically with those systems through simulations and models. For example, researchers can simulate experiments in the earth's core and view the core's response to changes in pressure, temperature, and material composition.

Astronomers use radio telescopes to "view" the beginning of time, visualizing the cosmos as it looked 13 billion years ago by peering at the edge of the universe.

At supercomputing centers, Internet-based high-fidelity simulations are being produced of complex, three-dimensional, computational fluid dynamics related to a variety of phenomena, such as the merging of neutron stars and the behavior of supernovas. The whole universe can be presented as a 3-D image, one through which viewers can voyage.

Much of the promise of these new techniques relies on the ability to access extremely large amounts of stored data and to link that information to displays over a network. The more information that can be streamed, the more detail that can be imaged. New display devices allow for super-high-definition screens with 2,500 by 2,000 pixels resolution.

High-Energy Physics

The high-energy physics (HEP) research community is one of the most demanding users of advanced networking, but it also is among the most innovative. For example, this is the community that developed the World Wide Web. HEP researchers conducting major projects at Fermilab use the Internet to pursue research that is defining how the universe works at its most fundamental core. They are at the leading edge of the international HEP community in experiment (colliding beam and fixed target) design, development, implementation, and utilization. The Collider Detector at Fermilab (CDF) is Fermilab's major colliding beam experiment. The researchers use the Fermilab instruments to examine charge parity violation (the attribute of matter that determines the universe's balance of matter and anti-matter and, therefore, the existence of "matter"). To accomplish these tasks, they need to gather, process, and analyze enormous amounts of data, tens of terabytes, which must be communicated over high-performance digital networks.

Teleimmersion

Some applications incorporate many different types of capabilities. Such applications are valuable to network developers because, as they are modeled and specified, they provide insights into optimal designs. One such application, which has been studied by designers of advanced networks, is teleimmersion.

Digital technologies also provide the capabilities for creating and experiencing new worlds. No technology has taken this concept further than teleimmersion. Teleimmersion provides an insight into the future of advanced applications that will take advantage of next-generation digital communications. Teleimmersion and other advanced virtual-reality (VR) technology is being developed by Tom DeFanti and the Electronic Visualization Laboratory at the University of Illinois, Chicago. These technologies are now implemented directly or as derivative technology at more than 100 sites around the world. The core of that technology is the CAVE (Cave Automatic Virtual Environment), which enables applications that are, in a word, compelling. Even technologies based on real needs can lead to extraordinary developments through imaginative insight—a description that is appropriate for CAVE technologies.

The CAVE is an immersive VR environment in which the viewer is allowed mobility through a room-sized VR space, created through projected images. This "holodeck" type of VR supports a wide range of visualization applications, including interactive virtual environments, the dynamic steering of high-performance, scientific computations through VR interfaces, utilizing distributed computation and imaging. A related technology is the CAVERN, a CAVE research network.

Teleimmersion is a CAVE application that allows collaborative VR sessions to take place over high-performance networks. It provides for a new type of interactive space that supports human-to-human interaction across the world, as well as simultaneous, shared, real-time data (including data from data-mining processes), digital video, computational process, and model sharing. Current teleimmersion research is exploring new ways for people to interact easily with heterogeneous, distributed resources across the world, including instrumentation, visualization of massive amounts of data, simulated architectural spaces, and planetary surfaces. CAVE technology can provide a quantum extension of human vision to the farthest limits of human imagination.

Collaborative Spaces

The CAVE can be used for multi-functional collaborative spaces, digital rooms that provide support for different functions (research, teaching, informal discussion, and lab experimentation) by providing for each function complete sets of resources that are called up on demand—data, access to real or virtual instrumentation, software, and analysis tools that change depending on the requirements of the user at any given moment. EVL researchers have created a Narrative, Immersive, Constructivist/Collaborative Environment (NICE). One NICE application enables children at multiple locations to cultivate a three-dimensional garden and control its environment.

A five-sided CAVE is being used in Japan (at the University of Tokyo) for many applications including urban planning. One application in the United States, as an experiment in real-time dynamic data exploration, demonstrates computational fluid dynamics and the imaging of these flows within a CAVE. It may be possible to use red-shift data from astronomical digital surveys to create a CAVE-based virtual universe to allow VR travel to, and through, any galaxy in the universe. Such data is being collected at Fermilab through the Sloan Digital Sky Survey project, which is being conducted under the auspices of the Astrophysical Research Consortium, to produce a detailed photometric map of half the northern sky to about 23rd magnitude. The project will create a 3-D map of the 1 million brightest galaxies in the universe and will survey the properties of 100 million fainter galaxies.

General Application Requirements

The requirements of the applications described here, as well as related applications, all vary to some degree. Some application requirements do not coexist well, and others are mutually exclusive. Collectively, the complete set of next-generation applications provides for a large number of challenging, complex advanced networking requirements, including the following:

- Access to any type of information, for example, real-time applications such as multimedia

- Ability to communicate information from anywhere to anywhere, world-wide

- Ability to ensure the integrity of information

- Ability to transform information into knowledge, for example, special analysis tools

- Convenient access to data in extremely large amounts of digital information, for example, not simply accessible but also directed, intelligent searches, in distributed repositories

- Access to specialized instrumentation, for example, virtually any device that uses or generates information anywhere in the world

- Extensions of human sensory perception

- Ability to integrate different types of digital information

- Allowing different applications to use the same suite of network services, as opposed to having network services tightly coupled to applications

- Ability to ensure the integrity of information

- Enhanced monitoring and management of network resources

General and Core Technical Requirements for the Next-Generation Internet

For most types of advanced technical architectures, a set of general requirements must be met, for example, high quality, high performance, exceptional reliability, modularity, open standards, scalability, expandability, manageability at all technical layers, operability at increasingly higher performance (and other improvements over time), security, and resource efficiency. The next-generation Internet will be distinguished from the first by how it addresses these requirements and by how it meets a set of core requirements.

Differentiated Services

The current Internet essentially provides for a best-effort IP service. The core requirements for the next-generation Internet center on mechanisms for providing for differentiated services. By stating that the provisioning of differentiated services is a requirements goal, a number of issues must be addressed, as follows:

If services are differentiated, a scheme must be developed to define different classes and levels, or qualities, of services and their parameters.

A mechanism must be created to allow for applications to signal specific requests for services.

Because services are no longer common, the requests for services must be carefully managed, through enhanced mechanisms for identification, authentication, authorization, and resource utilization.

A mechanism must be established for services provisioning, to fulfill requests, to link the requests with specific allocations, or reservations of network resources, through some type of contractual guarantee.

The ability to fulfill specific guarantees implies a need to know precisely what network resources are available for allocation at what time.

Provision of differentiated services requires policy mechanisms to adjudicate for priorities, priority queuing, conflict resolution, and contingencies for unexpected circumstances.

Mechanisms must be implemented to ensure performance of established contracts and to provide for enforcement of noncompliance with established contracts—allowing for a measure of restraint among applications and processes (rationed resource allocations, priority queuing, scheduling, millisecond adjustments, etc.).

Management mechanisms must be implemented to monitor all processes related to service and resource provisioning, especially resource utilization, and to respond dynamically to needs for adjustments.

Next-Generation Internet Middleware

The next-generation Internet will have sophisticated capabilities for addressing the needs of applications, especially with regard to matching the requirements of advanced applications to the resources provided by the network. These interlinking/brokering tasks, processes, and services will be accomplished through a midlevel set of technologies and capabilities. The aggregate collection of many of these mechanisms has been termed *middleware*, or advanced Internet middleware, the processes that live between the next-generation Internet applications and the infrastructure.

To some degree, many of these types of processes have existed in some form within the existing Internet. The next-generation Internet, however, will require a substantial new level of complex middleware processes. The delivery of optimal network capabilities that fully support advanced applications is currently problematic, in part because the power of the network is underutilized as a result of the fairly primitive nature of existing middleware, where it exists at all.

Advanced middleware networks will do more than allow for the reservation of required network resources and for guarantees that network performance will match the resources requested by the application; they will also provide links to other types of network services, such as directory and security services (including identification, authorization, authentication, and resource usage auditing).

When these features are implemented in the Internet fabric, the applications they support will be far more capable of providing functionality to Internet applications. Recently an IETF Middleware draft has been developed (Aiken 1999).

General Networking Economic Requirements

Network economic considerations are particularly important because no technology is designed, developed, and implemented with an unlimited budget. All technology designs require some form of economic trade-off, and it is not always clear which trade-offs are the best, especially given rapid technology change. Resource values (ratios measuring requirements against resources) must be projected. The "macroeconomic" resource utilization policy providing balances among many resources must be determined, including (a) applications, (b) networks, (c) computational processing, (d) peripherals, and (e) secondary processes.

Providing for network resource optimization is particularly complex in a dynamic environment. For example, choices projected for trade-offs among computational processing at various points at various levels and bandwidth based on current assumptions of economics are not straightforward. A matrix model projecting alternate scenarios of free versus scarce computational processes and bandwidth yields dramatically different results under different circumstances. Moore's Law specifies that processor power doubles every 18 months, yet bandwidth demand is accelerating at a far greater pace. Large gains are possible by distributing multiple processors within a system, and large gains are possible by over-provisioning bandwidth as those costs decline.

Conclusion

The development of the next-generation Internet is being driven by dynamic, interactive processes in which aggressive application requirements shape technical design and development—even as technical design and development influence the evolution of the applications that they support. This process consists of a large number of constantly changing variables. Consequently, the implementation of advanced digital communications systems has not always followed predictable paths. Increasingly, an important design goal is provisioning for optimal interactions among a wide range of integrated, highly distributed resources. Therefore, while increased bandwidth is important, it is also important to provide for differentiation among multiple requests for network resources and to optimally allocate available resources among those requests, especially those that are highly distributed and those that require sustained allocations.

References

Much of the information in this chapter is derived from provisioning for advanced applications on advanced networks. Some of the best sources for this type of information can be found on Web sites at national high-performance computing centers, at national research labs, and at advanced university research labs.

Aiken Bob et al. 1999. Internet Draft. ID: draft-aiken-middleware-reqndef-01.txt

URLs

Corporation for National Research Initiatives: www.cnri.reston.va.us

Electronic Visualization Laboratory, University of Illinois, Chicago: www.evl.uic.edu

National Computational Science Alliance and the National Partnerships for Advanced Computing Infrastructure: www.ncsa.uiuc.edu

San Diego Supercomputing Center: www.sdsc.edu

CHAPTER 4

Next-Generation Internet Initiatives

Overview

The goal of developing a ubiquitous, advanced digital communications network based primarily on a next-generation Internet will succeed only through the same spirit of cooperative partnership that developed the first Internet. Future challenges in advanced digital communications will be overcome only through cooperative efforts by the best research and development teams worldwide. Currently, the effort to create the next-generation Internet is a global partnership, comprising many different areas of networking research and development activities, undertaken by corporations, government agencies, nonprofit research labs, professional and standards organizations, academic research centers, and individuals.

This chapter describes a wide range of these next-generation Internet cooperative-development projects in the United States. These projects are not all-inclusive, but rather they have been selected to illustrate contemporary formulations of next-generation Internet development. Chapter 5 describes international next-generation Internet projects. The first part of Chapter 4 describes several next-generation Internet initiatives and events that were formulated in the early-to-mid 1990s. The second part of this chapter describes those that were established more recently.

In the United States, Internet-related research and development partnerships include not only entities that are directly focused primarily on Internet development, such as the IETF, or even on more general networking development; they also include many members of the broader information technology research and development community and general standards organizations, such as the Institute of Electrical and Electronics Engineers (IEEE) and the American National Standards Institute (ANSI). They also include participants from among large-scale, advanced, information-technology projects that are extending the edge of innovation, such as the National Science Foundation's Partnerships in Advanced Computational Infrastructure (PACI), the National Partnership for Advanced Computing Infrastructure (NPACI), the Department of Energy's Alliance for Strategic Computing Initiatives (ASCI), and the Department of Defense's High Performance Computing Modernization Shared Resource Centers. One important initiative is the Federal Next Generation Internet (NGI) project, which was formulated as a cooperative effort among a number of government agencies. Two others are academic projects formulated by a number of research universities and corporate associates, namely, the Internet2 project and Abilene, a network infrastructure project, both of which are discussed in this chapter.

Finally, this chapter describes a visionary concept related to next-generation Internets called the Grid—or as it was described in the title of a recent book, *The Grid: Blueprint for a New Computing Infrastructure* (Foster 1999).

The National Science Foundation

As noted in Chapter 2, in the mid-1980s, the National Science Foundation through a series of programs began funding projects directed at designing and building a national Internet backbone to allow for interconnection among researchers, especially at academic institutions and national research centers, and to provide remote access to supercomputer centers.

In 1994, the NSF began to address part of the national need for advanced Internet capabilities by providing investment funding to allow, initially, for remote access to national supercomputing centers for members of the research community with meritorious applications. The NSF also wanted to ensure the ongoing development of advanced Internet technologies. Consequently, in 1994, the NSF's Directorate for Computer and Information Science and Engineering (CISE) established a subsequent program that established a national, advanced, high-performance network—the very-High-Speed Backbone Network Service, or vBNS.

The NSF CISE Directorate was established to support research in a wide number of disciplines related to computing, information sciences, and engineering. It was also established to assist in the development of leading-edge national computing and networking infrastructure for research and education, and it contributes to educating computer scientists and engineers.

The NSF Very-High-Speed Backbone Network Service

The contract for the development of the NSF-sponsored very-High-Speed Backbone Network Service (vBNS) was awarded to MCI vBNS (at the time a division of the MCI Telecommunications Corp., now a division of MCI WorldCom) and provided for a national OC3c (now OC12c) backbone linking major research centers. Testing for the vBNS began in 1994, and the production network entered service on April 1, 1995. The previous model of the NSFnet was a three-tiered hierarchy consisting of (1) local networks (often widely dispersed campus networks), (2) regional networks that interconnected those campuses, and (3) a national backbone (NSFnet) that connected the regional networks. The new model assumed the existence of the numerous interconnected commercial Internet providers, interconnected at national interchange points (national access points, or NAPs), along with a special network for the advanced research and education community. The vBNS, therefore, was designed to interconnect supercomputing centers, research and education institutions, and national interchange points.

Later, through the NSF High Performance Connections Program, universities having meritorious applications were provided grants that allowed them to connect to the vBNS. The vBNS also allowed for substantial additional leveraging through institutional investments, especially by universities. By early 1999, the vBNS had 12 core nodes, more than 75 operational connections and another 25 planned.

The vBNS provided access to remote instrumentation nationwide, not just to supercomputers, but also synchrotrons, telescopes and scanning electron microscopes, located at directly attached sites or reachable through interconnections with other research networks developed by federal agencies. More information on the vBNS is presented as a case study in Chapter 10.

Other Early Next-Generation Internet Initiatives

An earlier section of this book noted that in the late 1980s and early 1990s many testbed, advanced networks were established by consortia, including government agencies, universities, and corporations, for example, those that were developed by the Corporation for National Research Initiatives (CNRI). Also, an earlier section noted that national conferences and showcase events, such as SIGGRAPH 92, SC '92, and SC '93 continued to advance the state of the art. Furthermore, in the early to mid-1990s, a new type of regional network was designed, based on emerging principals in advanced networks. The first of these was the Metropolitan Research and Education Network (MREN).

Metropolitan Research and Education Network

In 1993, a consortium of universities and federal research laboratories in the upper Midwest developed a strategic plan for advanced networking to meet the needs of research scientists. This project led to the establishment of the Metropolitan Research and Education Network (MREN), which began production in 1994 and later became one of the world's most advanced, innovative, regional high-performance networks. The MREN network spans seven states and has national and international high performance links. MREN is a collaborative effort undertaken as an interdisciplinary, interorganizational, cooperative partnership.

MREN's technical design is based primarily on extensive analysis of multiple requirements of leading-edge scientific applications. MREN allows real-time, state-of-the-art applications to actively use the latest, multisite, advanced-networking technologies. MREN was developed to support a wide range of advanced research applications, requiring high performance and high bandwidth, including some of those applications described in Chapter 3. Research applications that utilize MREN include high-performance computing, advanced digital video, advanced medical imaging, computer-aided diagnostics, high-energy physics, computational biology and chemistry, astronomy and astrophysics, and advanced networking research.

Currently, a number of MREN-related regional, national, and international projects have been established, ranging from aggressive bandwidth-utilizing applications to research and development. Many of these research and development projects center on advanced network architecture, methods, experimentation, and tools. In Chapter 10, MREN is discussed as a case study.

The Supercomputing 95 I-WAY Project

An important experimental project that provided a number of early insights into the requirements for next-generation Internets was the I-WAY (Information Wide Area Year) project. In 1995, during the development of the Supercomputing 95, the I-WAY project was developed as a demonstration of distributed high-performance computing. Although this project was focused on advanced computation, it also provided important insights into the future of advanced networking.

The Supercomputing 95 conference brochure announced "I-WAY—The Next Generation of Internet debuts at SC '95." The I-WAY project was a particularly important historical event for advanced networking and, as is usually the case for such events, one of the least noticed. This project was led by Argonne National Laboratory, the Electronic Visualization Laboratory, and the National Center for Supercomputing Applications.

As part of the I-WAY project showcase, an innovative national testbed network was temporarily implemented (for one month) as the first-of-its-kind national broadband network. The I-WAY was a unique national 1 gigabit testbed developed as a cooperative research venture that designed a high-performance network linking a number of the nation's highest-performance computers and advanced visualization environments. For the first time, some computers were not transported to the conference but were left at research centers and linked to the conference over the I-WAY network. The I-WAY supported a wide range of distributed applications, interactive video, and remote computations for virtual environments, including those based on the CAVE technology described in Chapter 3.

I-WAY was based on an interlinking of existing networks along with some additional connectivity and services provided by many national communications services corporations. The existing high-performance research networks included AAInet (ACTS ATM Internetwork); ATDnet (Advanced Technology Demonstration Network); CalREN (California Research and Education Network); CANARIE (Canadian Network for the Advancement of Research Industry and Education); CASA (Gigabit Testbed); DREN (Defense Research and Engineering Network); ESnet (Energy Sciences Network); MAGIC (Multidimensional Applications and Gigabit Internetwork Consortium); MREN (Metropolitan Research and Education Network); and vBNS (very-High-Speed Backbone Network Service). The other linked networks were provided by a number of carriers, including MCI, AT&T, Sprint, Ameritech, and Pacific Bell.

Globus

Another important project in the development of the next-generation Internet that has its roots in the SC '95 I-WAY project is Globus. The two principal architects of Globus are Ian Foster of Argonne National Laboratory and Carl Kesselman of the Information Sciences Institute, the University of Southern California. The I-WAY showed that distributed computational testbeds were extremely promising but that they required a prodigious effort in programming, system management, and performance stability. As a consequence of observations made during the I-WAY project, the researchers involved realized that a new type of capability was required as a middle layer between advanced applications and advanced computing infrastructure. Subsequently, Globus was established to develop such middleware components.

Although this project is focused on advanced distributed computing, its architectural approach and early implementation has implications for development of next-generation Internet middleware.

The Globus project is a multi-institutional research initiative centered within Argonne National Laboratory's Distributed Computing Laboratory and the University of Southern California's Information Science Institute. The goal of the Globus project is to design, develop, and implement software infrastructure that would allow "pervasive, dependable, and consistent access to high-performance computational resources."

The Globus project is developing an integrated set of basic services for computational infrastructures called the "Globus toolkit." This toolkit allows for applications to be developed and implemented without being constrained by a particular programming model. The toolkit consists of software components that allow for applications to utilize services for resource management, information access, security, communications, system status, remote data access, and management of executables. The Globus project is funded by the Department of Energy (DOE) and the Defense Advanced Research Projects Agency (DARPA) and several other organizations.

Federal Computing, Information, and Communications Research and Development Programs

The federal government has long been involved in networking research initiatives, before the ARPANET Project. Its involvement is motivated in part because of its specialized needs, for example, to coordinate data communications across the nation among its laboratories and agencies and because of the particular requirements of government agencies. Also, because development of networking as a national resource is crucial to national interests, the federal agencies, in partnership with universities and the private sector, undertake long-term, high-risk projects, which are generally outside the domain of private research. As a consequence, several federal agencies funded extremely important networking research initiatives in the 1990s, which have accomplished much to provide a foundation for the next-generation Internet. Many of these projects are ongoing today.

Since the Internet began as a Defense Advanced Research Projects Agency project, the federal government has been a major contributor to its research and development. The federal government has also been a major contributor to many other areas of research and development in computing, communications, and information technology, even though these contributions are a modest portion of its overall budget. The return on these investments, however, has been significant, especially with regard to its support for basic science and long-term research in technology.

Currently, federally funded research and development in information technology is coordinated through Computing, Information, and Communications Research and Development programs, which have succeeded the High Performance Computing and Communications (HPCC) program. These programs are organized into several program component areas (PCAs), including: High End Computing and Computation (HECC), High Confidence Systems (HCS), and Large Scale Networking (LSN), which incorporates the Next Generation Internet (NGI) initiative. The NGI initiative is a recently established government initiative in which major agencies are cooperating to create next-generation Internet capabilities to allow for enhanced support for their core missions, as well as to advance the state-of-the-art in advanced networking.

Large Scale Networking

The Large Scale Networking (LSN) research and development project is directed at ensuring ongoing leadership in high-performance network communications by advancing networking technologies, services, and performance. LSN projects coordinate the operation and peering of advanced federal networks, including the Department of Defense's Defense Research and Engineering Network (DREN), the Department of Energy's Energy Sciences Network (ESnet), NASA's Research and Education Network (NREN), the multiagency, Washington, D.C.-based Advanced Technology Demonstration Network (ATDnet), and the vBNS. Research areas of special emphasis for FY98 and FY99 included network-based applications, satellite technologies, specialized connectivity programs, network security, and global communications.

The primary focus of the LSN initiative in 1998 was the Next Generation Internet (NGI) program, which was announced in 1996 by the federal government as an initiative to do the following:

> Demonstrate new applications that meet important national goals and missions: Higher-speed, more advanced networks will enable a new generation of applications that support scientific research, national security, distance education, environmental monitoring, and healthcare.

Next Generation Internet

The federal government's Next Generation Internet (NGI) initiative was established to ensure continued national leadership in high-performance communications and networking through a wide range of specific projects. The NGI initiative is directed at developing the foundation for twenty-first century networks—communications systems that are significantly more powerful than the current Internet with speeds that are at least 100 times those of the current Internet. This program, part of the broader Large Scale Networking (LSN) program, provides funding to federal agencies for research that will advance communications and networking technologies, primarily through innovative research and development and through the experimentation, testing, and early deployment of advanced networking systems and infrastructure.

The general goals of the NGI are to develop revolutionary new applications—capabilities not possible on the current Internet—and to conduct research and development in the key areas of advanced, high-performance networking. The intent is to provide for a networking infrastructure that will meet the needs of next-generation networks, for example, as described earlier in this book.

The general goals of this initiative are formulated in three primary goals:

1. To conduct research on advanced end-to-end networking technologies, including differentiated services, particularly for digital media, network management (including allocation and sharing of network resources), reliability, robustness, and security.
2. To prototype high-performance network testbeds for testing scalability of networks and advanced applications.
3. To develop revolutionary new applications.

The first goal consists of efforts, led by DARPA, to conduct research and development in advanced networking technologies and to undertake experiments with those technologies.

The NGI program also prototypes high-performance network testbeds for systems scale testing of advanced technologies and services. The second goal, which is led by the National Science Foundation, therefore, provides for the coordinated development of the NGI network infrastructure to interconnect various NGI sites. Specifically, this goal is directed at accomplishing two primary objectives: connecting 100 sites at 100 times the speed of the general Internet, end-to-end, through all network components linking those sites and connecting 10 sites at speeds 1,000 times the current Internet—over 1 gigabit per second. The objective of connecting these 10 sites is to be achieved in the second phase of the development of the NGI infrastructure. Ultimately, the goal of this program is to provide for terabits per second (Tbps) and even terabytes per second networks.

Initially, the vBNS is providing much of the infrastructure to accomplish the first goal. This part of the NGI project provides for agency participant networks to be interconnected, including DREN, NREN, and ESnet. This part of the NGI project also provides for participant sites to have interconnectivity to advanced research networks such as DARPA's terabit SuperNet, to advanced academic networks, and to international advanced research networks—through the STAR TAP.

The third major goal of the NGI program is to develop advanced applications that will utilize the enhanced power and capability of these networks. The broad spectrum of advanced applications described in Chapter 3 are examples of the applications that are targeted by this part of the NGI project. Also, part of this effort is the creation of an environment for the development of those compelling applications.

In 1999, NGI funding was provided to DARPA, NSF, NASA, the Department of Energy (DOE), the National Center for Standards and Technology (NIST), the National Library of Medicine (NLM), and the National Center for Research Resources (NCRR).

The National Science Foundation and NGI

As noted earlier, the NSF is a major participant in the NGI, especially the vBNS. Within the NSF, the Directorate of CISE's Advanced Networking Infrastructure and Research division (ANIR) Advanced Networking Infrastructure program provides for the national high-performance infrastructure required by the scientific research and education community in the United States. An applied research program supports the development, implementation, and evaluation of leading-edge experimental high-performance networks and related technologies. Many projects provide support for distributed information technology, such as remote use of specialized facilities, including instrumentation and supercomputers.

The ANIR supports two basic research programs (Networking Research and Special Projects in Networking Research) and one experimental facility program, the Advanced Networking Infrastructure (ANI) program. The goal of the first two programs is to support research in technical areas that will lead to an enhanced understanding of the global information infrastructure and to create a foundation for future advancements.

The focus of the Networking Research program is the fundamental science and technology required to facilitate efficient high-performance transfer of information through networks and distributed systems. Special Projects in Networking is a program that focuses on network research areas that emphasize the importance of those technologies to the convergence of communications and computing, for example, multidisciplinary theoretical and experimental networking research projects. The NSF also assists in the development of leading-edge and experimental advanced networking infrastructure to enable its use in support of research and education.

Defense Advanced Research Projects Agency

The Defense Advanced Research Projects Agency (DARPA) also has established a number of key NGI projects. From the time of the origin of the ARPANET, DARPA has been on the leading edge of advanced networking innovation. Its role in the NGI initiative is to create innovative network capabilities that will enable revolutionary new applications. Projects include a wide range of experimental research for advanced networking technology, segmented into two parts, Network Engineering and Quorum.

The Network Engineering initiative is designing and implementing a network architecture that will provide for network growth by a factor of 100 and reduce costs by automating network planning and reducing the need for support. The Quorum initiative is developing a model of network computing that is dynamically adaptive to the requirements of applications. Its goal is to develop an architecture that takes into consideration the total network system from application through network interfaces, enabling network services, operating systems, middleware, and resource management layers.

DARPA research projects tend to be those that are established to provide for major innovative technology advances—major leaps forward rather than incremental improvements in technologies.

DARPA's SuperNet, Extensible Networking, and Other Projects

Another Defense Advanced Research Projects Agency NGI initiative is the development of a foundation for terabit per second (Tbps) networks, the SuperNet project, which will require research and development related to the design and creation of ultra-high-speed, multiplexing, switching, and transmission technologies. The SuperNet initiative will also develop advanced technologies for configuration management and functional control and for providing distributed network-based resources to tens of sites across the Tbps network.

Other DARPA initiatives are directed at Extensible Networking, which allows for new modes of advanced networking, for example, wireless gigabit per second (Gbps) networks and Internets that integrate low orbiting satellites. Another set of projects involves deeply networked systems, which allow for innovative technologies and techniques for application and network system integration. DARPA has also established a number of projects in optical networking using WDM, especially through the Broadband Information Technology program. Most of these projects support development leading to Tbps networks.

Advanced Technology Demonstration Network

The Advanced Technology Demonstration Network (ATDnet), which is based in the Washington, D.C., area, is an ATM over SONET OC48-based testbed network for research and experimentation related to developments required by Gbps networking technology and advanced applications. Although its initial fastest path was OC12 (622 Mpbs), it serves experiments that are not possible on other types of advanced research networks. It is used by federal agencies and research partners. ATDnet is linked to other testbeds, a DREN testbed and the Multi-dimensional Applications Gigabit Internet-working Consortium (MAGIC) testbed, by the Advanced Communications Technology Satellite ATM Internetwork.

ATDnet is a regional testbed; a number of others that have been established are national in scale.

Collaborative Advanced Interagency Research Network

Collaborative Advanced Interagency Research Network (CAIRN) is a national networking research testbed that allows for advanced research and experimentation with gigarouters and other advanced facilities. CAIRN replaced an earlier testbed, the DARPA Research Testbed (DARTNET), established in 1991. It is funded primarily by the Information Technology Office of DARPA but also by the NASA EOSDIS Office and the National Science Foundation. Almost all "research networks" that primarily provide production support for advanced applications also support some form of networking research. Although they also support network technology research, research networks are expected to be highly reliable and therefore can support only limited types of network experimentation. They cannot allow for the type of experiment that would cause outages or performance problems. CAIRN provides a testbed for advanced computer network-protocol research and development—a network that "can be broken," which is a particularly rare and valuable asset for network researchers.

Experiments have been conducted on this network with many new and emerging protocols, including those that were also deployed on the vBNS and ESnet, such as native multicast, a native mode IPv6 implementation with related protocols, with resource reservation methods (RSVP), IP security, and new techniques for supporting latency-intolerant applications. A GATED v6 implementation is also planned. Another major area of activity is mobile environments for wireless communications.

Multiwavelength Optical Networking Technology

A cooperative NGI project involving Bell Labs is the Multiwavelength Optical Networking Technology (MONET) testbed on the East Coast. This project is focused on developing capabilities for optical networking, based on DWDM (Dense Wave Division Multiplexing), including component development and management techniques. The MONET initiative was established to determine the optimal means to provide multiwavelength optical networking nationally that will support commercial and government applications. The primary objective is to integrate network architectural concepts, advanced technology, network management, and business drivers to achieve transparent multiwavelength optical networking that is high capacity, high performance, cost-effective, and reliable.

National Transparent Optical Network Consortium

The National Transparent Optical Network Consortium (NTONC) consists of NORTEL, Pacific Bell, Sprint, Columbia University, Hughes, Lawrence Livermore National Laboratory, United Technologies, Uniphase Telecom, Case Western Reserve University, University of California, San Diego, and Rockwell. NTONC is managing a testbed, prototype, next-generation network (NTON). It is being built on the West Coast as an experiment in creating an all-optical network, based on WDM and using SONET as its foundation technology. Eventually, this network will attempt to communicate data at multiple Tbps.

Lawrence Livermore National Laboratory Photonics Program

Many advanced networking projects have been established at the Department of Energy's national laboratories. The work at Argonne National Laboratory has been noted in Chapter 3 (also see discussion of Globus at the beginning of this chapter). Another example is the Lawrence Livermore National Laboratory (LLNL) Photonics Program, which works with the LLNL Advanced Telecommunications Program and the NTONC; it is focused on innovation in optical components for high-speed optical-fiber data links. The lab has capabilities for modeling system components and network configurations; fabricating semiconductor optoelectronic devices and other components; and packaging, testing, "ruggedizing," and integrating components into systems. The lab's approach is based on a concept of hierarchical methods for multiplexing data, including the use of time division multiplexing (TDM), WDM, and subcarrier multiplexing (SCM).

Research and development projects at LLNL include those focused on minimizing dispensation and loss in high performance (for example, OC48 and

OC192), long-distance optical transmissions (including projects focused on semiconductor optical amplifier technology), all optical switching technologies for TDM, secure systems, innovative DWDM chips, SCM and WDM devices optimized for minimal dispersion, high-speed interfaces, multiple separate transmissions over separate wavelengths, and specialized monitoring equipment such as high-sensitivity external modulator links.

Advanced Networking in Higher Education

Higher education has always had a prominent role in the development and deployment of the Internet, especially those activities related to the deployment of NSFnet starting in 1987. In the early 1990s, the U.S. higher-education community noted the inadequacies of the existing commodity Internet for advanced applications and research, and it began to address the issue by developing a number of policy papers setting recommendations for solutions. Some of these policy papers were developed by EDUCOM (now EDUCAUSE). These included several documents developed by an academic networking policy conference in 1995, which produced, in September 1995, a proceedings report entitled *Higher Education and the NII: from Vision to Reality*. As a subsequent activity, a small committee, the "Monterey Futures Group," developed a policy paper urging the creation of a new advanced Internet (Educom 1995). These reports noted that the privatization and widespread commercialization of the first-generation Internet led to congested conditions that significantly hindered advanced research and education.

Also, these reports pointed out that new network infrastructure and technologies were required to develop next-generation Internet applications. This community noted that Internet applications traditionally tended to be produced as additions to advances in networking research and development. Increasingly, however, network applications were beginning to outpace existing network capabilities in many areas, especially performance. Subsequently a few early, advanced networks were established to provide for the needed capability, such as the vBNS and MREN, but it was clear that a national higher-education effort was required as well.

University Corporation for Advanced Internet Development

On October 1, 1996, representatives from 34 research universities met in Chicago to establish a process to create and implement next-generation network applications and technologies for research, education, and other activities associated with research universities, such as health care and digital library capabilities. Later, they were joined by more than a hundred other universities. This effort, the Internet2 project, was later reorganized as the University Corporation for Advanced Internet Development (UCAID). The initial organizational effort was led by Gary Augustson of Pennsylvania State University. Subsequently, in 1997, UCAID was formed, with Doug Van Houweling as president.

The goal of UCAID is to assist the coordination of advanced networking development within higher education. UCAID's mission is to do the following:

> Facilitate and coordinate the development, deployment, operation and technology transfer of advanced, network-based applications and network services to further U.S. leadership in research and higher education and accelerate the availability of new services and applications on the Internet.

Currently, UCAID has almost 150 university members and more than 40 corporate members.

UCAID has established two major projects, the Internet2 (I2) project, which is focused on applications, and a related infrastructure project, Abilene, a national networking infrastructure project, described later in this chapter.

Internet2

Some of the more specific goals of UCAID, beyond encouraging corporate and governmental partnerships, pursued in part through the Internet2 project, are to demonstrate new applications that can enhance education and research, including the ability to conduct and collaborate on experiments, to enhance the network delivery of educational services enabled by an advanced infrastructure.

To accomplish its mission, UCAID initially formulated an Applications Working Group and an Engineering Working Group. In addition, the Internet2 Applications Group was established to focus on developing tools for distance learning, applications sharing, digital video, instructional systems, virtual labs, digital libraries, real-time simulation and modeling, large-scale computation, large-scale database processing, and teleimmersion. Internet2 development projects are planned to utilize object-oriented programming, component-based software, object request brokering, and dynamic run-time binding. The Internet2 project also explores concepts of directory services, authorization and authentication services, APIs for application support and services, metadata services, and network service negotiation (applications will negotiate for levels of network resources, such as bandwidth, QoS, and other services).

One Internet2 project is developing a national digital video network (I2-DVN, led by iCAIR; see text that follows), which will provide services for video-conferencing, video-on-demand, and live transmission over a multicast cloud supported by an advanced infrastructure. Another project is the Internet2 Distributed Storage Initiative (I2-DSI at the University of Tennessee), which is developing capabilities for network-based services such as caching and replication.

Abilene

With regard to network infrastructure, UCAID's goals, which are pursued primarily through the Abilene project, include facilitating the development, deployment, and operation of an affordable high-performance network infrastructure capable of differentiated services (QoS), experimenting with new network technologies, and encouraging interoperability and technology transfer.

Abilene is a partnership involving several corporations, including Qwest Communications International, Inc., Northern Telecom Ltd. (Nortel), and Cisco Systems Inc. Its principal goal is to develop and deploy an IP over OC48 (2.4 Gbps) SONET high-availability, national backbone network that will connect UCAID GigaPOPs and support the advanced applications being developed by UCAID (see Figure 4.1).

The Abilene Project was established to give UCAID members a cost-effective, high-performance backbone network capable of supporting advanced applications. It also offers facilities that support advanced network research, including exploration of alternative network designs and facilities for testing new capabilities before they are generally deployed. This project was established in part to stimulate industry to advance the state of production

Abilene Network
February 1999

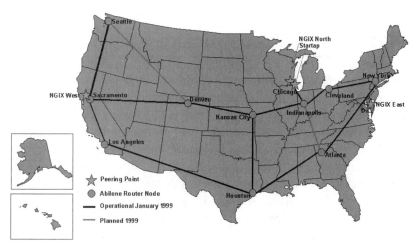

Figure 4.1   Initial Abilene backbone. (Permission of UCAID.)

networking and to allow for more rapid technology transfer so that advanced capabilities would be widely deployed.

GigaPOPs, which provide for regional connectivity, will be able to use Abilene for interconnectivity among GigaPOPs and for providing their region with access to Internet2 services. Although initially the backbone will be OC48, Abilene is also implementing a few OC192c (9.6 Gbps) routers. In the early phase of Abilene, GigaPOPs will have OC12c and OC3c links.

Another goal is to provide for a separate testbed network that would allow for testing of advanced network capabilities before they are introduced into the production network. Network services currently being developed for the Abilene network are differentiated services (a QoS implementation, with an initial testbed experiment planned for the mid-1999), multicasting, advanced security, and capabilities for authorization and authentication.

To support this project, Qwest Communications International, Inc., has contributed the use of a portion of its national high-capacity fiber network and a significant number of points of access throughout the continental United States. Nortel supports the project by contributing to the development and provisioning of Abilene, while Cisco provided 12000 Series routers.

UCAID also supports access to other advanced networks, such as the vBNS and other federal research networks. In 1998, the NOC for the Abilene network was established for the Abilene network at Indiana University.

One of the projects closely related to the Abilene network deployment is a Qbone testbed (that is, a quality-of-service testbed), which is implementing a version of DiffServ as a research project. Part of this project is a test implementation of a model of a bandwidth broker, which will provide for network resource signaling and allocation techniques across separate network domains.

Global Information Infrastructure

Researchers, and other communities, require high-performance connectivity to remote sites, including international broadband network connectivity, for example, to the European Center for Nuclear Physics (CERN) in Switzerland—and even to extremely remote instrumentation sites. Such connectivity is required also for international collaborative projects and for sharing of large amounts of data. The Global Information Infrastructure (GII) international initiative was established by the federal government to encourage the advancement of global communications and infrastructure development and collaborative applications development. The initiative has sponsored a number of innovative international showcase projects.

Science, Technology, and Research Transit Access Point

In 1997, Tom De Fanti, director of the Electronic Visualization Laboratory of the University of Illinois at Chicago, proposed to the National Science Foundation (under the International Division's High Performance International Internet Services program) the development of the Science, Technology, and Research Transit Access Point (STAR TAP) as a means to enhance collaborative research among scientists worldwide. De Fanti, working with collaborators throughout the world on supercomputing projects, was among the first to recognize the crucial importance of international advanced connectivity. The STAR TAP interlinks international advanced research networks and national networks at the Ameritech Advanced Data Services Network Access Point (the AADS NAP), a high performance ATM switching facility in Chicago.

The STAR TAP is the only facility in the world that allows for a cooperative interconnection point among numerous international advanced networks. Early connections to the STAR TAP were established by CA*Net (managed by CANARIE, the Canadian advanced research, industry, and education network), TANnet (Taiwan), SINGAREN (Singapore), and the vBNS. Later, they were joined by the Asia Pacific Advanced Networking organization (APAN) through the TRANsPac project, led by Mike McRobbie, CIO of Indiana University as well as SURFnet, NORDUnet and a high performance link to CERN.

International Center for Advanced Internet Research

In July 1998, Northwestern University, IBM, Ameritech, and Cisco Systems announced the creation of the International Center for Advanced Internet Research (iCAIR), providing a focal point for leading-edge Internet research and innovation. iCAIR undertakes cooperative projects with corporations, universities, and regional, national, and international research and education networks. It focuses on large-scale projects in advanced, next-generation Internet research, innovation, and experimentation. iCAIR has established projects to develop advanced applications, advanced network middleware and metasystems, and new types of network infrastructure. Currently, iCAIR is developing advanced applications (including those based on large-scale multimedia), advanced Internet middleware, and infrastructure capabilities. One project is a large-scale international quality-of-service testbed, as part of the Qbone project. Many of these projects have been undertaken in partnership with advanced networking organizations worldwide.

The Next-Generation Internet Enterprise

If the new economy is based on digital information flowing over high-performance networks, then individual organizations must also undergo a communications transformation to provide for ubiquitous, advanced, digital communication services for its members. The macrocosm convergence of digital information will inevitably be reflected within the microcosm of the twenty-first century organization. At the organizational level, and especially at the local level, next-generation Internet projects must deal with basic issues of ensuring end-to-end performance. These issues include transition strategies from legacy networks, management policy options, shared governance of resources among multiple organizational units, resource allocation policies, priorities, and implementations of organizational QoS definitions and management tools.

Just as in wide area networks, a common organizational architectural strategy has been to begin with a new organizational backbone; often these have been based on ATM switches (IP over ATM, although Gigabit Ethernet is beginning to appear). For example, the new high-performance external connection is attached to an ATM switch attached to a router that is interconnected to the legacy network. The coexistent legacy network continues to be operational as the new backbone is built out.

Initially, when an organization is upgrading to a high-performance network, the backbone network is brought through links into areas where it is most needed, for example, in a research lab or media center, with the understanding that the legacy network will slowly be replaced with the new system as resources allow. Fiber to the desktop is not always required. Most end-stations require only 100 Mbps and can utilize 100BaseT; few require 155 Mbps ATM.

High-performance NICs for desktop units are currently reasonably priced, two to several hundred dollars, and one day such functionality will probably be part of the standard chip set within a computer. For large-scale high-performance applications, OS tuning may be required, that is, tuning TCP stacks for large windows and implementing other adjustments. Public information on OS tuning for high-performance networks is still fairly scarce, although some Web sites post such information (www.ncne.net).

Delivering the Next-Generation Internet to the Home

A frequently asked question about the next-generation Internet is "When will the capabilities of the next-generation Internet be available within the home?" Given that the Internet is one of the most rapidly proliferating technologies in history, deployment to the home should occur quickly, more quickly than the deployment in the past of utilities, such as the telephone, which are now commonplace. In a few areas, 10 Mbps to the home is available today. Singapore already has a widely deployed national fiber infrastructure and, therefore, may be the first nation in the world with virtually universal advanced data communications (described in Chapter 5).

Future scenarios involve planning for networks that will provide speeds of gigabits per second to the home. This deployment will follow a traditional technology development and implementation cycle, with initial production occurring within specialized sites, such as research centers, selected universities, government agencies, and corporate sites, as well as related locations.

After that first phase, the advanced Internet will more likely be deployed to large government, university, and corporate organizations, then to large population centers and areas of commercial concentration. Finally, the advanced Internet will generally be deployed to other areas. Of course, by then the current "next-generation Internet" will be advanced only in terms of today's technology and capability, so it will actually be the previous-generation Internet. Meanwhile, newer generations of Internet technology will be cycling through the technology spiral (mentioned in Chapter 2).

Future Tasks

The advanced infrastructure requirements for a national next-generation network remain largely conceptual; consequently the technical specifications that will meet those requirements are also still in initial stages of formulation. Theoretical approaches to the problems implicit in tens of billions of easy-to-use IP devices sharing a global digital grid can be formulated. The behavioral reality in implementation, however, often has proven to be quite different than the projections of theoretical models. Much more needs to be accomplished in the area of requirements analysis, not only with regard to specific emerging advanced applications, but also with regard to the specific behavior of multiple advanced applications utilizing the same infrastructure, especially as those applications increase in volume and complexity of use. Additional research, simulation, prototype development, and testbed experimentation of advanced components and systems are crucial.

Also, in Internet time, design, development, and early implementation cannot wait for complete requirements analysis and testing. Rapid development and early implementation of advanced technologies are two more critical imperatives. Early deployment must be accomplished even as the core technologies utilized undergo rapid change. Similarly, mechanisms must be developed to provide for the ongoing management and continuous improvement of dynamically changing infrastructure.

The GRID: Blueprint for a New Computing Infrastructure

Some of the major implications for the information infrastructure that will support the twenty-first-century digital economy were explored in a recent book, entitled *The GRID: Blueprint for a New Computing Infrastructure*, developed and edited by Ian Foster and Carl Kesselman, the principal architects of Globus 1999 (Foster 1999). The title is a metaphoric description of a distributed high-performance computing infrastructure—regional and national "computational grids" that provide ubiquitous computational power. The analogy is derived from the power grids that provide universal electrical services. Larry Smarr, Director of NCSA, has presented this concept of an Alliance National Technology Grid in a number of forums, and has contributed as a first chapter to *The Grid* an essay on "Grids in Context," which notes that "it will become clear that the development and deployment of interconnected and persistent [information technology] national-scale grids are one of the major activities helping to shape the 21st Century" (Smarr 1999). Such Grids will depend on a universal digital-communication Grid, which provides for access to an almost infinite range of digital information, services, and powerful, new information-based capabilities.

Components of the Grid will include advanced applications, as well as the tools and environments for creating and maintaining them, including those based on high-performance distributed computation; real-time, widely distributed, instrumentation systems; data-intensive computing; and advanced VR, such as that based on CAVE technology (described in Chapter 3). The Grid will provide for a wide range of core services on which those applications will depend for such capabilities as scalability, performance, reliability, security, and interoperability. In part these capabilities will be provided by new generations of sophisticated middleware, that is, advanced network-based services. Other Grid, or Grid related, initiatives include the NASA Information Power Grid, the NPACI metasystems project, DOE Collaboratories, and the DOE ASCI DISCOM. Also related is the iGRID project at the Electronic Visualization Laboratory at the University of Illinois, Chicago, which demonstrates international collaborations using distributed resources over high speed networks and STAR TAP facilities.

As noted earlier, the Globus project is developing an integrated set of basic grid services, the "Globus tool kit," which indicates how such systems will be designed. Globus provides for functionality without being tied to a particular programming model, provides services traditionally supplied by commodity computing, and supports an information-based approach to performance requirements. The Globus Metacomputing Directory Service

(MDS) provides a mechanism that allows for information about system components and states within the grid to always be available to applications. Eventually the grid may rely on a complete suite of services, for example, one that may be provided through metasystems.

Metasystems

Currently, researchers at NPACI and at a few other research centers are investigating metasystems. A metasystem provides applications with a large number of highly distributed computing and network resources (computational processors, databases, files, instruments, and I/O systems), as if they were local and provides them with a high degree of transparency, so that utilization does not require complex procedures. NPACI does not support basic research into metasystems, but rather implements emerging components developed elsewhere and provides for hardening and integration of those components.

Advanced Infrastructure: A World of Intelligent Fiber

Fiber will be everywhere, supplemented by broadband wireless where necessary (such as with 20 Mbps to 1 Gbps and higher Local Multipoint Distribution Networks). Optical networks were developed for long-distance transmission (optimizing fiber capacity through multiplexed SONET signals), but the components developed for those purposes now are increasingly attractive for almost any distance. Researchers discovered that DWDM technology allowed for light to be divided into a few wavelengths, then several, then several dozen, and now well over 100; perhaps several hundred are possible (although not currently commercially available). At the same time, researchers are finding ways to allow each wavelength to carry increasing volumes of bits, first a few gigabits, then tens of gigabits per wavelength. Also, various intelligent, dynamic means of controlling that volume of traffic—ultimately multiple terabits per second (Tbps)—are being devised.

Advanced Network Management

Network management is a special challenge for advanced, high-performance Internets. IP has been declared as the Convergence Layer; consequently functionality that had been at Layers 1 and 2 are being migrated to Layer 3. Layer 3 functionality may provide for the type of reliability, self-healing, interface adaptability, traffic management, and routing management capabilities that are currently the domain of Layers 1 and 2. Some hybrid management schemes have also been proposed, with functionality at multiple layers.

Network Weather Service

Given the high volume of traffic and high speeds of the next-generation Internet, one question concerns how it can quickly recover from fault conditions. It seems as if it is necessary to know that the error condition will happen before it occurs. This concept is one of the premises behind an innovative project called the Network Weather Service (NWS), under development by Richard Wolski at the University of California, San Diego, which provides for the dynamic forecasting of network and computational performance over a specified time period. NWS is currently utilized to gather information on the performance of the vBNS by assessing current status data that is then analyzed by complex numerical algorithms to project future conditions. Predictions are gauged against real results to calibrate the system continually.

Conclusion

Information technology will be the basis of the twenty-first century economy, and, in anticipation of its needs, the evolution of a second-generation Internet is now well underway. These multiple initiatives and projects are important, and with other substantial quality efforts, have moved the development of the Internet forward. Continual advances in digital communications technology will allow for the creation of numerous new applications and infrastructures.

Yet, the movement toward the twenty-first-century digital communications revolution has barely begun. Much remains to be accomplished—the blueprint for future digital communications is still in development. Many key areas remain only partially addressed, and some major challenges have not been dealt with at all. There are many difficult technical and other challenges to overcome before this vision of a ubiquitous, national, high-performance broadband infrastructure can become a reality.

References

This chapter describes multiple advanced networking initiatives, each of which comprises numerous projects and secondary initiatives. Many of the best sources of information on these rapidly progressing projects are Web based. In addition, the development of core technologies can be tracked through computation and networking technology journals.

The Committee on Computing, Information, and Communications publishes key documents that guide federal technology research projects.

Networked Computing for the 21st Century. 1998. A Report by the Subcommittee on Computing, Information, and Communications R&D, Committee on Technology, National Science and Technology Council Office of Science and Technology Policy: Washington D.C.: www.ccic.gov

Metropolitan Research and Education Network (MREN): www.mren.org

National Science Foundation: www.nsf.gov

Next Generation Internet project: www.ngi.gov

Very-High-Speed Backbone Network Service (vBNS): www.vbns.net

Globus

The I-WAY Project and the subsequent Globus project have been well-documented. The following information provides sources of overviews and additional references.

Foster, Ian and Carl Kesselman. 1997. "Globus: A Metacomputing Infrastructure Toolkit." *International Journal of Supercomputing Applications.* 11(2):115-128.

Korab, Holly and Maxine Brown, ed. 1995. *Challenge Applications on the I-WAY, Virtual Environments and Distributed Computing at SC '95*; "GII Testbed and HPC." December ACM/IEEE Supercomputing '95. New York.

1998 Proceedings from the Second Annual Globus Retreat August Chicago, Illinois, can be found at the Globus Web site: www.globus.org

Additional information can be found at the Mathematics and Computer Science Division Web site at Argonne National Laboratory: www.anl.gov

Major National Testbeds

Collaborative Advanced Interagency Research Network (CAIRN): www.cairn.net

Multiwavelength Optical Networking Technology (MONET) Project: www.bell-labs.com/project/MONET

National Transparent Optical Network (NTONC) Project: www-phys.llnl.gov/H_Div/photonics/NTONC.html

Included among the early policy documents that led to establishing a national research and education network are the following:

1992 *Proceedings of the NREN Workshop*. September 1992. Washington D.C.: Interuniversity Communications Council, Inc.

1995 *Higher Education and the NII: From Vision to Reality*. September 1995. Monterey Conference Proceedings. Washington D.C.: Educom.

Information on the University Corporation for Advanced Internet Development (UCAID) and its various projects can be found at www.ucaid.edu

The International Center for Advanced Internet Research and its initiatives are described at www.icair.org

There are a number of first rate publications on the concept of a national technology grid. An excellent recent publication that addresses issues of advanced next-generation infrastructure is this title:

Foster, Ian and Carl Kesselman, ed. 1999. *The Grid: Blueprint for a New Computing Infrastructure*. San Francisco: Morgan Kaufmann. This title contains an extensive useful bibliography.

Smarr, Larry. 1999. "Grids in Context," in *The Grid: Blueprint for a New Computing Infrastructure*, pp. 1–13. San Francisco: Morgan Kaufman.

An article that presents the paths from the I-WAY project to the Grid is:

Stevens, Rick, P. Woodward, T. Defanti, C. Catlett. 1997. "From the I-WAY to the National Technology Grid." *Communications of the ACM* 40 (11).

URLs

American National Standards Institute: web.ansi.org/public.iisp

Computer Research Association: www.cra.org

Electronic Visualization Laboratory, University of Illinois, Chicago: www.evl.uic.edu

Internet Society: info.isoc.org/home.html

National Computational Science Alliance: www.ncsa.uiuc.edu

National Telecommunications and Information Administration: www.ntia.doc.gov

CHAPTER 5

International Next-Generation Internet Initiatives

International Advanced Networking: Overview

A general observation about international communications is that it is being transformed not only by technology but by privatization and restructuring. For most of the twentieth century, the majority of the world's telecommunications services and infrastructure were owned by governments and communications organizations provided services as protected monopolies. The United States has been fairly distinctive in having a communications system run by private companies. Currently, throughout the world, telecommunications organizations are being privatized to allow for more rapid response to new customer requirements and changing technologies.

One result of this global transformation is that more opportunities worldwide to design and deploy advanced Internets are occurring, and many initiatives have been established to take advantage of those opportunities. It is notable that almost all are academic, industry, and government partnerships. The information in this chapter about these worldwide initiatives is intended to be selective and illustrative, not comprehensive. Other international, advanced-networking projects have been established that are not described here. It is notable that the STAR TAP is an important facility for international interconnections among these facilities. A related effort is the Coordinating Committee for Intercontinental Research Networking (CCIRN), a consultative organization that promotes worldwide cooperation in research networking.

Canadian Network for the Advancement of Research, Industry, and Education

CANARIE, the Canadian Network for the Advancement of Research, Industry, and Education, is a not-for-profit research consortium that has been on the forefront of advanced network innovation for many years, including advanced network design and implementation. Because of CANARIE and its partners, a high-tech area near Ottawa has been referred to as Silicon Prairie North. This consortium is a partnership with more than 140 members, including the Canadian government, educational research institutions, and commercial companies. CANARIE is committed to advancing the information highway in Canada and has undertaken the funding and deployment of several major networking initiatives in Canada. Beginning in 1993, CANARIE established special programs for designing, developing, and deploying advanced communications infrastructure throughout Canada. The CANARIE program in advanced networking is directed by Bill St. Arnaud.

CA*net

In 1990, a Canadian national Internet, CA*net, was established to provide Internet services and interconnectivity among a wide range of participating member organizations. CA*net was the initial Canadian Internet backbone, and because it primarily served universities, it was funded by the National Research Council. This infrastructure is used for production as well as test-bed networks for advanced applications and technologies and facilities for interoperating with advanced networks developed by other nations at international connectivity points. In 1993, CANARIE undertook responsibility for upgrading CA*net (as discussed later in this chapter).

ITS

In 1995, the Board of CA*net noted that these types of general Internet services should be provided by commercial carriers and other network providers, who were beginning to offer a wide choice of connection and backbone options. In April 1997, CA*net, like the NSFnet before it in the United States, was commercialized. It was renamed Bell ITS, and its operation and management were assumed by Bell Advanced Communications (BAC) Canada. The backbone was upgraded to an IP over ATM OC3c network, and four links were provisioned to interconnect with the United States.

National Test Network

In 1995, CANARIE designed, deployed, and managed one of the world's largest ATM testbed networks—the National Test Network (NTN). The NTN project, which was established as a partnership with Bell Canada and AT&T Canada, interlinked 11 regional ATM test networks across Canada. NTN provided for Internet (TCP/IP) and asynchronous transfer mode (ATM) over DS-3/OC3c (45 Mbps/155 Mbps). Its primary goal was to test and to implement ATM services, technologies, and advanced applications. The NTN initiative was motivated by CANARIE's mandate to accelerate the development of Canada's advanced networking capabilities.

When completed, NTN was one of the largest high-speed test networks in the world, spanning over 3,000 miles from St. John's, Newfoundland, to Vancouver, British Columbia. High-performance connectivity was provided to Europe through Teleglobe and to remote areas through ATM satellite provided by Telesat Canada. Teleglobe is a telecommunications company with significant global transoceanic links and satellite systems. Tests of advanced applications and trials included advanced video and audio streaming, videoconferencing and other multimedia, virtual reality, distance education, and medical imaging. High-performance international links were also established and used for interoperability and applications testing.

CA*net II

In June 1997, the NTN was decommissioned, replaced by Canada's next-generation Internet initiative—the new CA*net II network. CANARIE designed and implemented the nationwide CA*net II as Canada's first national next-generation network. CA*net II provides for connections among 13 GigaPOPs, with IP over ATM (OC3c), and for international connectivity at the STAR TAP in Chicago and has an STM-1 (OC3c) connection to Sylt, Germany. Like MREN, CA*net II is built on commercial network facilities provided by BAC and AT&T Canada, not from a separate private network with leased links.

The CA*net II project parallels related projects in the United States noted in earlier chapters—the federal Next Generation Internet (NGI) initiative, including the vBNS, and the academic Internet2 project. The mission of CA*net II is to test and implement next-generation Internet applications, network services, and technologies, as well as to provide support for related advanced, meritorious research, especially those projects that cannot be supported through commercial Internet services. CANARIE supports advanced network-based applications through its Advanced Networking Applications

(ANA) Competition. These CA*net II research and development projects, as well as general management, are coordinated by an engineering group at the Advanced Research Development Network Operations Center (ARDNOC), a facility jointly managed by Bell Canada and CANARIE. CANARIE was one of the first international connections at the STAR TAP, in 1997, at DS-3, and later upgraded to an OC3c connection.

CA*net III

In February 1998, the Canadian national government announced a $55 million commitment to CANARIE to build a National Optical Internet network. In March 1998, CANARIE issued a request for information (RFI) to a few potential industry partners to design, develop, and implement this optical Internet network. CANARIE is currently provisioning for CA*net III, a Canadian Optical Network based on wave division multiplexing (WDM), with a potential for OC768 (40 Gbps), but with probable early deployment at OC192 (10 Gbps), although the router ports are OC48c. CA*net III is currently being developed as a testbed that showcases Canadian industry strengths in next-generation Internet products and services. In conjunction with CA*net II, the Optical Network provides exceptional communications support for advanced research and education applications.

CANARIE and its Bell Canada consortium (which includes Cisco Systems Canada Co., JDS Fitel, Newbridge Networks Corp., and Nortel) will develop and deploy the core of this third-generation network across Canada (east to west). CANARIE's collaborative approach provides opportunities for other carriers to participate in the associated research and development and to provide regional services. Unlike existing optical transport networks, which have been built primarily to support voice communications, CA*net III is being built specifically as an Internet network with voice traffic treated as just another form of data. With its substantial capacity to carry multimedia traffic, CA*net III will enable numerous health, research, educational, and commercial applications not possible on today's networks.

Asia Pacific Advanced Networking

There are many advanced networking initiatives in Asia Pacific, and a number of them are interconnected through the Asia Pacific Advanced Networking (APAN) initiative (described later in this chapter). The following section lists only a few, mainly those related to advanced Internets.

Japan

Japan has generally ranked second in listings of computers on the Internet, after the United States. Internet usage is fairly pervasive throughout the country, and adoption continues to accelerate. There are a number of next-generation network initiatives in Japan.

Japan's telecommunications industry is undergoing a significant transformational change as a result of its privatization. Prior to 1996, the industry was managed by the government; afterward it moved toward privatization and restructuring (to be completed in 1999). For example, before 1996, the Nippon Telegraph and Telephone Corporation (NTT) provided the majority of domestic communication services, while Kokusai Denshin Denwa Co., Ltd. (KDD) provided international services to 232 countries and territories worldwide.

In 1996, these two companies were authorized to enter into each other's markets. During that year, an agreement between the Ministry of Posts and Telecommunications (MPT) and NTT provided for the restructuring of NTT into three companies: NTT long-distance and two government-regulated companies, NTT East Japan and NTT West Japan. One consequence of this restructuring was a series of mergers and alliances among various communications carriers.

KDD owns and manages the transoceanic fiber links that are the basis of its international connections. KDD was one of the first Internet developers in Japan, and it is creating the Japan Information Highway, based on a 100 Gigabit fiber in Japan using WDM. KDD is also developing the KTH21 project—the KDD Terabit Highway for the twenty-first century, which will have a terabit per second (Tbps) backbone and international connections.

The National Center for Science Information Systems (NACSIS), which reports to the Ministry of Education, Science and Culture, has developed two networks. One is the Science Information Network, SINET, the largest research network in Japan, interlinking 600 institutions nationally and others internationally (including the United States, Europe, and Asia Pacific), and providing a range of services including X.25, frame relay, and ATM. The core network is approximately equivalent to OC3c, with some links at lower speeds, for example, DS-3 and 6 Mbps. A testbed project was established to connect five primary cities and eight associate cities with an OC3c ATM ring.

NACSIS provides for international connectivity. Japan is also a founding partner of APAN (described in a later section), through APAN-JP, and therefore is connected to the STAR TAP in Chicago, with a 45 Mbps link. In 1996,

NACSIS worked with DANTE (a European network described in a later section) to create a 2 Mbps link to Europe (EuropaNET). Japan also has established a 2 Mbps link to Thailand. And Singapore has a noncommercial 2 Mbps link to Japan. Japan also has established a few other low-speed links to other countries.

APAN-JP partners include the following:

- Imnet, an interministry network owned and operated by the Science and Technology Agency (or STA), which supports national science and technology policy development and coordination and supports advanced projects, especially large-scale advanced research projects).

- APII, International Joint Research and Experiment for Establishment of an Asia Pacific Information Infrastructure (an APEC Telecom network owned by the Communications Research Laboratory of the Ministry of Post and Telecommunications).

- RWCP, a distributed computing network owned by MITI.

- MAFFIN, a Ministry of Agricultural, Forest, and Fishery network owned by that Ministry, MAFF.

- WIDE, an academic network devoted to Internet research.

- SINET, advanced networking for research and education owned by MESS.

- WIDE, SINET, TISN/Genome, and related networks also interconnected to university networks such as the University of Tokyo Network (Utnet), which has a computing center that manages the TRAIN (Tokyo Regional Academic Internet).

IEEE 1394 over IP

Japan has established numerous projects in advanced networking. One particularly interesting example is presented here. Researchers at the WIDE project, with researchers at Keio University, are conducting interesting experiments with digital video streams on IEEE 1394 encapsulated over IP for long-distance transmission. The IEEE 1394 provides for a high-performance serial bus (cable and backplane) capable of 100 Mbps (soon perhaps 400 Mbps and above) that can simultaneously transmit asynchronous and isochronous data. It is a standard with a fairly simple architecture, aimed at small devices such as computer peripherals, consumer electronic devices, and specialized industrial instrumentation. This dynamically configurable protocol provides for mapping SCSI-3 commands to serial bus frames. Its limitation has been considered its transmission distance limitation. Encapsulated within IP, however, distance no longer is a factor.

During SC98 (Supercomputing 98), the first demonstration was held of streaming high-quality digital video from a digital video camera to a digital video television between the United States and Japan, using IEEE 1394 encapsulated within IP. IEEE 1394-based technology has the potential to allow for worldwide communications among ubiquitous consumer electronic devices that are capable of very high performance and speeds. If based on 1394, consumer devices linked to the Internet can intercommunicate freely—a handheld camera in the United States can send its data over the Internet to a PC storage device in Japan, and a display device in the United States can receive a digital video signal from a DVD appliance in France.

Nippon Telegraph and Telephone

Japan's Nippon Telegraph and Telephone (NTT) also supports a variety of advanced research laboratories and special projects, including those directed at optical networks, advanced media applications, and related technologies. NTT is currently developing an advanced digital network in Asia Pacific with a number of partners in other AP nations. Recently NTT also announced that it was linking GEMnet, its international experimental network, to the STAR TAP in Chicago to conduct experiments in advanced virtual reality between the University of Tokyo and the University of Illinois. This dedicated 6 Mbps link will use the CAVE technology from the EVL lab (see Chapter 3) and a specialized transmission technology called Media Cruising developed by NTT, Sony, and Keio University.

NTT recently announced the initiation of a two-year trial of a high-performance, advanced-service aggregation technology, multiple access over SONET/SDH (Mapos), which will interconnect five locations in Tokyo with fiber links. Ten companies and universities are taking part in the experiment.

Singapore

Singapore is one of the most forward-looking advanced-networking nations. SingAREN, the Singapore Advanced Research and Education Network, established in November 1997, is being developed by a consortium of academic, government, and industrial researchers to provide advanced application and networking research and development. SingAREN is being developed by a wide coalition of partners, the National University of Singapore (NUS), Nanyang Technology University (NTU), several other universities and four polytechnics, a number of research institutes and centers, the project team for the High Speed Network Testbed II, the Broadband Competency Center, and industrial partners. SingAREN is managed by the SingAREN Technology Center (STC) within Kent Ridge Digital Labs (KRDL, the largest government IT research organization in Singapore), along with NUS and NTU, especially the Center for Internet Research at NUS and the Network Technology Research Center to NTU.

SingAREN also has a partnership with the National Science and Technology Board (NSTB, one of its funding agencies), which has the mission of developing Singapore's capabilities in science and technology in support of designated industrial sectors. SingAREN is also funded by the Telecommunications Authority of Singapore.

SingAREN was one of the first international network connections at the Chicago STAR TAP (November 9, 1997), at 14 Mbps, and it has a 2 Mbps link to Japan and through that a link to Korea.

A particularly interesting project is Singapore ONE, the world's first nation-wide broadband network. One of SingAREN's missions is to provide advanced technology support for Singapore ONE, with regard to research and development of new technologies, early implementation, testing, international connectivity, and global collaborations. This project is a joint initiative being undertaken by the Telecommunication Authority of Singapore, the National Science and Technology Board, the National Computer Board, the Economic Development Board, and the Singapore Broadcasting Authority.

The goal of Singapore ONE is to provide advanced digital data services to every home, school, and office in the country, as well as to public spaces such as airport terminals. The Singapore ONE project provides both a production services environment and a test environment for advanced services. Digital services include various communication services, e-commerce, online shopping, online banking, entertainment ticketing and interactive entertainment, information services, educational services, digital libraries, and government services.

The backbone of the service is a core ATM-based broadband infrastructure configured for integrated digital communication services (data, voice, video), which is being built by 1-Net Singapore Pte Ltd. Local links are operated by Singapore Telecom and Singapore Cable Vision utilizing ADSL and hybrid fiber coaxial cable.

Republic of Korea

Advanced networking in the Republic of Korea is led in part by the Korea Advanced Institute of Science and Technology. Many advanced-networking initiatives in Korea are developed by government, industry, and academic consortiums. Korea is one of the leading APAN institutions; it is active in many of its projects, and it has a number of AP links. Through these efforts, Korea is involved with a large number of international collaborative development projects, including some with U.S. partners. Korea is connected to the STAR TAP through APAN.

The Development of the Asia-Pacific Advanced Network

The Asia Pacific Advanced Network (APAN) was established in June 1997 as a nonprofit international consortium. The importance of advanced networking services for research and development, especially for advanced communication technologies and applications, was recognized both at the Asia Pacific Economic Community (APEC) Testbed Forum in June 1996 and at the APEC Symposium for Realizing the Information Society in March 1996.

As a consequence of these considerations, a consortium was formed to design, develop, and implement an advanced network that would assist in the creation of advanced technologies and applications for leading-edge communications. The mission of APAN is to conduct research and development for advanced applications and services and to provide an advanced network environment for local research communities and for international collaboration. The founding members were Australia (ACSys), Japan (APAN-JP Consortium, APII/CRL, IMNet/STA, KDD, MAFFIN/MAFF, RWCP/ETL, SINET/NACSIS, WIDE/AI3), Korea (APAN-KR Consortium, APII/MIC, KT, Pubnet/NCA), and Singapore (SingAREN).

There are four major components of APAN: an AP hub; an AP highway, which interconnects countries; a Eurasian bridge; and a Pacific bridge. The APAN hubs are exchange points, initially in Seoul, Korea, and Tokyo, which use a common, advanced network meet point for traffic exchange and other services. The principal technology used is ATM cell exchange based on PVPs and PVCs, supported by routers and specialized application servers such as those for Mbone and caching services.

To create the Pacific bridge, APAN formed a partnership with the STAR TAP and with Indiana University to create the TransPAC project, led by Mike McRobbie at Indiana University. The project allows for interconnectivity with U.S. national research networks such as the vBNS and Abilene, as well as with advanced regional networks such as MREN. TransPAC provides for a 35 Mbps link (scheduled for a 100 percent increase in capacity in 1999) from the APAN countries to the STAR TAP, partially funded through an HPIIS award and partially through the Japan Science and Technology Corporation, which implements policies developed by the Science and Technology Agency (STA) of Japan. The initial TransPAC activities involved networks in Japan, Korea, Singapore, and Australia. The primary international carriers are AT&T and KDD.

Taiwan

Taiwan also has a number of major advanced-networking programs, including TANet II, the Taiwan Academic Network, an advanced research and education network established in 1990 to support advanced applications and network technology research. TANet II is supported by the National Center for High Performance Computing (Taiwan's supercomputing center), which is funded primarily by the National Science Council (equivalent to the U.S. National Science Foundation), Academic Sinica (AS), and the Ministry of Education, which is the network operator. (The National Science Council is responsible for next-generation Internet activities in Taiwan.) TANet II is ATM-based, with some network segments at OC12 and others at OC3. SIPNet, the Science Industrial Park Network, is a Taiwan NII project. International connectivity for advanced networking is provided by a 45 Mbps TANet II link to the STAR TAP. A second connection is a 45 Mbps link to MAE-West. Recently, Taiwan established a second-generation Internet project.

European Advanced Networking

The European Community (EC) began the process of deregulation of much of its telecommunication industry in 1997. The European Community provides for general international programs in advanced networking and national programs. An extensive testbed infrastructure dedicated to advanced research, including projects related to communications and networking, is funded by the European Advanced Communications Technologies and Services (ACTS) program. In addition to these efforts, many European National Research Networks (NRNs) have established national high-performance advanced network infrastructures, especially to interconnect universities and research institutes. The European Networking Policy Group (ENPG), comprised of representatives of European national governments who are responsible for policy development and funding for research networks, is an organization that provides a forum for information exchange and policy coordination.

Also, a number of European corporate efforts are directed at deploying experimental, preproduction or production advanced networks. For example, recently, Global TeleSystems Group (GTS) initiated a plan to create a European IP-based DWDM network on its Hermes Europe Railtel (HER) network. "EuroLink" is a consortium comprised of the Electronic Visualization Laboratory at the University of Illinois, Chicago, four charter European National Research Networks (described in following sections) and CERN, which link to the STAR TAP—NORDUnet, SURFnet, Israel's InterUniversity Computation Center (IUCC), and the CERN transatlantic network.

DANTE, TEN-34, TEN155, EuropaNET, et al.

Beginning in 1996, the European National Research Networks (NRN) established a project to design and build a high-performance (at 34 Mbps) Trans-

European Network Interconnect (TEN-34)—an IP network—with support from DG-XIII, Telematics for Research, and DG-III, Esprit, of the European Commission. EuropaNET was established to provide backbone services. The establishment of TEN-34 was an important event in European research networking because it created the first network that provided the whole European research community with high-speed IP. The core of the TEN-34 network was operational in April 1997; the project was funded through July 1998.

DANTE (Delivery of Advanced Technology to Europe, Ltd.) was selected as project manager for the TEN-34 network operations and management service. DANTE is a not-for-profit organization that has Research Association status with Cambridge University (U.K.). DANTE, which is owned by a large number of European National Research Networks, was established to coordinate and manage advanced network services for the European research community.

The central DANTE has overall responsibility for the Network Management Service; the Network Operations Center function for TEN-34 was provided by UKERNA (United Kingdom Education and Research Networking Association), the organization responsible for the operation and development of the UK NRN), centered at ULCC (University of London Computer Center, or ULCC). In the United Kingdom, advanced networking is provided by UKERNA's SuperJANET, which was also part of the TEN-34 project.

The primary role of DANTE has been to provide high-performance, best-effort IP service for the European academic and research community by operating an international backbone. The TEN-34 IP backbone service interconnected the NRN services in all Western European countries and several in Central Europe. It was based on IP over ATM at 34 Mbps using PVPs—PNOs provided the leased circuit capacity; for example, Unisource provided significant capacity with through access ports in the following countries: Sweden, Netherlands, Switzerland, Spain, and with Belgium sharing the Netherlands' access via a separate link to Amsterdam. In addition, Unisource also provided connectivity to the United Kingdom and Germany. In three places (London, Geneva, and Frankfurt), the basic service network interconnected with an ATM-based subnet that linked Austria, the Czech Republic, France, Germany, Greece, Hungary, Italy, Luxembourg, Slovenia, Switzerland, and the United Kingdom. A number of NRNs provided access capacities that allowed for speeds up to 45 Mbps.

As part of its EuropaNET service, DANTE provided for the coordination of some intercontinental connectivity. For example, as noted previously, in 1996 DANTE developed a 2 Mbps link from EuropaNET to NACSIS, the Japanese research network organization.

Task Force TEN

TEN-34 used its access to ATM to undertake various projects related to researching functions and features of ATM technology, primarily to develop a path to a successor network to TEN-34. For example, TEN-34 built an ATM testbed, with initial experiments carried out on the JAMES network (Joint ATM Experiment on European Services), using PVPs on leased lines—primarily 2 Mbps capacity—provided by European Public Network Operators (PNOs) that were the basis of the JAMES consortium. These efforts, conducted by Task Force TEN, were established within the activities of the Lower-Layer Technology Working Group of the Trans-European Research and Education Networking Association (TERENA—an organization that was established to support the development of high-quality international information and telecommunications infrastructure for research and education).

These experimental projects focused on IP over various ATM services. The TEN-34 network employed ATM CBR (constant bit rate) and, in a more limited way, VBR (variable bit rate), for production services. VBR could be used only on international links because it was not available in most local regions. Experimenters noted that if VBR services were to be used to carry IP traffic, for optimal results, the service should be configured with PCR-SCR (peak cell rate-sustainable cell rate) and MBS (maximum burst size) as large as possible. TCP-UDP over CBR, and IP and ARP over ATM, and basic ATM network management were fairly straightforward to implement and well understood.

Like other early adopters of SVCs, TEN-34 found a number of issues that made production implementation problematic, especially when directly linked to end-user applications. Only precise configurations or specialized management of the TCP would avoid operational instability. Some problems were circumvented by tunneling signaling information by using static CBR PVPs. IP routing over ATM with NHRP (Next Hop Resolution Protocol) was found to be too problematic for production. European ATM addressing was noted as an unresolved issue because E.164 (the ITU specification number for ATM address formats) and NSAP (Network Service Access Point) were both to be implemented requiring a universal translation mechanism as a basic network service. One experiment that transited CDV (cell delay variation) over concatenated ATM networks demonstrated that each switch in the path led to an increase in the variation of cell interarrival times on a CBR service. A potential solution was to allow for reshaping on long paths on ATM networks or to provide for more general traffic descriptors.

These experiences demonstrated the value of innovative initiatives such as TEN-34. Allowing for early experimentation within advanced networking provided information that has been invaluable to network providers.

TEN-155/QUANTUM

In July 1998, the original TEN-34 contracts among the NRNs and service providers expired. As a subsequent project, a number of the TEN-34 members prepared a proposal in response to the European Commission's Telematics for Applications Programme, Esprit, and ACTS (DGXIII). The proposal was to build an STM-1 (or OC3 speed, 155 Mbps) network. This capacity was already available in a number of European NRN nations. The QUANTUM project (QUAlity Network Technology for User-oriented Multimedia) was established to take advantage of multimedia services, especially QoS, for example, over native ATM, but also RSVP and IPv6. The consortium was formed by 16 national research networks and included DANTE, Renater (France, supported by GIP Renater and France Telecom), Deutsches Forschungsnetz (DFN, Germany, supported by Deutsche TeleKom), SWITCH (Switzerland), Telebit (Denmark), CSIC/RedIRIS (Spain), GRNET (Greece, supported by the Ministry of Development and OTE), and INFN (Italy, supported by the Ministry of Research and Telecom Italia).

Other European International Networking Projects

DANTE is the coordinating partner in the Q-MED project that is exploring potentials for interconnecting, through high-performance links, the research networks of Israel and Cyprus (MACHBA/ILAN and CYNET) to the TEN-155 network. Other partners are MACHBA/IUCC (the Israeli InterUniversity Computation Center) and CYNET/University of Cyprus (GRNET, and INFN/GARR). This project is related to the QUANTUM initiative, especially with regard to trial services testing, such as streaming media using ATM native QoS. The CAPE consortium, which comprises DANTE and DFN, is exploring the potential for additional connectivity between Europe and Asia Pacific.

Other European Research Networks

Other European research networks include ACOnet (Austria, supported by the Federal Ministry of Science and Post and Telekom, Austria), ARNES (Slovenia, supported by the Ministry of Science and Technology), BELNET (Belgium supported by the Ministry of Science Policy and UBN Belgium), CESNET (Czech Republic, supported by Telecom PTT), GARR (Italy, supported by the Ministry of Research and Telecom Italia), HEANET (Ireland), HUGARNET (Hungary, supported by MATAV), RESTENA (Luxembourg, supported by Enterprise des P&T), JANET/UKERNA (United Kingdom, supported by HEFCE and BT Worldwide), NASKand POL34 (Poland, supported by KBN), NORDUnet (Scandinavian countries), FCCN (Portugal, supported by FCCN), and SURFnet (Netherlands).

Netherlands: SURFnet

In the Netherlands, SURFnet, through its headquarters in Amsterdam, has been providing support for national and international connectivity for the Dutch research and education community for a number of years. SURFnet provides implementation of leading-edge techniques and infrastructure. Currently, SURFnet is leading an Innovative GigaPort project, which is a next-generation Internet, international-networking project. One recent link is an OC3 equivalent to New York, which continues to the STAR TAP via a DS-3 link. SURFnet is also supporting the innovative MESH project (Multimedia Services on the Electronic Super Highway), which is funded by the Dutch Ministry of Economic Affairs. The mission of this project is to enable advanced methods of collaboration over long distances through innovative applications in advanced network-based media.

Other collaborators on this project are Lucent Technologies, the Telematics Research Center, the Center for Telematics and Information Technology, and KPN Research. The Telematics Research Center is an independent research institute involved in a wide range of advanced networking projects. The Center for Telematics and Information Technology at the University of Twente undertakes scientific research in advanced telematics applications, including optimal designs for intersections among infrastructure, applications, and end-user environments. KPN Research is a technology organization that is part of the Royal Dutch PTT (Koninklijke PTT Netherlands), with a focus on advanced technology such as ATM.

Germany: Deutsche Forschungsnetz

In Germany, DFN operates a high-performance ATM-based national backbone network, B-WiN, based on a mesh of PVCs. This network has a link from an ATM switch in Frankfurt, Germany, to the United States. Reliability is enhanced for the transatlantic links through redundancy of equipment, for example, duplicate routers and switches.

Italy: GARR-B

Italy's NGI effort, INFN, managed by the Italian Ministry of Research, is developing the Italian research and education network, GARR-B, which is ATM OC3c based (The "B" represents broadband). This network provides services to approximately 65 universities, the National Research Institutes (including CNR, ENEA, and INFN), instrumentation sites (such as astronomical observatories), and other research centers. It was a participant in TEN-34 and is discussing participation in the successor initiative. Its point of origin for its next-generation link to the United States is Naples.

NORDUnet

A Scandinavian partnership, NORDUnet, provides for advanced networking for research and education networks for Denmark, Finland, Iceland, Norway, and Sweden, interlinking them and also providing them with international connectivity. Through a special arrangement, NORDUnet also provides for international connectivity to research and education networks in Estonia, Latvia, Poland, Ukraine, and Russia. The Scandinavian countries have one of the largest and fastest-growing Internet populations in Europe, on a per capita basis.

NORDUnet has supported connections to the United States for a number of years and now connects to the STAR TAP in Chicago from the NORDUnet operations center at Kungliga Tekniska Högskolan in Stockholm with a 45 Mbps link. NORDUnet and its partner organizations anticipate developing a next-generation NORDUnet, based on a proposal that was successfully presented to the Nordic Council of Ministers. Like the other next-generation network projects, this initiative would organize advanced network and applications research and development projects and international collaborations. One OC3 equivalent link is carried by Teleglobe to New York with a provision for a subset of traffic to be carried to the STAR TAP—DS-3 equivalent.

RENATER

Similarly, in France, RENATER, which supports advanced research and education networking, is designing and deploying a next-generation RENATER2 project along with other members of Groupement d'Internet Publique (GIP). The project provides for metro networking, national networking, European networking, and other international connectivity. RENATER2 has supported international broadband ATM connectivity to several other countries, including the United States, for several years. A new DS-3 equivalent link to the United States has also provided for a subset of traffic to be connected to the STAR TAP. Funding for RENATER is provided by the French Ministry for Research and the French Ministry for Industry.

SWITCH

Advanced, ATM-based networking in Switzerland is provided by SWITCH, which also works with CERN on advanced networking projects, including international connectivity. SWITCH is planning to provide an STM-1 (OC3c equivalent) to the United States in 1999. CERN, which is near Geneva, Switzerland, is a high-energy physics research center, where the World Wide Web was first created by Tim Berners-Lee. CERN established a link to the STAR TAP in 1999.

Other National Networking Initiatives

Russia, Eastern Europe, and the Middle East are also developing a variety of advanced networking initiatives. Several selected examples follow.

MirNET

There are several advanced networking initiatives in Russia. A primary Russian high-performance network links Moscow and St. Petersburg, but it is being expanded to other locations, including scientific research centers in Siberia. One is MirNET, which was developed by the Russian Institute of Public Networking, the Friends and Partners-Russia Foundation, and the Moscow State University with an American partner, the University of Tennessee, and funding from the National Science Foundation and the Russian Ministry of Science and Technology of the Russian Federation. (In Russian, "Mir" has several meanings—world, peace, and a community of individuals living and working together.) The Ministry of Science and Technology develops science and technology policy, provides legal and organizational support for science and technology transfer to the private sector, and supports national science and technology programs.

Rascom is MirNET's Russian carrier, and Teleglobe is its U.S. carrier. At this time, MirNET is a 6 Mbps link from Moscow to the STAR TAP funded in part by an HPIIS award made to the University of Tennessee, Knoxville, specifically its Telecommunications and Network Services (TNS) and its Center for International Networking Initiatives. An initial objective was to provide for interconnectivity to the vBNS.

Networking in Israel

Israel is developing a variety of advanced networking projects, in part to support its growing high-tech industrial sector. Among the advanced research projects are those focused on component development, including Java code for telecommunications. Its InterUniversity Computation Center has a DS-3 equivalent link connected to the STAR TAP. The potential to connect to the European TEN-155 (see Chapter 6) research network is being explored through the Q-MED project, led by DANTE, with MACHBA/IUCC (the Israeli InterUniversity Computation Center) as a partner, along with CYNET/University of Cyprus.

Project OXYGEN

Project OXYGEN, undertaken by CTR Group Ltd., is a $14 billion infrastructure project building a global Internet capability with 320,000 km of optical fiber cable, primarily under the ocean. Many thousands of miles have already been laid. This capability will allow communications carriers to purchase only required capacity, rather than excessive capacity in anticipation of provisioning for sudden spikes in demand. This project will bring advanced Internet capabilities to many areas of the globe where they currently do not exist. The impact of this project and related capacity development initiatives can already be seen in reduced trans-oceanic rates.

Conclusion

The next-generation Internet will be much more global than the current Internet. There is significant, important activity around the world, not only directed at expanding the current Internet but also at designing, developing, and implementing advanced Internet technologies and capabilities. These activities are giving rise to major opportunities for multi-international partnerships in advanced Internet applications, technology development, and deployment of advanced services.

References

The following sites referenced are primarily those related to research networking. Not all of these URLs reference next-generation Internet initiatives; some are national RENs that are candidates for participation in such initiatives.

Coordinating Committee for Intercontinental Research Networking: www.ccirn.org

International Connectivity Facility: Science and Technology Transit Access Point (STAR TAP): www.startap.org

The Internet Society: www.isoc.org

Canada

Canadian Network for the Advancement of Research, Industry, and Education (CANARIE): www.canarie.ca

Asia Pacific

AARNET 2 Australia Academic and Research Network: www.aarnet.edu.au

AI3 Asia Internet Interconnection Initiative: www.ai3.wide.ad.jp

APAN-Japan: www.apan.net/japan

APAN-Korea: www.apan.net/korea

Asia Pacific Advanced Network Consortium (APAN): www.apan.net

Asia Pacific Networking Group: www.apng.org

Australia (APAN member): www.acsysweb.com, www.aunic.net

CASNET China Academy of Science Network: www.cashq.ac.cn

CERNET China Education and Research Network:
www.wdu.cn/cernet/index.html

China (APAN member): www.bta.net.cn, www.edu.cn, www.cnc.ac.cn

HARNET Hong Kong Academic and Research Network:
www.hku.hk/jucc/harnet.html

Indonesia (APAN member): www.apjii.or.id

KREN Korea Education Network: www.kren.nm.kr

KREONet Korea Research Environment Open Network: www.kreonet.re.kr

Related networks in Japan: www.jst.go.jp, www.sta.go.jp, www.kdd.com

Related networks in Korea: www.kren.nm.kr, www.kreonet.re.kr, www.kor-
net.nm.kr, www.kria.or.kr, www.krnic.net

SINET Science Information Network Japan: www.sinet.ad.jp

SingAREN (APAN Member): www.singaren.net.sg

TANET Taiwan Academic Network: www.nchc.gov.tw

WIDE Project Japan: www.wide.ad.jp

Eastern Europe and Russia

Academic and Research Network of Slovenia (ARNES): www.arnes.si/

Azerbaijan Academy of Sciences: www.ab.az/texts/antaas.htm

Belarussian Academic and Research Network (UNIBEL):
www.unibel.by/index.asp

Croatian Academic and Research Network (CARNet): www.carnet.hr/

Lithuanian Academic and Research Computer Network (LITNET): neris
.mii.lt/litnet.litnetmii.html

Russia

MirNET: www.mirnet.org, www.friends-partners.org/fiends/mirnet/
home.html

Ukrainian Academic and Research Network (UARNet): alpha.icmp.lviv.ua/
UARNet/

Europe

Belgian Research Network (BELNET): www.belnet.be/

CESNET Internet Provider (Czech Republic) (CESNET): www.cesnet.cz/

Danish Research Network (DENet): info.denet.dk/

DANTE ATM experiments: www.dante.net/ten-34/DELIVERABLES/D11.3,
www.dante.net/ten-34/tf-ten/D14.1/D14.1-970606v3.ps

Delivery of Advanced Network Technology to Europe (DANTE) (trans-
European): www.dante.net, www.dante.net/ten-34/ten-34 broch.html

Deutsche Forschungsnetz (DFN): www.dfn.de

FCCN (Portugal): www.fccn.pt/RCCN/

Finnish University and Research Network (FUNET): www.funet.fi/

Greek Research and Technology Network (GRNET): www.grnet.gr/

Higher Education Authority Network (Ireland) (HEANet): web.hea.ie/

NORDUnet: www.nordu.net

Norwegian Academic Network (UNINETT): www.uninett.no

Red Nacional de I+D—National Research Network (Spain) RedIRIS:
www.rediris.es/

SuperJanet The UK Academic and Research Network: www.ja.net

SURFNET (the Netherlands): www.surfnet.nl, www.surfnet.nl/surfnet/
projects/surf-ace/sn4applarea.html, www.tik.ee.ethz.ch/~walter/
Telepoly/Telepoly.html

Swedish University Network: www.sunet.se/

Swiss Academic and Research Network (SWITCH): www.switch.ch/

TERENA (trans-European): www.terena.nl

United Kingdom Education & Research Networking Association (UKERNA):
www.ukerna.ac.uk

Middle East

Egyptian Universities Network (EUN): www.frcu.eun.eg/

CHAPTER 6

Next-Generation Internet Technical Architecture and IP

Introduction

Chapters 4 and 5 provide an indication of the extensiveness of worldwide advanced Internet initiatives. It is particularly notable that a core architecture that has been widely implemented among most of the networks developed by those initiatives is IP over ATM over SONET. The next several chapters provide descriptions of the core components of this architecture. This chapter focuses on IP (in a TCP/IP context), the next focuses on BGP, and the following two discuss ATM.

Next-Generation Internet Design Requirements

Chapter 3 describes next-generation Internet application requirements and notes that architectural designs that can address those requirements vary. A wide range of architectural models has been proposed as potential logical extensions to, and substitutes for, current networking architecture. This result is not surprising, given the uncertainties of rapidly changing networking technology, innovation, changing economics of components and services, new application requirements, and the balances that must be achieved among numerous dynamic parameters.

Despite these multiple options and their variability, the majority of early instantiations of next-generation Internets have been implemented with the same basic architecture—essentially best-effort IP version 4 (IPv4) over ATM over SONET. Although these standards developed independently, in combination they provide a powerful framework for a general, advanced, digital communications architecture, especially by incorporating a number of components that address the basic application requirements described in Chapter 3. This chapter describes the basic components of this architectural framework. Later chapters present case studies of advanced networks that have implemented an architecture based on IP over ATM over SONET. Also, this chapter discusses the degree to which this architecture meets the needs specified in Chapter 3, and it indicates where improvements are necessary. Later chapters expand on these topics and provide additional details.

Summary of General Technical Requirements

Best-effort IPv4 over ATM over SONET meets the majority of general technical requirements of many of today's advanced applications.

The following list of the requirements, expanded here from those covered in Chapter 3, is taken directly from the design requirements of an initial prototype advanced regional network (that is, the Metropolitan Research and Education Network, or MREN), described in a case study presented in Chapter 10):

Standards-based. The network had to be based on widely accepted standards formulated within an open architecture. Interoperability among numerous institutions and applications was a key requirement.

High performance. High speed was required as well as high end-to-end quality of service.

High reliability. Given that these networks are mission-critical for the organizations that depend on them, they must be production, industrial-strength networks, not experimental; high reliability is critical, that is, 99.999 percent uptime, especially for core components.

Modularity. A modular architecture creates an interoperability framework within which components can be placed and allows for the exchange of components at any level, as part of management procedures, or to take advantage of new technology without affecting the rest of the system. This characteristic should apply to as many components and protocols as possible.

Scalability. Given the growth in traffic volume, scalability in architecture is particularly critical. A network should be scalable at all levels, particularly with regard to traffic volume, because of growth in demand for capacity and in number of additional applications. A modular architecture is useful in meeting this requirement because components can be swapped without major effects on the rest of the network. Scalability includes not only the ability to handle more traffic at higher speeds and to add more connectivity, but also to take advantage of alternate technologies, for example, that enhance bandwidth management of higher volume traffic.

Expandability. The network architecture should provide for adding numerous additional sites easily and cost-effectively by immediately acquiring economical high-speed access through a connection to the network. Expandability also means provision of options to interconnect, through various line speeds and protocols if required (the common bearer service is still IP), to other advanced networks, commodity Internet providers, national and international networks, specialized single purpose networks, and testbeds.

Manageability at all technical layers. The network had to be manageable as a totality and within its component parts.

Reasonable security. Reasonable security for components and traffic has to be provided.

Architectural Framework Implementation Considerations

The IPv4 over ATM over SONET architecture also provides for many of the mechanisms to implement much of the functionality required by next-generation digital communication and many related to ensuring quality of service through an ability to differentiate those services. There are six key functionality requirements:

1. A capability for matching requests for the network resources to the resources that are available, within the context of specific policies.

   This capability implies that at the system level there is a collection of basic information about those requests, their individual characteristics (especially what is standard as opposed to customized), their aggregate behavior, their priorities, their claims on specific services (especially priority claims and guarantees), their authorization to claim services, and so on.

   This function also implies that at the same system level there is an understanding of what network resources are available at a given time (type of service, class of service, quality of service, specialized functions and processes, etc.). This capability should also provide for resolving conflicting claims, that is, contention for the same resources. This capability also implies some understanding of an end-to-end path, i.e., signalling.

2. A capability for the allocation of known available resources among the requests for those resources—optimally separate from any type of forwarding function.

   This capability implies a right to provide for an allocation of specific resources throughout an end-to-end path, including across multiple domains, for example, intranets, extranets, and the general Internet.

3. A capability for optimal forwarding (for example, Layer 3) based on the results of a process for matching between claims on resources and available resources, formulated within predetermined policies and processes.

4. A capability for providing extremely efficient, high-performance switching and transmission at the core of the system.

5. A capability for receiving, assessing, and delivering transmitted information and for monitoring results.

6. Various capabilities for scaling and extension, customization, and multiple access paths—at multiple speeds, from various devices and locations—as well as sufficient flexibility to integrate innovative new technology.

7. Various capabilities for management, performance measurements, and reporting.

Although this architecture provides various mechanisms for achieving these results, in practice, they are achieved more through over-provisioning of bandwidth than through use of those mechanisms.

IP over ATM over SONET

For a period beginning in the mid-1990s, the most common technical architecture implemented to address the goals of large-scale advanced Internets was best-effort IPv4 over ATM built on a SONET infrastructure. IPv4 is scalable, ubiquitous, and flexible; asynchronous transfer mode (ATM) is a connection-oriented, cell-based switching and multiplexing technology, which was becoming increasingly rich in function and features; and SONET provides for a robust, reliable, manageable core infrastructure. This describes the basic design of advanced Internets from the mid-1990s until recently.

Even for more general purposes, implementing IP over ATM for large-scale, high-performance networks has become fairly common. Although both protocols developed independently, this architecture provides for a wide range of capabilities, by combining the multiple strengths of IP with those of ATM and SONET.

IP: Powerful and Ubiquitous

The TCP/IP protocol suite has become a ubiquitous standard, and its multiple, powerful characteristics have been almost universally recognized. IP is common to all next-generation Internets. The exponential adoption of IP is gratifying to those who believe in IP "over everything" and "everything over" IP. For purposes of the architecture described in this chapter, IP is the protocol of the edge node, providing for various standardized and customized enterprise services and applications.

As noted in Chapter 2, digital communications can be divided into two basic categories: circuit-switched and packet-switched. Circuit-switched networks operate essentially by providing fixed resources in order to establish a dedicated circuit between two points.

The Internet is based on the concept of a packet-switched network, an innovation when it was first developed and still a dynamic force behind the current revolution in digital communication. Packet-switched networks segment data into variable-sized segments called packets. Routers then transmit the packets across the Internet, where they share available resources. A packet, which usually contains a few hundred bytes of data, carries information that enables network hardware to send it to its specified destination.

Chapter 2 noted that the TCP/IP protocol suite was developed as core protocols for data transmission across the Internet. Also as noted, IP is a particularly powerful and flexible protocol. It has remained so as traffic volumes have increased, as data types have become diverse, and as access and backbone speeds have increased from 56 Kbps to 1.5 Mbps to 155 Mbps, to 622 Mbps, to 2.4 Gbps.

Because of the explosive growth of the Internet and IP-based enterprise networks, IP is now ubiquitous. IP is used by large multinational corporations, small businesses, home office operations, and even some households for general, personal networking. At the higher levels of the OSI Reference Model, many protocols are still used. IP, however, is the one most commonly used. It has become the standard packet-switched protocol for both LANs and WANs.

Packet connections take place at many layers of the OSI Reference Model. At Level 2, IP is widely supported (IP over ATM, Frame Relay, and SONET are discussed in later chapters). It is notable that lower-level services such as frame relay and ATM use circuit-switching techniques because they use circuit creation mechanisms similar to the public-switched telephone network. These networks, though, provide only bit forwarding for IP packets and often just provide links between router ports. The dynamics of providing IP over these protocols give rise to a set of particularly important issues that are central to the development of the next-generation Internet. One such issue is the long term viability of the current support layers for IP.

Internet Protocols

The Internet is sometimes referred to by two contradictory names: the "network of networks" and the "dumb network." Both are true and provide an interesting insight to its underlying architecture. The network is often called "dumb" because the protocols of IP and TCP have intentionally been designed with simplicity in mind (Black 1992). IP is concerned primarily with addressing packets so that they can be transmitted across the Internet. Because the addressing scheme is universal, it is possible for one network operator to pass packets to another operator and for the packet to be successfully delivered. Therefore, the reference to the Internet as the "network of networks" also holds because, while there is no central authority, the system continues to operate, even though information is transferred across multiple network domains.

The TCP/IP protocol suite provides two types of services that all application programs use. First, it provides a packet-routing service, which means that the Internet routes messages from one computer to another based on addressing information carried in each individual packet. Second, the suite provides a reliable streaming transport service. The reliable transport service in TCP/IP protocols handles transmission errors, lost packets, or incorrectly ordered packets. It allows an application on one computer to establish a virtual connection with another computer, as if it were a direct, hardwired connection.

Some of the protocols in the TCP/IP suite of protocols provide low-level functions needed for many applications. These include IP, TCP, user datagram protocol (UDP), and Internet control message protocol (ICMP) (Minoli 1991). Other protocols are designed for undertaking specific tasks, such as transferring files between computers, sending mail, or finding out who is logged in on another computer. The primary features that distinguish TCP/IP are these (Minoli 1999):

Network technology independence. Although TCP/IP is based on conventional packet-switching technology, it is independent of any particular vendor's hardware.

Universal interconnection. TCP/IP allows any pair of computers with appropriate drivers to communicate. Each computer is assigned an *address* that is universally recognized throughout the internet/Internet.

End-to-end acknowledgments. The TCP/IP Internet protocols (specifically TCP) provide acknowledgments between the source and the destination, even when they do not connect to a common physical network.

Application-level protocol standards. The TCP/IP protocols include standards for many common applications including electronic mail, file transfer, and remote login.

TCP/IP protocols are normally thought of as being implemented in individual layers where each layer has a unique responsibility (Perlman 1992). The four different layers can be subdivided into the following categories: data link, network, transport, and application (see also Minoli 1999).

1. The *Data Link layer* is responsible for the interface between the networking application software and the physical network interface. This function is implemented in what is called a device driver. The device driver plays a critical role in that it provides a consistent interface to the higher-layer software so that regardless of the physical interface, the IP protocol operates in the same manner.

2. The *Network layer* is chiefly responsible for addressing and moving packets as they traverse the network. It is at this layer that packets are given their addresses before being passed to the Data Link layer. The actual address for the packet is determined by higher-layer applications.

3. The *Transport layer* provides error correction, detection, and flow of data between two computers. In the Internet protocol suite there are two main transport protocols: The Transmission Control Protocol (TCP) and the User Datagram Protocol (UDP). TCP has been designed to check the flow of inbound packets, asking for retransmission when errors are found, and subsequently providing a reliable flow of data between two hosts. It is also responsible for segmenting data from applications into packets, acknowledging received packets, reducing the transmission rate when congestion is encountered, and setting time-outs to make certain the other end acknowledges packets that are sent. TCP allows a process on one computer to send a stream of data to a process on another computer. Because TCP makes the network behave like virtual wire, it is called connection-oriented. Therefore, before transmitting data, participants establish a connection and negotiate parameters. In addition, because data can be lost in the intermediate networks, TCP can detect lost data and request retransmission(s) until the data is correctly and completely received.

   Because the Transport layer provides this reliable flow of data, the Application layer can ignore all those details. UDP, on the other hand, provides a much simpler service to the Application layer. It sends packets of data called *datagrams* from one host to the other, but there is no guarantee that the datagrams will be delivered to the other end. The Application layer must add any desired reliability.

4. The *Application layer* handles the interface between the user applications and the transport layers. At this level, users invoke application programs to access available services across the TCP/IP Internet. The application programs choose the kind of transport needed, TCP or UDP. Example applications that would interface to this layer are the Simple Mail Transfer Protocol for electronic mail or the HyperText Transfer Protocol for WWW browsers.

As described above, in the TCP/IP protocol suite, IP is responsible for relaying packets of data from node to node. TCP is responsible for verifying the correct delivery of data from the sender process to the receiver process and for providing a reliable mechanism for computers to transmit data over one or more interconnected networks. Often data must be delivered reliably, in sequence, completely, and with no duplication, in spite of the fact that there may be multiple networks along the way. In these cases, the IP's job is to move—specifically, forward—blocks of data over each of the networks that are situated between the computers that need to communicate.

IP Version 4

IP provides the network-layer protocol support in the Internet to transfer information between computers. The current version of the IP that is implemented in the Internet is known as IP version 4, or IPv4.[1] Like any network-layer protocol, IPv4 makes the underlying network transparent to the upper layers, TCP in particular. Being a network-layer protocol, IPv4 is a connectionless protocol where each packet is treated independently. IP provides two basic services: addressing and fragmentation/reassembly of long TCP datagrams. IP in itself adds no guarantee of delivery, reliability, flow control, or error recovery. If these are necessary, IP expects the higher layers to handle these functions. IP may lose PDUs, deliver them out of order, or duplicate them; IP defers these problems to the higher layers (TCP, in particular). Effectively, IP delivers PDUs on a "best-effort basis." IP maintains no network connections, physical or virtual.

To provide its services IPv4 contains various header fields that help implement its various functions:

Addresses (source and destination). IP address of sending host and of receiving host.

Protocol type. Protocol specified.

Data unit ID. Unique integer that identifies the datagram, allowing the destination to collect datagram fragments into an integral datagram.

Type of service. Parameters set by the endstation specifying, for example, expected delay characteristics, expected reliability of path, and so on.

Time-to-live. Parameter used to determine the PDU's lifetime in the interconnected system.

Options. Parameters to specify security, timestamps, and special routing.

Header checksum. A two-octet field used by IP to determine PDU integrity (however, no corrective action is supported).

IP provides for the carriage of datagrams from a source host to destination hosts, possibly passing through one or more gateways (routers) and networks in the process. An IP protocol data unit (datagram) is a finite-length sequence of bits containing a header and a payload. The header information identifies the source, destination, length, handling advice, and characteristics of the payload contents. The payload is the actual data transported. Both computers and routers in an Internet are involved in the processing of the IP headers. The hosts must create and transmit them and process them on receipt; the routers must examine them to make routing decisions and modify them as the IP packets make their way from the source to the destination.

IP has become the de facto standard of network interconnecting protocols. Although the Internet is the most well-known IP network, it is just one of the millions of such networks now deployed, public or private. As IP networks have become ubiquitous, the business community has become sophisticated about utilizing IP networks as a cost-effective corporate tool, first in data communications, now for other applications. Organizations favor developing internal networks based on IP because of its flexibility and vendor support.

IP protocols are supported over a variety of underlying media, such as ATM, Frame Relay, dedicated lines, ISDN, Ethernet, Token Ring, and so on. Although TCP and IP were developed initially for basic control of information delivery across the Internet, Application layer protocols have been added to the TCP/IP suite of protocols to provide specific network services. It is particularly advantageous that intranets use the same WWW/HTML/ HTTP and TCP/IP technology used for the general Internet.

Addresses

IP addressing provides a way to identify a device on the Internet. A PDU coming down the stack of a host connected to the network contains the IP address of the origination as well as the address of the destination. If the destination device is on the same network as the originating device, the PDU will directly go to that destination. If the network is different from the network of the originating device, the PDU must first be routed to that remote network (or some intermediate network), where it will go to the intended device.

An IP address consists of a network address used to identify the network to which a device (also called host) such as a PC, terminal, or computer is connected, and an *identifier for the device itself*. It is 32 bits in length. An IP address can be represented as follows:

AdrType | netID | hostID.

The IP address must be and is unique because of the requirement to interconnect a multitude of networks with a worldwide backbone (the Internet). Traditionally there have been five standardized ways of describing how the 32 bits are to be allocated; these are referred to as Classes A, B, C, D, and E. These classes are used to accommodate different requirements in terms of enterprise size.

IP utilizes a simplified notation to represent, for ease of use and reference, the 32 binary bits. This notation is known as Dotted Decimal Notation (DDN). Finally, the IP address is represented as 126.97.254.57. In fact, this notation can be used directly when specifying routing tables because there is an internal translation function, so that the DDN number is automatically translated to binary.

Subnetwork Addressing

Typically organizations have subnetworks that subdivide the larger network. This is done for performance or administrative reasons. The establishment of subnetworks can be done locally, while the whole network still appears to be one IP network to the outside world. As discussed above, the IP addresses consist of the pair:

<network address>< host address>

IP allows a portion of the host/device field to be used to specify a subnetwork (the network ID portion cannot be changed). Subnetworks are an extension to this scheme by considering a part of the <host address> to be a "local network address," that is, the subnetwork address. IP addresses are then interpreted as follows:

<network address><subnetwork address><host address>.

Subnetwork masks are used to describe subnetworks; they tell devices residing on the network how to interpret the device ID portion of the IP address. The address-checking software in each device is informed via the subnetwork mask not to treat the device ID exclusively as a device identifier, but as a subnetwork identifier followed by a (smaller) device identifier. Naturally, because the address space is finite, there is a trade-off between the number of subnetworks that can be supported and the number of devices on each subnetwork. The mask contains a bit for each bit in the IP address, although the "active ingredients" portion of the mask is really contained only in the section describing the device ID. If the bit is set in the IP address mask, the corresponding bit is to be treated as a subnetwork address. All unaffected bits in the left portion of the mask are set to 1. Bits set to 0 represent the actual extent of the device address.

IP and Routing

IP networks are interconnected via routers. Routers are found at several boundary points on subnetworks. In practice, a router is used for internetworking subnetworks that use the same Network layer but have different Data-Link-layer protocols. Internetworking products, including routers, represent a large fraction of the sunk enterprise network cost, as well as a large portion of the yearly network deployment and operating budget. This is true because the routers themselves have been relatively expensive, particularly at the high end and/or for newer protocols and also because the number of such devices in the network has increased over the last few years. Routing entered enterprise networks in the mid-1980s and has supplanted a large portion of the previous multiplexer-based technology. Today network administrators spend a lot of time in deciding which routing technology to use, by way of the products they purchase, and in analyzing how to refine the router's metrics to consistently support optimal routes. Furthermore, network design tuning follows from topology changes, such as adding locations, links, and access technologies (Minoli 1993).

Routers have become the fundamental and the predominant building technology for data internetworking. Routers permit the physical as well as the logical interconnection of two networks. With the introduction of ATM, however, the role of routers in enterprise networks could theoretically change. For example, devices enabling connectivity between locations based on router technology may, conceivably, no longer be obligatory elements. The concept of forwarding frames at the Network layer of the protocol model will continue to exist. In addition, routers work well for traditional data applications, but new broadband video and multimedia applications need different forwarding treatment, higher throughput, and tighter QoS control (Ferguson 1998). Of course, none of these requirements imply that ATM is an optimal solution, and various configurations have been implemented to address them including IP over ATM and IP over SONET.

The connectivity provided by routers is supported at the Network layer of the OSIRM. Routing entails the use of network-layer (topology) information as part of the process of deciding how to forward Network layer PDUs and deciding which PDUs to forward (and where). Source and destination addresses within the Network layer PDU identify the sending and receiving networks. The use of routers allows the establishment of distinct physical and logical networks, each having its own network address space. Routing methodologies are becoming increasingly sophisticated, as topologies become larger and more complex. A variety of protocols are supported by various LAN subnetworks that need to interwork to make end-to-end connectivity feasible. As noted, the most common network layer protocol is IP. Routers can be used to connect networks in building/campus proximity or to support wide-area connections. The communication technologies that can be used include low-speed, high-speed, and broadband dedicated-line services, as well as low-speed, high-speed, and broadband-switched services.

Basic Routing

When IP packets are moved from source to destination on the Internet, two mechanisms are at work, *forwarding* and *routing*. Each of these processes takes place within the routers. Forwarding deals with moving a packet along a route after the decisions have been made as to what is the correct next hop, that is, what interface the packet should leave. Forwarding of packets is done within the router by referencing a *forwarding table*. The forwarding table can be quickly searched. It contains information such as pairs of IP addresses, router output ports, and encapsulation type. The table is searched to find the best match for the packet, and then it is forwarded. Routing deals with determining where to move packets based on their network layer addressing (Perlman 1992). This section describes basics of how routing decisions are made and of two underlying functions: determination of forwarding, routes and movement of routing information through the Internet.

Routers build their routing tables with information gathered through *routing protocols*. These protocols allow routers to learn reachability information such as what routers are adjacent to one another and the optimal way(s) to reach attached networks. Routers can interconnect different physical types of networks (FDDI to ATM, or Ethernet to Token Ring) and have the ability to determine the best route to reach the destination. Path determination is accomplished through the use of algorithms that take as input network parameters such as hop count, available bandwidth, path cost, and path QoS. Values determined by the route calculation algorithms are then stored in router tables. Each of the entries of the table is populated through local as well as remote information that is circulated around the network. Routing protocols are the adjunct mechanism by which routers obtain information about the status of the network. That is to say, routing protocols are used to populate routing tables and calculate costs.

All IP datagrams contain a source and a destination address. Routing in the Internet uses the destination address as the primary means for selecting routes. Ideally, or in next-generation Internets, the routing decisions will take into consideration the type of service, network congestion, or network costs, but for the most part these capabilities do not exist today. Forwarding packets based on the IP destination address alone, while efficient, has some undesirable consequences. The most obvious from an ISP's perspective is that all traffic follows the same path. This means that if there are multiple paths to the destination, utilizing this capacity is very difficult. In other words, it is not possible to do traffic engineering with IP alone.

Routers operate by distributing reachability messages to their peers, signaling their presence. These reachability messages also carry information about other destinations that are reachable through the router or via links to its neighbors.

Routers communicate with other routers for the purpose of propagating the view of the network connections they have, the cost of connections, and the utilization levels. Different techniques are used to populate the routing table.

Static routing requires the network manager to build and maintain the routing tables at each router or at a central route server. This implies that once configured, the network paths must not change. A router using static routing can issue alarms when it recognizes that a communication link has failed, but it will not automatically update the routing table to reroute the traffic around the failure.

Dynamic routing allows the router to automatically update the routing table and recalculate the optimal path based on real-time network conditions. Dynamic routing is the most popular because it takes into account real events such as link failures. Although no router protocols in widespread use employ congestion metrics, it is an area of ongoing research. Routers implementing dynamic routing exchange information about the network's topology with other routers. Dynamic routing capabilities are the most desirable because they allow the Internet to adapt to changing network conditions.

In order to keep traffic smoothly flowing on the Internet, updating routing tables must occur rapidly. For this reason, dynamic routing regularly updates the view of the entire network to reflect any changes, and this view also includes a map of devices operating at or below the network layer. While the specifics of the various routing algorithms differ, the goals are common. First, they try to determine the optimal path to a destination and collect values for metrics that consistently result in the best route. Second, they minimize network bandwidth required for routing information propagation and also minimize router processing required to determine optimal routes. Third, after a topological change, they rapidly determine optimal routes that should be implemented for the subsequent steady-state condition.

With its routing tables, routers forward to given destination prefixes as soon as that information is available, quickly forwarding packets that arrive on its interfaces. The process of forwarding is divided into several steps. First, the specific data-link-layer information, such as Ethernet headers, is removed from the packet. Next the network layer (IP) address is examined, and a routing table lookup is performed. The routing table lookup will result in an interface value corresponding to the port on which the packet should leave the route. The routing table contains pairs of the IP address of a destination network and the IP address of the next-hop router along the path toward the destination. Each entry in a routing table points to a router that is physically connected to one of the segments on the router. That is, the next-hop router must be accessible over a local area network or a wide area network connection and must not reside on a network with an intermediate router in between. The router then formats the packet into the correct data-link-layer packet and transmits the packet on the physical interface toward the next hop.

Routing Modes

Two types of routing protocols are used to create routing tables, Interior Gateway Protocols (IGP) and Exterior Gateway Protocols (EGP). This chapter focuses on EGPs because they are most often used for interprovider communication. For now it is best to consider each as a unique application for interior topology control and exterior reachability communication. Regardless of whether the protocol is interior or exterior, its principal job is to populate the reachability information. When a datagram is ready to be transmitted, IP routing software locates the best-match entry in the routing table. From the IP address the forwarding process determines where to send the packet next and utilizes whatever the physical media may be to transmit the packet to the next-hop router.

Understanding routing protocols and understanding how to correctly configure IP routers are not trivial tasks. One of the most important things for network engineers to understand is when and when not to use the tools they have been given. Many of the protocols described throughout this chapter are powerful and flexibly configurable. This creates a double-edged sword because it allows ISPs to create ingenious ways of solving their problems, but it also has historically created some very difficult-to-diagnose problems.

Some examples of instances when IGP or EGP protocols are unnecessary can be found in networks that do not have multiple paths for data to traverse. In these cases, the designer can create what is called a *default* or *static* route. Static routing refers to routes to destinations being listed manually in the router. Default routing refers to a *route of last resort* to a destination that the router will use as an outlet for all networks for which it does not have reachability information.

These terms are used to define the technique where the router is instructed that it has only one possible path, the default, to forward packets. This type of configuration is useful in sites with only one connection to the rest of the Internet. For example, a simple case would be a small business, with one LAN, where there is a single ISP and a single router. That router has only one possible choice for forwarding packets; therefore, it does not need to be involved in complicated routing topology updates.

Static routes are also used in small ISP networks because the address space that has been allocated throughout the network can be manually disseminated throughout the ISP's routers. For example, if a small ISP has only six routers and a dozen subnetworks, it is unlikely that there will be many topological changes. For this reason the ISP may not need to run a routing protocol, and it would be best served with static routing. In many cases, for smaller ISPs, the most stable configurations utilize static routing, and it would be best for these customers to avoid using BGP.

Finally, *dynamic* routing is a term used to describe the implementation of routing protocols so that the network can automatically learn routes. Dynamic routing implements either an internal or an external routing protocol and can be realized by running, for example, BGP or Open Shortest Path First (OSPF) (RFC 1583).

Routing Protocols

To support effective communication, the exchange of appropriate routing and status information among routers is required. The routers exchange information about the state of the network's links and interfaces, and available paths, based on different metrics. Metrics used to calculate optimal paths through the network include cost, bandwidth, distance, delay, load, congestion, security, QoS, and reliability. Routing protocols are used as the means to exchange this vital information.

As discussed previously, there are two routing protocol types for status dissemination. First, protocols that operate within an autonomous system (AS) are called Interior Gateway Protocols. An autonomous system is typically a collection of subnetworks under a single administrative domain. Second, protocols that operate between autonomous networks are called Exterior Gateway Protocols. Within an autonomous system any protocol may be used for route discovery, propagation, and validation; however, autonomous systems must make routing information available to other autonomous systems using a common protocol. So, outside and between autonomous systems an exterior routing protocol is used. The three commonly used protocols in the TCP/IP context for private enterprise networks are RIP, IGRP, and OSPF.

Two methodologies are used for information dissemination: *distance vector* and *link-state*. Routers that employ distance-vector techniques create a network map by exchanging information in a periodic and progressive sequence. Each router maintains a table of relative costs (hop count or other weights such as bandwidth availability) from itself, to each destination. The information exchanged is used to determine the scope of the network via a series of router hops. After a router has calculated each of its distance vectors, it propagates the information to each of its neighbors on a periodic basis, such as once every 60 seconds. If any changes have occurred in the network, as inferred from these vectors, the receiving router modifies its routing table and propagates it to each of its own neighbors. The process continues until all routers in the network have converged on the new topology.

Routers using link-state protocols learn the topology of the internetwork infrastructure and update each other's tables by periodically flooding the network with link-state information. This generally happens on demand, when topology changes, with infrequent "full topology refresh." This information includes the identification of the links or subnetworks directly connected to each router and the cost of the connection. Routers using the Shortest Path First algorithm send link-state information to all routers on the Internet; in turn, these routers use the information to populate a table of routers and link/subnetwork connections. After this, each router calculates the optimal path from itself to each link: Indirect paths are discarded in favor of the shortest path. Link-state protocols include protocols such as OSPF and the Intermediate-System to Intermediate-System (IS-IS) protocol.

Link-state routing is a newer form of dynamic routing. Here routers broadcast their routing updates, which are generated only if information changes, to *all* routers within the administrative domain. Because routing information is flooded, rather than just sent between neighboring routers as in the case in distance-vector environments, each router can develop a complete map of the network topology. Given the topology map, each router can then calculate the best path to each destination. Link-state protocols transfer routing information using Link State Packets (LSPs). The transmission of an LSP is also called *route advertisement*. LSPs are broadcast usually every 15 or 30 minutes. An LSP is also broadcast when a communication link to a neighboring router changes state, or when the metric of a link changes, or when a new router is added to the network.

Link-state routing may well be the preferred choice in the future because it requires less bandwidth than distance-vector routing and converges much faster following a topology change. The higher processing requirement for link-state routing algorithms becomes less important as processor performance increases and price per (millions of) operations per second continues to go down. Link-state protocols are indicated for rules-based routing and support of Type of Service or Quality of Service features. These protocols tend to be resistant to the creation of routing loops. In addition, they enjoy low overhead to support the routing function; bandwidth frugality is achieved through the use of more-intensive computing resources and higher memory requirements for the router.

Open Shortest Path First

Open Shortest Path First (OSPF) is a link-state internal gateway protocol developed by the Internet Engineering Task Force (IETF). OSPF is an open protocol specification, and version 2 is defined in Requests For Comments (RFC 1583); it has full Internet-standard protocol status. OSPF aims to allow more-optimized routing compared to distance-vector protocols by supporting user-definable, least-cost, multipath routing. Each router contains a routing directory that identifies the router's interfaces that are active, along with status information about adjacent routers. OSPF supports the definition of contiguous networks and systems as isolated network segments ("areas"), in order to reduce the amount of information required at each router related to its autonomous network. A router using OSPF calculates the shortest path to the other routers in the autonomous system by considering itself as the root. Although OSPF does not propagate route information, it does propagate topology information. Each router calculates its own routes using the topology database. This information is periodically proliferated to all routers in the same autonomous system. OSPF does the following:

- Authenticates routing update information to ascertain it is valid
- Converges rapidly on network topology changes
- Is resilient to routing loops
- Supports load balancing across multiple communication links/services because OSPF can store multiple routes for a destination
- Supports Type of Service routing, such as link bandwidth or expected link latency, although this is almost never implemented

OSPF routers use a number of advertisement techniques (Black 1992):

Router links advertisement. An area-specific advertisement carrying information about links in one area; the advertisement is flooded only throughout that area.

Networks links advertisement. Employed by a broadcast network to transmit a list of all routers connected to a network; the advertisement is flooded only throughout an area.

Summary links advertisement. Employed by border routers to proliferate information on routes inside an autonomous network; the advertisement is flooded only throughout an area.

Autonomous system extended links advertisement. Used by boundary routers to contain information on routes in *other* autonomous systems; they are flooded through autonomous system.

Classless Inter-Domain Routing (CIDR)

Closely related to routing are the issues involving IP address allocation and management. Throughout the Internet's history, IP address use has been associated with *classfull* allocations, discussed in the previous section. Classfull allocation, as described, is typically referred to as Class A, Class B, Class C and is a way of looking at the address space where each class has a predefined number of addresses and is easily identified by its prefix. For example, a Class C address is restricted to a single octet, therefore, and can accommodate 254 hosts.

Classfull IP addresses posed two critical problems to the Internet. First, by 1991, the rate at which addresses were being consumed was accelerating dramatically, and there was a fear that the pool of free addresses would disappear. The second problem posed by classfull IP addresses is that each requires an entry in the router's forwarding table. This is a critical problem for ISPs because until 1995 routing tables were growing at an alarming rate.

The Internet community has adopted a scheme, called Classless Internet Domain Routing (CIDR), that will preserve addresses by abandoning the old class rules. CIDR is expected to provide relief until well into the 21st century, when a new scheme will be required. The IETF is working on the next generation of the IP suite of protocols. In its current draft state, the next generation of IP is shown as IP version 6 (IPv6). The class-based scheme may continue to be used in some enterprise networks.

To cope with the problems associated with classfull address allocation, a new means of utilizing addresses was required. The new technique is called *classless inter-domain routing*, or CIDR, which simply allows a network in the Internet to be represented by a prefix and a number representing the subnet mask length. CIDR's allocation scheme creates the ability for address *aggregation*, that is, the practice of aggregating a contiguous block of addresses into a single routing table entry.

The CIDR allocation of IP addresses is then very different from IP Classes A, B, and C. For example, 198.100.0.0/16 is the notation for a CIDR allocation in which 198.100 is the beginning of a collection of aggregated Class C networks. The "/16" notation designates that the subnetwork mask contains 16 bits; therefore, a total of 256 traditional Class C networks will be aggregated into this block.

When a traditional classfull IP address is allocated into a larger aggregate than legally possible in the classless domain, as a product of CIDR's use, the result is called a *supernetwork*. Supernetworks are possible only with a CIDR allocation and are easily identifiable because the new CIDR network mask is larger then the classfull allocation's natural mask.

One of the key advantages of CIDR supernetwork aggregation that can be seen in the previous example is that the ISP routing table entry for the individual classfull networks would be substantially larger than without the CIDR aggregate. Networks that are subsets of an aggregate are sometimes said to be *more specific* because they provide greater detail for routing reachability. If there were more than one entry in the IP routing table for the subnetwork, then the forwarding process always selects the longest match, that is, it selects the most specific routing entry.

This efficiency of routing table utilization, in the previous example of replacing 256 entries with just one, has successfully curbed the growth of Internet backbone routing tables. There are two potential pitfalls to CIDR aggregation. First, the IP addresses used by customers must be taken from their ISP's address space. If a customer subscribes to one ISP's service and is allocated IP addresses, then decides to change to a different provider while keeping the same addresses, the CIDR block will no longer be aggregated. The second possible problem with CIDR involves customers who are connected to multiple ISPs. Because they are *multi-homed*, that is, connected more than once, each ISP must advertise reachability to the customer, and this therefore may lead to routes that are not in aggregated blocks.

IP Routing Tables

A key function of the Internetworking layer is to support routing. Basic IP routers (also known as *gateways with partial routing information*) have information only about the devices directly attached to the physical networks to which this gateway is attached. The IP routing table contains information about the locally attached networks and IP addresses of other gateways located on these networks, in addition to the networks to which they attach. The table can be extended with information on IP networks that are further away, and it can contain a default route, but it still remains a table with limited information. Hence, this kind of gateway is called a gateway with partial routing information. Gateways (routers) with partial information are characterized by the following:

- They do not have knowledge about all interconnected networks.
- They allow local autonomy in establishing and modifying routes.
- Routing entry errors in one gateway may introduce inconsistencies, thereby making part of the network unreachable.

Some configurations require more than just the basic routing function; these configurations require a gateway-to-gateway (that is, router-to-router) communication mechanism to relay routing information. A more sophisticated gateway (router) system is required if the following conditions apply:

- The gateway (router) needs to know routes to all possible IP networks.

- The gateway (router) needs to have dynamic routing tables. Dynamic routing tables are kept up to date with minimal or no manual intervention.

- The gateway (router) has to be able to convey local changes to other gateways.

If the destination device is attached to a network to which the source host is also attached, information can be sent directly by encapsulating the IP PDU in the physical network frame. This is called *direct delivery/direct routing*. When the destination device is not on a network directly accessible to the source host, *indirect routing* occurs. Here, the intended destination must be reached via one or more IP gateways. The address of the first of these gateways (the first hop) is called an *indirect route*. The address of the first gateway is needed by the source device to initiate the delivery of the information.

This simple view of the world makes the routing table relatively straightforward. A gateway keeps tracks of two sets of addresses in the IP routing table:

Devices attached to networks that are directly accessible. These devices have the same IP Network ID address as the IP Network ID of the source gateway/host itself.

"Indirect" hosts. The only knowledge required is the IP address of the "next gateway," that is, a gateway leading to the destination "IP network."

Additionally, the table contains a default route, which contains the (direct or indirect) route to be used in case the destination IP network is not otherwise identified.

IP relaying is based on the Network ID portion of the destination IP address. The Device ID portion of the address plays no part at this stage. On the incoming side, arriving IP PDUs are checked to determine if the IP address on the PDU coincides with the IP address of the local network (that address can be thought of as being assigned to the IP router, rather than something more abstract as a network). If the addresses match, the PDU is passed up to the upper portions of the protocol stack. If the address does not match, the IP router checks its routing tables to determine to which physical outgoing path the PDU should be directed.

The fundamental operation for gateways is as follows: An incoming IP PDU that contains a "destination IP address," other than the local host or gateway IP address (or addresses), is treated as a normal outgoing IP PDU. Any outgoing IP PDU is subject to the IP routing algorithm of the gateway/host in question. The host/gateway selects the next hop for the PDU (the next device/gateway/

host to send it to) by checking its routing table. This new destination can be attached to any of the physical networks to which the gateway/host is connected. If this network is a different physical network from the one on which the gateway/host originally received the IP PDU, then the net result is that the local gateway/host has forwarded the IP PDU from one physical network to another.

IP Protocol Data Unit

The format of an IP protocol data unit (PDU) is shown in Figure 6.1. It is 20 or more octets long. The VERS field describes the version of the IP protocol, for example, version 4. The LEN field is the length of the IP *header* counted in 32-bit units. The Type-of-Service field describes the quality of service requested by the sender for this IP PDU. It has this format:

Precedence | D | T | R | xxx

Precedence is an indication of the priority of the IP PDU; D specifies whether this IP PDU can be delayed (0) or cannot be delayed (1); T indicates the type of throughput desired (0 = normal, 1 = high); R specifies whether a reliable subnetwork is required (1) or not (0); and xxx is reserved for future use. The

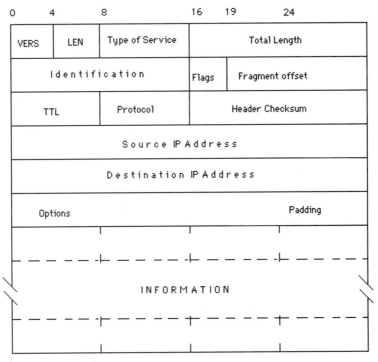

Figure 6.1 IP PDU.

precedence options are: Routine (000); Priority (001); immediate (010); Flash (011); Flash Override (100); Critical (101); Internetwork Control (110); and Network Control (111).

Refer to Figure 6.1, the Total-Length field specifies the length of the entire IP PDU. Because the IP PDU is encapsulated in the underlying network frame (for example, LLC and then MAC), its length is constrained by the frame size of the underlying network. For example, as mentioned, the Ethernet limitation is 1,500 octets. IP itself, however, deals with this limitation by using fragmentation and defragmentation. IP does require, however, that all underlying networks be able to handle IP PDUs up to 576 octets in length without having to use fragmentation capabilities. Fragments of an IP PDU all have a header, basically copied from the original IP PDU, and segments of the data. They are treated as normal IP PDUs while being transported to the destination. If one of the fragments gets lost, the entire IP PDU is declared lost because IP does not support an acknowledgment mechanism; any fragments that have been delivered will be discarded by the destination. More information on segmentation is provided in the text that follows.

The Identification field contains a unique number assigned by the sender to aid in reassembling a fragmented IP PDU (all fragments of an initial IP PDU have the same and unique identification number). The Flags field is of the form 0 | DF | MF where DF specifies if the IP PDU can be segmented (0) or not (1); and MF specifies if there are more segments (1) or no more segments, the present one being the last (0).

The Fragment-Offset field is used with fragmented IP PDUs and aids in the reassembly process. The value represents the number of 64-bit blocks (excluding header octets) that are contained in earlier fragments. In the first segment (or if the IP PDU consists of a single segment) the value is set to 0.

The Time-to-Live (TTL) field specifies the time in seconds that this IP packet is allowed to remain in transit. However, in practice the key variable is the number of router hops not time. Each IP gateway through which this IP PDU passes subtracts from this field the processing time expended on this IP PDU (each gateway is requested to subtract at least one unit from this counter). When the value of the field reaches 0, it is assumed that this IP PDU has been traveling in a loop and is therefore discarded.

The Protocol field indicates the higher-level protocols to which this gateway should deliver the data. Approximately 40 protocols are currently defined, but more are being added every year. For example, a code of decimal 6 (=00000110) means TCP; 29 is for ISO TP4; 10 is for BBN's RCC; 22 is for Xerox's IDP; 66 MIT's RVD; and so on.

The Header-Checksum field is a checksum covering the header (only). It is calculated as the 16-bit 1s complement of the 1s complement sum of all 16-bit words in the header (for the purpose of the calculation the Header-Checksum field is assumed to be all 0s).

The Source IP Address field contains the 32-bit IP address of the device sending this IP PDU. The Destination IP Address field contains the destination for this IP PDU. These addresses conform with the format described earlier.

The Options field (which must be processed by all devices in the interconnected network, although not all devices must be able to generate such a field), defines additional specific capabilities. These include explicit routing information, record route traveled, and timestamping.

Conclusion

This chapter has described basic principles of the reference model of different protocols used on the Internet. The Internet backbone routers are specialized high-performance computers with interfaces that have been optimized to forward IP datagrams at very high speeds. The process of routing involves the exchange of messages in a routing protocol and subsequently determining the topology of the Internet so that forwarding tables within the router can be populated. Chapter 7 discusses in detail the de facto standard for an exterior routing protocol, Border Gateway Protocol (BGP version 4).

End Note

[1]Portions of this section ("IP Version 4") and the following sections (through page 121) are based on a treatment in *Internet Architectures*, by Dan Minoli and Andrew Schmidt (1999, John Wiley & Sons).

References

Black, U. 1992. *TCP/IP and Related Protocols*. New York: McGraw-Hill.

Ferguson, P. and G. Huston. 1998. *Quality of Service: Delivering QoS on the Internet and in Corporate Networks*. New York: John Wiley & Sons.

May, John. 1998. *OSPF: Anatomy of an Internet Routing Protocol*. Reading, MA: Addison-Wesley Longman.

Minoli, D. 1991. *Telecommunication Technology Handbook*. Norwood, MA: Artech House.

Minoli, D. 1993. Designing Broadband Networks. Norwood, MA: Artech House.

Minoli, D. and A. Schmidt. 1999. *Internet Architectures*. New York: John Wiley & Sons.

Perlman, R. 1992. *Interconnections: Bridges and Routers*. Reading, MA: Addison-Wesley Longman.

RFC 1247. 1991. J. Moy. *OSPF Version 2*. ftp://ftp.isi.edu/in-notes/rfc1247.txt (draft standard, rendered obsolete by RFC 1583).

RFC 1583. 1994. J. Moy. *OSPF Version 2*. ftp://ftp.isi.edu/in-notes/rfc1583.txt (draft standard, rendered obsolete by RFC 2178).

RFC 2178. 1997. J. Moy. *OSPF Version 2*. ftp://ftp.isi.edu/in-notes/rfc2178.txt (draft standard).

URLs

RIPE Database: www.ripe.net

Routing Arbiter: www.ra.net

CHAPTER 7

Border Gateway Protocol

Previous chapters have described how Internet services and the underlying architectures are designed to move IP datagrams. This chapter focuses on the details of data movement in the Internet by describing how routers forward IP datagrams and the protocols that are used to communicate network reachability information.[1] Chapter 6 describes how routing takes place in the Internet, the concept of table-driven IP routing, and the different IP routing algorithms. This chapter covers the most common protocols for IP routing in Internet Service Provider (ISP) backbones, for example, interdomain routing, specifically the Border Gateway Protocol (BGP) (versions 2, 3, and 4 defined in RFCs 1163, 1267, and 1771 [1995] respectively).

BGP is a distance-vector exterior routing protocol developed by the IETF as a replacement for EGP (described in Chapter 2) for interdomain applications such as the Internet. In effect, BGP replaced EGP by providing additional features and eliminating some of EGP's limitations. The enhanced capabilities of BGP include (1) support for policy-based routing, for example, with fine-grained and powerful route selection techniques and (2) use of an authentication technique to guard against unauthorized updates to routing tables. BGP provides multiple methods for handling path selection, through selecting from various BGP attributes. BGP was designed so that the exchange of reachability information takes place only with other BGP gateways, limiting the amount of traffic that has to transit across the Internet; in steady state only changes to reachability information are exchanged. Also, the protocol supports the maintenance of a virtual connection between two endsystems for exchanging entire routing tables and table updates.

BGP routing updates consists of Network Layer Reachability Information (NLRI) or L3 prefixes, autonomous system paths, and additional attributes such as those that designate community values. Given that BGP enumerates the complete route to the destination, routing loops are avoided and convergence is expedited. To ensure reliable transfer of routing information, BGP utilizes TCP as its transport mechanism.

Routing Protocol Architectures

Earlier we explained that, from a high level of abstraction, routing protocols can be segregated into two categories, interior and exterior. One reason that a single protocol is not used globally is scalability. From the categories of interior and exterior it is possible to perform further segregation into the two main categories of routing protocol architectures called distance-vector protocols and link-state protocols.

Distance-vector protocols were designed for small networks; the name is derived from the fact that the protocol utilizes updates containing vectors of distances. These distances are actually the number of intermediate routers between subnetworks. The protocol operates by exchanging routing updates that contain tables showing which networks are reachable and how far the network is from the router. After this information has been flooded throughout the network, each individual router can calculate a new routing table. An example of a distance vector protocol is the RIP (Comer 1995).

Several problems are associated with distance-vector protocols. First, since the routers are calculating reachability information based on the flooded routing tables, the total topological distance of the network cannot be huge because it would become difficult to flood the tables, and it would become overly computationally intensive to calculate reachability. An additional problem with the distance-vector protocols is that, as the topological size of the network grows, the hop count can exceed the RIP maximum value of 15, as specified in the standards document, although this value is not intrinsic to the generic distance-vector category.

Link-state protocols were designed after distance-vector protocols and have addressed some of the deficiencies. The link-state protocols are driven by routers exchanging information called *link states* that inform link-state areas about the physical link and node conditions. LSAs are flooded throughout a link-state area, and flooded LSAs propagate along the adjacencies. The advantage of an update that contains only link and node conditional information is that, as opposed to distance-vector protocols, entire routing tables are not exchanged. An example of a link-state protocol is OSPF.

Link-state protocols have some clear advantages over distance-vector protocols. A few of the more important examples to Internet service providers are lack of reliance on hop count values, ability to better represent network bandwidth topology and delay, smaller load caused by routing information updates, and better support for network hierarchy.

Autonomous Systems

The final topic that needs to be reviewed prior to discussing Internet routing technology is the concept of autonomous systems (AS). An AS is a technique used to segregate the Internet into subsections with clear administrative and technical autonomy. Autonomous systems are collections of routers that maintain a single routing policy and are under the control of a single organizational entity, such as a corporation, and ISP, or a government agency. The Internet is a collection of thousands of autonomous systems where each autonomous system, from the outsider's perspective, is a distinctive entity. Routing protocols, like the BGP, are used to exchange reachability information between autonomous systems. Autonomous systems' numbers, like IP addresses, are acquired from an Internet registry.

Three different types of autonomous systems correspond to the three different possible ISP architectures (see Figure 7.1):

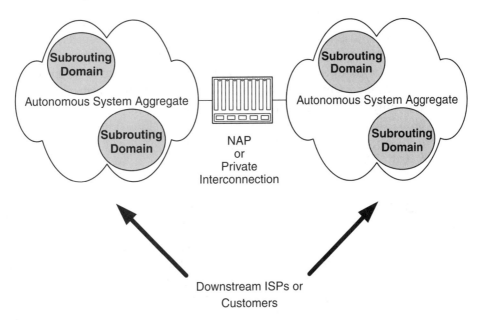

Figure 7.1 Autonomous system types.

Single-homed autonomous systems. These correspond to ISPs, corporations, or universities that have only one possible outbound route; that is, static or default routing usually will suffice.

Multi-homed nontransit autonomous systems. These autonomous systems are utilized by ISPs or corporations that have Internet connectivity to either two different ISPs or at two different locations in the Internet to the same ISP. The autonomous system is called nontransit because it advertises reachability only to IP addresses that are within its domain.

Multi-homed transit autonomous systems. These autonomous systems correspond to national ISP networks because they contain multiple entry and exit points and are used to carry transit traffic. The traffic is called transit because it contains source and destination addresses that are not within the transit provider's domain.

Strictly speaking, single-homed autonomous systems, sometimes called a *stub AS*, do not require an EGP such as BGP because they typically do not need to learn Internet routes. There are examples, however, where the internal use of a dynamic routing protocol may be used to make the network administrator's job easier. For example, if the domain contained several noncontiguous networks, it may be easier to distribute this information with a dynamic protocol as opposed to manual table entries. Single-homed autonomous systems that do utilize BGP can optionally use an autonomous system number from a private pool that does not need to be registered on the Internet. The private pool's values range from 65412 to 65535.

Some nontransit autonomous systems may not need to advertise their own routes and may not need to transmit routes learned from other autonomous systems outside of their domain. Therefore, multi-homed nontransit autonomous systems also may need to run BGP with their providers and would do so only in situations where some of BGP's functionality for routing policy control (that is, route filtering) was beneficial. On the other hand there are also strong arguments for using BGP in this context for flexibility and efficiency (Stewart 1998).

BGP Routing

The Border Gateway Protocol is the de facto standard for the dynamic routing protocol on the Internet. The version that is currently widely used is called Border Gateway Protocol version 4, or BGP4, and it went into production in 1993. BGP4 is widely used because it allows ISPs to control routing policy and support scalable routing calculations, and it understands techniques to reduce routing tables' size, such as CIDR aggregation. BGP4 made obsolete the previous versions of the protocol, BGP1, BGP2, and BGP3.

BGP is somewhat similar to distance-vector protocols. BGP operates by exchanging, or advertising, reachability information in the form of autonomous system (AS) path vectors. When BGP routers exchange collections of the autonomous systems they can reach, Network Layer Reachability Information (NLRI) with their associated path vectors and related attributes, each router can subsequently construct a directed graph corresponding to the total topology of the Internet. AS path vectors are used in part to avoid routing loops.

When two BGP routers form an adjacency, they are called *peers* or *neighbors.* Routers running the BGP protocol exchange routing information utilizing TCP. Therefore, the exchange of routing information is reliable, and the protocol does not need to provide transport-layer error correction. BGP message types that initialize routing tables are generated only at the beginning of a BGP session. Update messages are used throughout, to synchronize at the beginning of the peering session and to announce and withdraw changes. Therefore, the protocol is much more efficient than its predecessors because after transmitting the initial full routing tables, only routing additions or withdrawals are communicated.

The actual operation of BGP centers on the exchange of four fundamental message types. When two routers have been configured to be BGP peers, they will follow a predefined set of phases. The process is as follows: Initially, a peer will enter an initialization state; next the peer will exchange routing updates and keep alive messages (to determine if a peer still exists); and finally the peers may enter an error-reporting or session termination state.

Like static and dynamic routing protocols, within BGP routing updates may be created dynamically or statically. Dynamically created routes, sometimes referred to as *injected* routes, depend on the status of the network and are susceptible to route fluctuations and the instability of the operational Internet. Statically injected routes are created manually by the network engineer and will remain in place regardless of the state of the network. Two ramifications of these techniques are that BGP provides the ISP with the ability to utilize the protocol to inject static information into the global routing database and dynamic routing is acceptable; however, routes that change too frequently can be dampened and prevented from being advertised.

Finally, to help illustrate one of the key strengths of BGP4 over its predecessors, BGP3 and BGP2, refer to Figure 7.2: It shows the protocol's ability to accept routes from downstream autonomous systems and aggregate those advertisements into a single supernetwork.

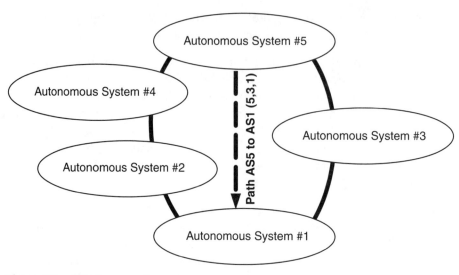

Figure 7.2 BGP4 aggregation.

BGP Message Types

The first message type described is also the first message that is used to establish neighbors between BGP peers. A BGP peering session begins with a TCP session initialization that includes TCP's three-way handshake. After the TCP session is established the BGP peers will transmit OPEN messages.

BGP OPEN and NOTIFICATION:

The OPEN message is intended to establish identity and optionally authenticate the other end of the connection. Following the BGP OPEN message, routing updates can be exchanged between BGP neighbors. After the OPEN messages have been exchanged, the routers will examine the autonomous system numbers to determine if they are within the same logical autonomous system. If they are, then the peers consider the interaction as a BGP session.

A BGP OPEN message contains six fields:

Version. This field is used to specify the version number, typically BGP4. When two BGP peers are establishing a neighboring relationship, they will attempt to negotiate the highest version number.

Autonomous system. This 2-byte field is used to transmit the source autonomous system number.

Hold time. This field specifies a value for a timer that is used to determine if the neighbor is still functional, in that if the neighbor does not transmit a routing update or a KEEPALIVE message before this timer value has expired, the peering session will be considered terminated. A KEEPALIVE message is typically transmitted at approximately one-third to one-half of the hold time interval and contains only a 19 byte BGP message header.

BGP identifier. This 4-byte value indicates the sender's identification and in order to be globally unique is usually the highest numeric IP address assigned to one of the router's interfaces.

Optional parameters. The BGP protocol supports extensions and exchanges of optional parameters specified in the standard Type, Length, and Value (TLV) format. An example of an optional parameter would be a session authentication key value or password.

Optional parameter length. This field is a single octet; it specifies the total length of the optional parameter field and if set to 0 designates that no optional parameters have been specified.

If for any reason during the OPEN process an error should occur or some condition after the OPEN has successfully completed should force termination, a NOTIFICATION message will be generated. A NOTIFICATION message comprises three fields: error code, error subcode, and a variable length error-data field.

The NOTIFICATION message is one of the key tools for diagnosing BGP peering session problems because the message provides, via the error code, a major category of failure, followed by the error subcode that provides information in a subcategory to help isolate the offending parameter. The variable-length error data section is used to convey information that may have caused the error, for example, a bad TLV value used as an optional parameter.

BGP UPDATE

The heart of the BGP protocol centers on the exchange of UPDATE messages. The UPDATE messages contain all the information necessary for the neighbor to determine which routes are being newly advertised, which routes are having their advertisement withdrawn, and which CIDR aggregates are accessible. This information is conveyed via three basic components of the UPDATE message: the Network Layer Reachability Information (NLRI), the path attributes, and the unreachable route section. An UPDATE message can advertise at most one route, which is described by multiple path attributes, but it can contain multiple routes to be withdrawn. (See Figure 7.3.)

Network Layer Reachability Information is critical to BGP's functionality because it is the mechanism for expressing reachability. NLRI updates con-

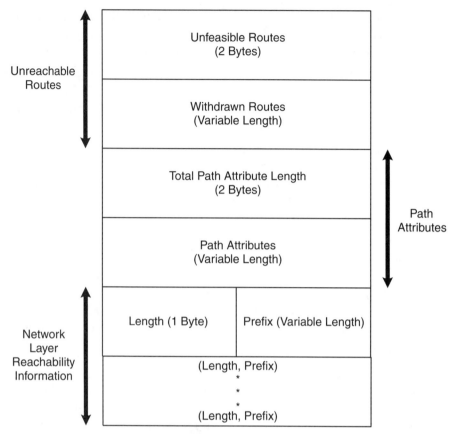

Figure 7.3 UPDATE message format.

tain an IP route prefix and the path attributes list. The path attribute lists the autonomous systems that are traversed to get from the present location to the advertised prefix. In other words, when a prefix is announced at one end of the Internet, that advertisement may traverse other autonomous systems as the advertisement crosses the Internet.

When the advertisement is passed from autonomous system to autonomous system, the path vector is updated with the last AS traversed. This information can subsequently be used to determine if a routing loop, or circular route, exists because an AS number would appear multiple times in the AS path list.

All BGP UPDATE messages contain a sequence of path attributes (see Figure 7.4). Path attribute categories (transitive characteristics, known information, etc.) are used to monitor route-specific information such as next-hop value, routes preference, and CIDR aggregation. In addition path attributes are used

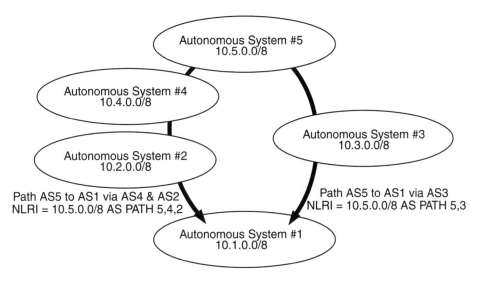

Figure 7.4 BGP routing update.

to facilitate making routing decisions and in the implementation of route filters. Path attributes are made up of a type, a length, and a value.

BGP Path Attributes

Several categories of path attributes are differentiated by the first two bits of
the path attributes type field, including:

Mandatory attributes. These attributes, such as the AS path, are required in
 BGP UPDATE messages, and all routers are required to recognize these
 attributes.

Transitive attributes. These attributes are required to be recognized by all
 BGP capable routers but are not required in every UPDATE message.

In addition to communicating feasible routes via Network Layer Reachability
Information, BGP4 has the capability of expressing withdrawn routes or
routes that are no longer feasible. Withdrawn routes take the format of a
CIDR announcement in that they are expressed as a subnetwork mask length
and an IP address. A BGP UPDATE message may contain multiple routes
that need to be withdrawn, and in its simplest form the UPDATE message
will not contain any NLRI advertisements—it will contain only routes to be
withdrawn.

There are currently 10 path attribute types used to control routing in the
Internet. The most common attributes are listed here:

NEXT _ HOP. (This is a well-known mandatory attribute.) The next-hop attribute contains the IP address of the neighbor that is announcing the route.

ORIGIN. (This is a well-known mandatory attribute.) It is used to convey where the Network Layer Reachability information was created. BGP uses this information when constructing its routing tables and can determine if the information originated within the autonomous system or outside of the autonomous system. BGP prefers internally generated information to externally generated information.

AS_ PATH. (This is a well-known mandatory attribute.) It contains a list of autonomous system numbers that the routes traversed before reaching this destination. As the routing information propagates through the Internet, each autonomous system is responsible for prepending the local autonomous system number into the AS path list.

Multi-exit discriminator. (This is an optional nontransitive attribute.) This attribute is used to convey preference for data flow between two ISPs interconnected at multiple locations. The MED can be utilized to express preferences over EGP information so that both providers and customers can load balance traffic over multiple links between their autonomous systems. Multi-exit discriminators are transmitted out of an autonomous system, but they do not traverse more than one autonomous system before being deleted.

Local preference attribute. (This is a well-known discretionary attribute.) This attribute is used to manage traffic flows leaving an autonomous system when there are clear preferences for which path is best to exit a multi-homed network. For example, if an autonomous system was multi-homed to the same ISP with a primary high-speed link and a backup low-speed link, the routers within the autonomous system can be configured with the local preference attributes to prefer routes learned from the high-speed link. The local preference attribute is communicated within the autonomous system. MED values often correspond to IGP metrics.

Atomic _ aggregate. (This is a well-known discretionary attribute.) When a downstream autonomous system is performing aggregation of multiple address blocks, specificity of where those blocks originated is lost. This attribute is required to be transmitted when that aggregation causes loss of information and is implemented to communicate the loss to the next autonomous system.

Aggregator. (This is an optional transitive attribute.) This attribute should go hand in hand with atomic _ aggregates and is used to notify the neighboring autonomous system of the router that has performed an aggregation. The attribute contains an AS number and the IP address of the router.

BGP Operation

With the preceding basic review of BGP components in mind, the BGP routing process can be reviewed from initialization through routing table establishment (see Figure 7.5). BGP routing messages are exchanged between BGP neighbors in UPDATE messages. The UPDATE message can contain a series of routes that are being withdrawn, that is, are no longer reachable, or a route that is being advertised as reachable. BGP UPDATE messages that are advertising reachability to a network do so by specifying the CIDR block and the

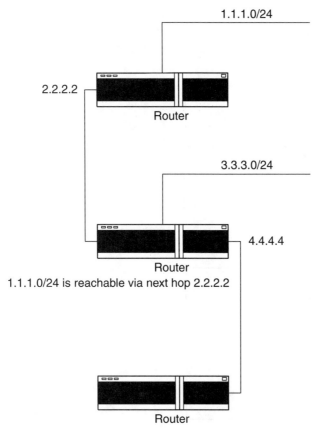

BGP NEXT_HOP

Figure 7.5 Attribute examples.

autonomous system path list between the current router and the original sub-network, along with mandatory and perhaps optional AS path attributes.

When a router running the BGP protocol receives an UPDATE message, it may optionally implement its own policy for routing modifications or rejections. Then it forwards a possibly modified UPDATE BGP message on to other adjacent neighbors. The modification may be the result of its locally configured policy. This capability is a subtle point but one of BGP's greatest strengths, in that the protocol is capable of applying policy decisions to input routes and then again generating unique policy-based routing decisions for advertised outbound routing information. The router that has received multiple BGP UPDATE messages will then examine the different messages, which may have come from different upstream routers, and it will determine what are the best routes that should be included in the local routing table that will be consulted when forwarding packets. (See Figure 7.6.)

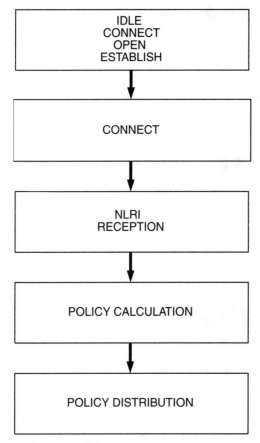

Figure 7.6   BGP operation.

Conclusion

The de facto standard for an exterior routing protocol on the Internet is BGP version 4. This protocol provides network engineers with the ability to capitalize on innovative technologies like CIDR and autonomous systems that produce manageable, loop-free, routing tables. BGP's main strengths are the rich diversity of attributes that can be used to control the way routes are advertised and the way inbound advertisements are interpreted. BGP also supports strong route filtering capabilities that, when combined with the attributes, provide a flexible network management tool. As the Internet migrates to its next generation, many of these capacities will migrate also, although with enhancements and extensions.

End Note

[1]Portions of this chapter are based on a treatment in *Internet Architectures*, by Dan Minoli and Andrew Schmidt (1999, John Wiley & Sons).

References

Comer, D. 1995. *Internetworking with TCP/IP.* 3d ed. Upper Saddle River, NJ: Prentice-Hall.

May, John. 1998. *OSPF: Anatomy of an Internet Routing Protocol.* Reading, MA: Addison-Wesley-Longman.

Minoli, D. and A. Schmidt. 1999. *Internet Architectures.* New York: John Wiley & Sons.

RFC 904. 1984. D. L. Mills. *Exterior Gateway Protocol formal specification.* ftp://ftp.isi.edu/in-notes/rfc904.txt (historic).

RFC 1163. 1990. K. Lougheed and Y. Rekhter. *Border Gateway Protocol (BGP).* ftp://ftp.isi.edu/in-notes/rfc1163.txt (historic).

RFC 1771. 1995. Y Rekhter and T. Li. *A Border Gateway Protocol 4 (BGP-4)* ftp://ftp.isi.edu/in-notes/rfc1771.txt (draft standard).

Stewart, John W. 1998. *BGP4: Inter-Domain Routing in the Internet* (The Networking Basics Series). Reading, MA: Addison-Wesley.

CHAPTER 8

The Internet and ATM over SONET

Introduction

This chapter focuses on asynchronous transfer mode, or ATM, which, although developed independently of IP, has become an important and growing support protocol for the Internet over the last several years. A gigabit ATM switch (scalable to many tens of gigabits) at the core of a high-performance network provides for a wide range of capabilities. The success of ATM partly results from its broadband service capabilities supporting enterprise LANs and WANs, at a national and international scale. Currently, the highest capacity Internet backbones provide for burst speeds up to OC48 (2.4 Gbps), many based on IP over ATM. Corporations, as well as top research universities, government laboratories, and large ISPs use IP over ATM to provide backbone access with burst speed rates up to OC12c (622 Mbps).

As noted, most advanced research networks today employ IP over ATM over SONET. In addition, ATM provides a wide range of potential capabilities for QoS and traffic management. ATM was designed with QoS components as core to its architecture. Traffic contracts can be established, and policing mechanisms provide assurances that the parameters specified in those contracts are met. Traffic can be accepted asynchronously although it is generally transmitted synchronously by layers under ATM. For high-bandwidth networks based on fiber, ATM is generally deployed with SONET as the underlying transport system. (SONET is described at the end of this chapter.)

Questions have arisen about the long-term future of the IP-over-ATM model. Some have asserted that this approach has reached its apogee, especially in the core of the Internet, and, that it introduces a needless performance tax, and have consequently declared ATM a technology without a future in the backbone. They note that high-end IP routers provide for the same type of performance, or better, than equivalent ATM switches. Also, while QoS was designed as a core ATM component, this feature has not been widely implemented in IP backbones, and the IETF DiffServ model as well as related techniques for quality provision are gaining momentum. A number of important, new advanced networking initiatives are developing OC48c and OC192c backbones that provide for IP over SONET; two have announced IP over lightwave. In addition, there have been a number of important developments in traffic engineering related to high performance IP. These issues are also explored in later chapters.

The IP-over-ATM model has been proliferating and will continue to do so for the next few years at least, although perhaps increasingly less within backbones. Nonetheless, it is useful to explore the model's various features. ATM is also evolving with the Internet, and high-end routers use ATM uplinks as well to reach the speeds required in backbones. Because of ATM's flexibility, many Internet backbones are ATM-based. In addition, IP over ATM services are being used in support of the core of traditional corporate enterprise networks as a way to provide increased bandwidth, functionality, and management capability. However, deploying ATM as an end-to-end solution, for example, to the desktop, is rare.

ATM platforms are now being utilized to support a variety of evolving applications such as these:

- Network interconnection over wide area network links
- Campus backbone support bridging legacy networks together at very high speed
- Multimedia conferencing and collaborative computing
- Video distribution using the Motion Pictures Expert Group (MPEG) standard over ATM
- Support of Internet service provider (ISP) high-capacity backbones
- Support of carrier multiprotocol backbones that support frame relay and other service integration (Spohn 1997)

The Development of Asynchronous Transfer Mode

ATM took shape through an international consultative process and through industry initiatives via the ATM Forum (ATM Forum 1993). Work on ATM began in the 1980s when researchers were looking at better methods to achieve high-speed data transmission.

ATM was essentially developed over many years by the telecommunications industry as a means of moving toward an integrated services architecture and services provisioning model, in anticipation of ubiquitous broadband capabilities. The ATM standard has been promoted by many standards committees, including the International Telecommunications Union (ITU-T, previously the Comite Consultatif International Telegraphique et Telephonique, CCITT), the European Telecommunications Standard Institute (ETSI), the American National Standards Institute (ANSI), and the ATM Forum.

ATM and ISDN

As a foundation, this work began with ISDN. A decision was made in the mid-1980s to seek a new standard that could be based, to some extent, on ISDN principles but at the same time support optical fiber; because of the media used, the supported speeds are much higher. The standard became known as B-ISDN (for Broadband Integrated Services Data Network).

Within the framework of the telephone industry's B-ISDN set of protocol stacks, ATM functions at OSI Layer 2 to transmit traffic across an enterprise, a city, a region, a nation, or the world. Although B-ISDN was formulated for public networks, ATM is used for both public and private networks. Both are digital, but ATM technology differs from ISDN insofar that ISDN is a synchronous transfer mode technology. In synchronous mode, data units within a specified channel tend to conform to more regular patterns and are identified by their position within the transmission frame. ATM, on the other hand, is an asynchronous transfer packet technology with statistical multiplexing gains. For multiplexed transmissions, the data units may have irregular behavior patterns and therefore traffic is adjusted to demand.

PNNI

An important part of ATM signaling is the Private Network to Network Interface (PNNI), which provides functionality related to various capabilities, including monitoring available network resources, matching requests to those resources, such as when providing for QoS, and managing the provision of those resources. There has been some discussion of using the PNNI specification to develop an Integrated PNNI (I-PNNI) that would also incorporate support for IPv4 and IPv6.

ATM Basics

The early proponents of ATM placed special emphasis on its voice and multimedia capabilities. Instead, ATM's ability to handle large amounts of data traffic has become its primary appeal. ATM was introduced as a protocol providing for cells of a fixed length (53 bytes, 5 bytes for the header and 48 for the data) that could handle both real-time (constant bit rate—CBR) and bursty traffic (variable bit rate—VBR)—in other words, voice, video, and data. ATM divides data into the cells prior to transmission across the network. ATM provides for cells delivered in the order sent, along a precisely defined, connection-oriented path.

With fixed-length cells, it is easy with ATM to get the maximum utilization of transmission resources. Longer cells can result in less efficient transmission because, for certain types of circuits such as for low speed access links, they can cause queuing delay and reduce possible QoS support. Short standardized cells allow multiplexing equipment at the link's endpoints to control jitter, and to some degree to occupy the link more efficiently with data and to vary priority data. In addition, cells of constant length improve, and help keep constant, the delay performance through the switches. At one time, it was argued that this type of switching technique would lead to improved overall performance relative to routing. In an IP environment, however, cellularization also implies a significant processing overhead; sometimes this overhead is referred to as an *ATM tax*. Also, IP routers have continued to improve significantly; some IP routers are now commercially available that provide for OC48c line forwarding for 40 byte packets.

ATM can be described as a packet-transfer mode based on asynchronous time-division multiplexing and a protocol engine that uses small fixed-length data units. ATM provides a connection-oriented service. Note that LANs such as Ethernet, FDDI, and token ring support a connectionless service. Hence, interworking must take this into account. Each ATM connection is typically assigned its own set of transmission resources (an example of an exception is UBR PVCs discussed later); however, these resources have to be taken out of a shared pool that is generally smaller than the maximum needed. ATM makes it possible to share bandwidth through multiplexing because multiple virtual channels can be supported on the access link and the aggregate bandwidth of these channels can be overbooked.

ATM supports two kinds of channels in the network: virtual channels (VC) and virtual paths (VP). Channels are communication paths of specified service capabilities between two ATM endpoints. Virtual channel connections (VCCs) are a concatenation of VCs to support end-to-end communication. VPs are groups (aggregations) of VCs. Virtual path connections (VPCs) are a concatenation of VPs to support end-to-end communication. In VC switching, each VC is switched and routed independently and separately. VP switching allows a group of VCs to be switched and routed as a single entity. ATM data units have headers with channel information fields, described in the next section.

ATM virtual circuits can be either switched (SVC) or permanent (PVC) (Minoli 1998). A switched connection is a dynamic allocation established through an ATM-defined mechanism called signaling, established with the carrier or private devices (Minoli 1994). PVCs provide for logical, statistically configured connections between two nodes. SVCs have not yet been widely implemented in large-scale networks because of issues related to management, especially during fault conditions. Specialized PVCs ("smart PVCs") can be set up by an ATM-defined mechanism called signaling, accomplished in part through the Service Specification Connection Oriented Protocol (SSCOP). SSCOP is a transport layer for both user-network interface (UNI) and network node interface (NNI) signaling.

A permanent connection is established through preprovisioning with the carrier or private devices. Quality of service parameters (described later in this chapter), such as inbound speed, outbound speed, and multipoint capabilities, are requested as a connection is established. A connection is established if the network is able to meet the request. If not, the request is rejected. Once the virtual circuit is defined, connection control for the call assigns an interface-specific virtual channel identifier (VCI) and a virtual path identifier (VPI) to the connection. These labels have only interface-specific meaning. Two different sets of VPIs/VCIs are assigned to the two endpoints of the connection. As long as the connection remains active, the assigned VCI and VPI represent valid pointers into routing tables in the network; the tables are used to accomplish cell routing through the network.

ATM Layers: An Overview

ATM is built from layers, for example, providing for an ATM Adaptation layer (AAL) that prepares protocol data units (PDUs) for specific services required (such as specific media) and ATM transfer services, by packaging them into ATM cells. An ATM PDU is a type of packet that consists of protocol control information and content data. After the PDU is prepared, it is partitioned into ATM cells and then transmitted. The header information of an ATM cell contains a VPI and a VCI. These designations allow for the setting up of dedicated virtual channels through the network that enable dependable high-quality transmission.

The Adaptation layer has three parts, two that receive the flows of different data streams from the upper layer of the protocol stack, which are (1) the convergence sublayer (CS) and (2) a lower layer, the segmentation and reassembly sublayer (SAR). The SAR receives the PDUs, chops them into cells, and sends them to the next layer down, which is the ATM layer. The SAR layer also receives cells and reassembles them.

ATM Adaptation Layers (AALs)

Initially there were four ATM Adaptation layers. AAL 1 was designed for constant bit rate and delay-bounded applications, such as voice and video. AAL 2 was designed for applications requiring variable bit rates and bounded delays. AAL 3 was designed for connection-oriented data applications, and AAL 4 was designed for connectionless data applications. Subsequently, AAL 3 and AAL 4 were combined (AAL 3/4) and evaluated as not appropriate for efficient transmission of data. AAL 5 was then developed for connection and connectionless data traffic. AAL 5 is generally used for IP traffic. In part, AAL 5 was designed to offer a service for IP communication with low overhead and good error detection.

ATM defines two classes of service for delay-sensitive traffic: (1) constant bit rate (CBR) and (2) variable bit rate (VBR). CBR ensures that network resources will be allocated to allow for performance levels specified by a predetermined contract, with specific parameters defined. AAL 1 has been used for CBR. VBR is divided into real-time and nonreal-time VBR, and it generally is used with AAL 5. In the near term, however, if ATM is to manage significant amounts of media traffic, that traffic will probably be IP-based and will flow over AAL 5 without taking advantage of native-mode ATM capabilities for managing such traffic. Currently, IP multimedia capabilities are being rapidly developed.

ATM Protocol Model

An extension of the conventional OSI seven-layer stack can be used to describe the structure of the ATM protocol: A reference model specific to ATM depicts its structure more clearly (see Figure 8.1). Beginning from the bottom, these are the Physical layer, the ATM layer, and the ATM Adaptation layer (AAL). From a high level of abstraction their tasks can be seen as placing data onto the physical media, controlling the flow of data before it is transmitted, and modifying data to fit the ATM's cell structure.

The Physical Medium (PM) sublayer interfaces with the physical medium and provides transmission and reception of bits over the physical facility. It

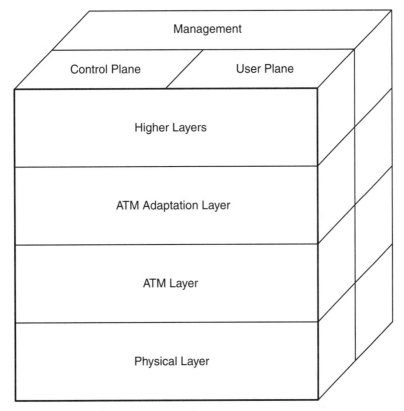

Figure 8.1 ATM reference model.

also provides the physical medium with proper bit timing and line coding. There will be different manifestations of this layer based on the specifics of the underlying medium (for example, for WAN/Internet applications a DS-1 link, a DS-3 link, a SONET link, etc.).

The Transmission Convergence (TC) sublayer receives bit streams from the physical media sublayer and passes it in cell form to the ATM layer. Its functions include cell rate decoupling (a mechanism that on the send side, inserts idle cells to adapt the rate to the transmission capacity and on the receive side, removes them), cell delineation (cell boundary recovery mechanism), generation and verification of the header error control (HEC sequence), transmission frame adaptation, and the generation/recovery of transmission frames.

The ATM layer controls the rate that traffic enters the network. It also encapsulates downward-coming data into cells from a number of sources and multiplexes the cell stream; conversely, it has the responsibility to de-encapsulate upward coming cells and demultiplex the resulting stream out to a number of sources. ATM, as a Data Link layer protocol, is independent of its medium:

It is capable of performing these functions on a wide variety of physical media. In addition, the ATM layer acts as an intermediary between the layer above it and the Physical layer below. It generates cell headers, attaches them to the data delivered to it by the Adaptation layer, and then delivers the properly tagged cells to the Physical layer. Conversely, it strips headers from cells containing data arriving on the physical layer before hoisting the data to the Application layer. The ATM layer ensures that cells are arranged in the proper sequence, but it does not identify and retransmit damaged cells.

The ATM Adaptation layer (AAL) allows various network layer protocols to utilize the service of the ATM layer, and it allows the Network layer to use ATM transparently. The AAL must segment the data from the Network layer (IP) into cells and, conversely, to reassemble cells into packets for the Network layer.

It is critical to understand that AALs are end-to-end functions (endsystem-to-endsystem). A network providing pure ATM will not be aware of, cognizant of, or act upon AAL information. The AAL used must be known in advance so that endsystems can agree. A number of AALs have been defined to meet different applications and quality-of-service requirements.

AALs utilize a portion of the ATM payload field of the cell to carry control information that is used for reassembly and error checking. In all AALs, the ATM header retains its usual configuration and functions. As noted, two sub-layers make up the AAL: the *Segmentation and Reassembly sublayer* (SAR) and the *Convergence sublayer* (CS). The SAR sublayer segments higher-layer information into a size suitable for cell payloads through a virtual connection. It also reassembles the contents of cells in a virtual connection into data units that can be delivered to higher layers. The CS sublayer performs functions like message identification and time/clock recovery (Minoli 1999). (See Figure 8.2.)

AAL 5 was designed to support data transmission and is by design a very simple protocol. In AAL 5 the CS sublayer creates a CS protocol data unit when it receives a packet from the higher application layer, namely IP. The first field in the PDU is the Information Payload field that contains user data. The PAD field fills in the number of bytes so that the payload is 48 bytes aligned. A two-byte Length field indicates the length of information payload.

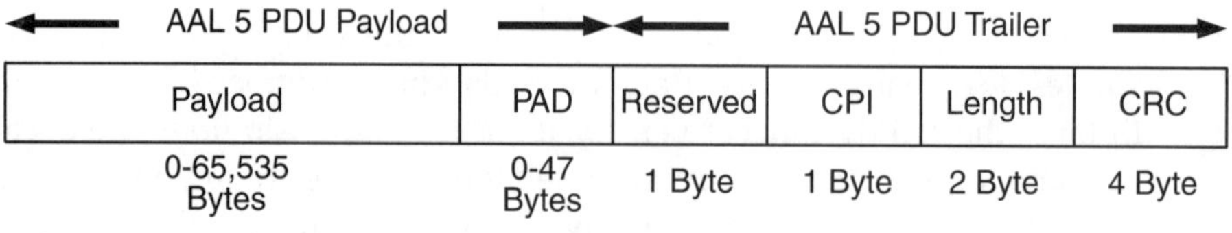

AAL 5 PDU Payload		AAL 5 PDU Trailer			
Payload	PAD	Reserved	CPI	Length	CRC
0-65,535 Bytes	0-47 Bytes	1 Byte	1 Byte	2 Byte	4 Byte

Figure 8.2   AAL type 5 CS-PDU.

This trailer is completed with a cyclic redundancy check field used to detect errors. The complete PDU is passed to the Segmentation and Reassembly sublayer of the AAL where it is segmented into cells. This layer also sets the *end of message* bit in the cell header. This bit along with the CRC can be used to detect and correct errors at the receiver. The cells are then passed to the ATM layer for transmission.

Classes of Service

Classes of service define ATM's basic support for quality of service by defining different types of traffic (video versus e-mail) and their respective behaviors. The different classes can be associated with different data flow, and as a consequence the ATM network can provide very good QoS support. ATM is one of the few technologies that can support a mixture of traffic classes in an effective manner. ATM's fine-grain QoS makes it a good platform for QoS-sensitive applications that need to share the network. For example, the ATM Forum started work on voice transport in 1993, and in early 1995 the Voice and Telephony Services over ATM working group published a document addressing both unstructured and structured circuit emulation specifications.

During the 1990s, ATM's place in supporting Internet backbones has been secure because of its ability to forward data at high speeds and to manage traffic, although links between IP and ATM management capabilities have not been implemented in backbones.

One of the key traffic-management features of ATM is support for negotiated connections with different QoS parameters such as peak cell rate, sustainable cell rate, delay, and cell loss. For ATM services, specifying the sustainable cell rate (SCR), the peak cell rate (PCR), and possibly the maximum burst size creates the circuit. The ATM network then allocates its limited resources using call admission control (CAC).

CAC involves the process of running an algorithm to determine if the new virtual circuit can be created. In the case where several switches are involved each switch can perform a CAC approximation on its downstream neighbors to determine the end-to-end likelihood of the call being accepted. Once the call has been established, the ATM switches use traffic shapers, traffic policing, and tagging for discard to keep traffic flowing smoothly. These switches also have the obligation to allocate enough resources to guarantee the type of requested service (for example, constant bit rate, variable bit rate, available bit rate, unspecified bit rate, etc.). It is notable that the functionality of these features has evolved to generic packet switching techniques, being implemented in IP routers along with certain aspects of ATM's "connection orientedness" through new methods such as Multi Protocol Label Switching (discussed in a later chapter).

Constant bit rate (CBR). This has a deterministic bandwidth requirement that makes it easy to provision and engineer. Sources that can make use of CBR generate cells at a fairly consistent rate, fully occupying the allocated bandwidth most of the time. The source rate corresponds to a peak transmission rate measured in cells per second. Conforming cells are typically guaranteed high priority because they are the products of latency-sensitive traffic such as video, voice, and circuit emulation.

Variable bit rate real-time (VBR-rt). The class is associated with so-called bursty data that has delay sensitivity. This type of class might be used for IP connectivity that carried a video payload.

Variable bit rate nonreal-time (VBR-nrt). This is bursty data without delay sensitivity. This type of class might be used for IP connectivity that carried general-purpose Internet traffic.

Available bit rate (ABR). This is the ATM Forum cell-based adaptive flow control. This class makes use of the ATM switch's ability to generate special congestion notification cells. When a traffic source receives the notification, it should reduce its offered load, in much the same way that the TCP slow start works.

Unspecified bit rate (UBR). ATM's best-effort category. The class is much like first-generation IP networks in that no guarantees are made and congestion loss is acceptable. This traffic call would be used on ISP backbones or at exchange points.

To ensure that the traffic arriving at a switch is conforming and is therefore not affected by the usage parameter control function, a traffic source must schedule traffic into the network according to the conformance definition. Two types of shaping are used: (1) ingress shaping, which is performed by the CPE source on the traffic before it enters the network, and (2) egress shaping, which is performed as traffic leaves the switch and enters another network. To be able to support the stated QoS, it is necessary to police the traffic according to the conformance definition to ascertain that nonconforming cells are discarded or tagged as low-priority cells. This guarantees that one connection is not able to affect the QoS of another connection. At the UNI, policing is done by a UPC function, which implements one or two instances of the GCRA (also known as *leaky bucket*) with the peak cell rate and the sustainable cell rate (ATM Forum 1995) (ATM Forum 1996a). At the NNI, policing is done by the network parameter control (NPC). UPC and NPC provide for similar capabilities but at different interfaces.

So, ATM switches that support QoS by policing their input traffic implement the leaky bucket algorithm. The leaky bucket provides a method of describing the rate of traffic when data is transmitted into the network in a frame or cell format. Each leaky bucket has an input rate and a limit parameter. The actual policing is done via vendor-specific code, and the leaky bucket is just a concept to help visualize the algorithm of policing (Schmidt 1998).

Call admission control for SVC service uses the traffic parameters discussed later in this chapter to make a best estimate of whether the network can carry data between clients at the desired bandwidth. ATM QoS is specified to the software implementing the call admission control as the performance that can be realized by the end devices via the negotiation of the following traffic description parameters:

Peak cell rate (PCR). The maximum number of cells that can be transmitted over a unit of time.

Cell delay variation tolerance (CDVT). The amount of so-called clumping that can be tolerated before a series of cells exceeding the PCR is deemed as violating the traffic contract.

Sustainable cell rate (SCR). A rate of cells that is near or slightly higher than the average over a unit of time.

Maximum burst size (MBS). The amount of cells on a virtual circuit that can burst at the PCR.

Minimum cell rate (MCR). The minimum rate at which a host using the available bit rate service category will always be able to transmit data. The default value is zero. When the minimum rate is set to zero, the network does not always promise that bandwidth will be available.

A successful call setup, and subsequent virtual circuit creation, involves selecting a set of values from the previously described parameters that are acceptable to the call admission control software running on the switches. If the desired resources exist then the switch will respond to the end devices that the call is established. The successful set of parameters is called the traffic contract because it specifies that the network will make some guarantees about performance if the network resources utilized are less than or equal to those specified in the call setup request (Schmidt 1998).

After the call has been established, the usage parameter control (UPC) software on the switch monitors the resources being used to determine if the traffic contract is being obeyed. For example, any usage parameter control algorithm that is policing the maximum offered load of the traffic contract uses the combination of the PCR and CDVT. The policing, on the values of the PCR and MBS, is done in the first leaky bucket. This bucket is allowed to accept logical cells until it overflows, in which case the overload feeds into subsequent measurement buckets.

In some cases, selecting the values for the traffic parameters can be difficult because most applications, like legacy LAN traffic, are not traditionally specified by these metrics. And in many cases network managers either specify no policing of LAN traffic or set the values of PCR/SCR only because their Internet provider is selling limited bandwidth. In that case, the Internet service provider (ISP) can utilize ingress policing on the ATM ports serving customers to check that only the allocated bandwidth is used (Schmidt 1998). For a virtual circuit requiring higher QoS, or at least a very consistent stream of cells, the sustained cell rate could be nearly identical to the bandwidth allocated. If the virtual circuit is carrying bursty data, the sustained cell rate requested is typically somewhat lower than the actual maximum because the call is more likely to be accepted, and the transmitting host's ATM layer should be able to shape the egress cell stream.

The SCR and MBS are the parameters used in constructing the second leaky bucket measurement device. The SCR is always chosen by the endsystem when signaling for the creation of the virtual circuit and can be lower than the PCR. MCR is used only with the available bit rate traffic category, described later in this chapter. When considering SCR values the network manager should consider values that will provide consistent good performance to applications over long periods of time. That way the data rate will be able to burst to the PCR for short periods but will always be able to depend on SCR performance (Schmidt 1998).

These traffic parameters are used by the network to determine which resources are required for the virtual circuit. In addition to those already discussed, the following QoS parameters are signaled in a call setup message:

Cell loss ratio (CLR). A measure that quantifies how much traffic has been lost compared to the total amount transmitted. The loss can be attributed to any cell-corrupting event like congestion or line-encoding errors.

Cell transfer delay (CTD). The measure of the time required for the cell to cross certain points in the ATM network. The primary concern to end users is the time required for the last bit of the cell to leave the transmitter until the first bit arrives at the receiver.

Cell delay variation (CDV). The measure of how the latency varies from cell to cell as the cells cross the network. Queuing and variation in switching speed are encountered and as they are transmitted cause variation. CDV is of concern in ATM networks because as the temporal pattern of cells is modified in the network, so is their traffic profile. If the modification is too large, then the traffic has the potential of exceeding the bounds of the traffic profile, and some cells may be dropped through no fault of the transmitter.

The signaled QoS parameters in the preceding paragraphs are used in the following fashion when requesting service:

- CLR applies to CBR, real-time VBR, nonreal-time VBR.
- For ABR, a value of CLR may be associated with the service but it is not signaled.
- CTD is carried in the call setup messages for CBR and real-time VBR services.
- CDV is carried in the call setup messages for CBR and real-time VBR services.

Compared with ATMF UNI 3.1, the UNI 4.0 specification supports the following additional features (Schmidt 1998):

Traffic parameter negotiation (TPN). Allows the SETUP to contain multiple information elements (IE) for the same object with the intent of reducing call admission control failures. If the first information element is unacceptable for call completion, the switch has the option of retrying the call admission control with the second IE.

Available bit rate (ABR). Utilizes ATM's closed-loop flow control by requesting in the signaling message that the service be associated with the new circuit. ABR also functions as a means of traffic parameter negotiation because it allows the user to establish a baseline, then request modification after the circuit is in service; applications can learn from the network how much data can be transmitted per second.

Virtual path switching (VPS). Permits the signaling of an entire virtual path instead of the usual VPI/VCI granularity.

Frame discard service (FDS). Allows signaling to request this service to be associated with a circuit so that during congestion the partial packet discard algorithms are employed. The technique of early packet discard (EPD) is discussed in a later section.

Signaling of individual QoS parameters. The UNI 4.0 specification diverges from the UNI 3.1 philosophy by selecting a QoS service category.

Multicast Connection Extensions

With these new features come a set of new information elements that evoke and control their behavior. The new information elements supported by UNI 4.0 are the following (Schmidt 1998):

Minimum acceptable ATM traffic descriptor. This field is used with the ABR service category. It sets the baseline for the ABR service and specifies the lowest bit/second that can be transmitted. ABR setup parameters include the various objects used to initialize ABR:

- Initial cell rate
- RM (resource management) round-trip time
- Data rate increment factor
- Data rate decrement factor
- Transient buffer exposure

Alternative ATM traffic descriptor. This field is used with the new feature of multiple information elements for the same parameter. If the ABR service is being selected, the alternative traffic descriptors are prohibited.

The ATM traffic category (CBR, VBR-nt, etc.) is selected by a new field, transfer_capability, in the broadband bearer capability information element. This IE also specifies whether the signaling message is point-to-point or multicast.

ATM Quality of Service

ATM provides for a wide range of capabilities for high-quality, advanced networking services. As noted, capabilities for provisioning *quality of service* (QoS) were developed as a core part of the ATM specification. These capabilities include a wide number of options from access control to resources controlling admission to resource-utilization privileges at a granulated level. Fine grain control is an issue at the core of the Internet.

ATM also allows for the development and implementation of a wide range of resource-allocation policy options, which can be flexible or restrictive, including provisions for dynamic changes, such as signaling for interrupts and resubmission of policies setups. Capabilities exist to define specific qualities of service, such as reference configurations (with baseline standards, performance references, and dependability parameters), defined through a variety of parameter variables, such as throughput speed, bounded delay, delay variance, priority, time schedule, cell error ratio, cell misinsertion rate, cell transfer delay, cell delay variation, cell loss ratio, and others. Provision is made for conflict resolution through negotiation rules.

These capabilities allow ATM to be used for the implementation of a highly specified QoS, and ATM QoS can be implemented directly, if the traffic is utilizing native ATM. Few of these advanced features, though, are currently utilized in IP over ATM implementations. Appropriate IP-ATM QoS mapping mechanisms are currently being developed; several IETF drafts exist on implementing controlled load and guaranteed services when implementing IP over ATM.

QoS in ATM Networks

ATM is a statistical multiplexing technology par excellence; yet, the statistical multiplexing is done in such an intelligent way that QoS is guaranteed to the user. Statistical multiplexing allows higher utilization of resources based both on allocating unused bandwidth to those that need it and on the intrinsic higher efficiency of pooled traffic. Furthermore, the use of overbooking also increases efficiency. Not only have standards been developed, but switches have been brought to market by many vendors supporting these standards. In general, support of QoS implies buffer management, a general packet-switching technique; in addition to algorithmic resources, this technique implies the presence of relatively large buffers.

Approaches to QoS in ATM

ATM networks have well-behaved operations in terms of predictable performance matching the expected level and minimizing congestion via strict traffic management. ATM's QoS support is useful not only in pure ATM networks, but in IP/RSVP-based networks that rely on ATM for Layer 2 transport. Today applications are not QoS-aware; but new voice, video, and multimedia applications may be developed with QoS in mind. QoS is achieved by managing the traffic intelligently. There are controls for the rate at which the traffic enters the network, at a VC level.

The parameters used by ATM to do traffic management are obtained at SVC or PVC setup time. As noted, the host signals its requirements to the network via the signaling mechanism. Each ATM switch in the path uses the traffic parameters to determine, via the CAC mechanism, if sufficient resources are available to set up the connection at the requested QoS level. In private networks the Private Network Node Interface (PNNI) protocol is responsible for determining if the required resources are available across the network. The CAC is used in each individual switch to determine if locally controlled resources are available, consistent with the request of the SETUP message. If the switch does have resources to support the call-request, it then reroutes the message to the next switch along a possible path to the destination.

To communicate QoS requests, the hosts or routers need a way to signal their requirements to the ATM network. In turn, individual switches must propagate requests across the network. The former is done via UNI signaling (for example, ATMF UNI 4.0); the latter is done via NNI signaling (for example,

PNNI 1.0). The signaling mechanism where the various QoS parameters are coded into the UNI 4.0 SETUP message supplement the *"QoS Class"* procedures defined in ATMF UNI 3.1 and ITU-T I.356. It is understood that the measurement of the network performance on a VC may vary slightly from the negotiated objective at any given time. This variance occurs because the negotiated objectives are the worst case of network performance that the network will allow, including peak intervals. Also, transient events may cause the measured performance to be worse than the negotiated objective.

QoS commitments are probabilistic in nature. Therefore, both users and carriers have to realize that statements like "guaranteed QoS"are subjective. The stated QoS is only an approximation of the performance that the network plans to offer over the duration of the connection. Specifically, because there is no limit to the lifetime of the connection and the resource allocation decisions are based on information available at connection time, the actual QoS may well vary over time. Transient events such as intermittent physical trunk failure, higher transient bit error rate, and even bursts of traffic from other sources when the UPC parameters are not properly set by the switch administrator can all impact QoS. Thus, the ATMF TM 4.0 document indicates that "QoS commitments can only be evaluated over a long period of time and over multiple connections with similar QoS commitments." Although this implies that in the long term the QoS is met, it could also mean temporary problems with real-time traffic such as voice, particularly if CBR services are not used.

ATM Forum Service Quality Parameters

The ATMF TM 4.0 supports the six QoS parameters, previously described:

Peak-to-peak cell delay variation (ptpCDV). Measures the jitter of delivered cells.

Maximum cell transfer delay (MaxCTD). Maximum delay to traverse the network.

Cell loss ratio (CLR). Lost cells/total transmitted cells.

Cell error ratio (CER). Errored cells/(successfully transferred cells + errored cells).

Severely errored cell block ratio (SECBR). Severely errored cell blocks/total transmitted cell blocks.

Cell misinsertion rate (CMR). Misinserted cells/time interval.

Using these metrics, the first three parameters can be negotiated as part of the call setup, while the last three are functions of the network's performance. Negotiation may entail specifying one or more of the parameters in question; also, the QoS could be set up differently for the two directions of a

VC. By definition, QoS call setup can be established on a per-call per-VC basis. In the network, QoS support is achieved by appropriate dynamic routing of the connection or by implementation-specific mechanisms. What may well fit in this last category is the current tendency of carriers to over-engineer the network to make sure that QoS can be achieved and sustained. It should be noted, however, that carriers may provide a small set of discrete choices for the negotiable parameters, rather than accept a continuum of request values. The size of the set of choice is, in part, limited by the finite number of bits used to specify each parameter.

Maximum cell transfer delay and peak-to-peak cell delay variation have to be defined very exactly, also using the reference model. A service agreement for ATM services involves a traffic contract. In the traffic contract the user's traffic is described via traffic parameters (see the previous discussion for PCR, SCR, MBS, and MCR).

Specified QoS Classes

A *specified QoS class* provides a quality of service to an ATM connection in terms of a subset of the ATM performance parameters discussed previously. For each specified QoS class, there is one specified objective value for each performance parameter. Initially, each network should define objective values for a subset of the ATM performance parameters for at least one of the following service classes from ITU-T Recommendation I.362 in a reference configuration that may depend on propagation delay and other factors:

- Service class A: circuit emulation, constant bit rate video
- Service class B: variable bit rate audio and video
- Service class C: connection-oriented data transfer
- Service class D: connectionless data transfer

Unspecified QoS Class

In the *unspecified QoS class*, no objective is specified for the performance parameters. The network may, however, determine a set of internal objectives for the performance parameters. In fact, these internal performance parameter objectives need not be constant during the duration of a connection. Thus, for the unspecified QoS class, there is no explicitly specified QoS commitment on either the CLP = 0 or the CLP = 1 cell flow.

Services using the unspecified QoS class may have explicitly specified traffic parameters. An example application of the unspecified QoS class is the support of a best-effort service (that is, UBR). For this type of service, the user selects the *best-effort capability*, the unspecified QoS class, and only the traffic parameter for the PCR on CLP = 0 + 1. This capability can be used to support users that are capable of regulating the traffic flow into the network and to adapt to time-variable available resources.

ATM Management Functions

ATM provides for a particularly rich set of management tools. Capabilities are provided for implementing traffic and managing contracts, for example, through validation procedures for QoS requests, measuring performance against contract baselines, service-class segmentation by session, shaping specific traffic patterns, and managing for delay intolerance.

ATM also provides tools for ensuring cell conformance and connectivity compliance through enforcement mechanisms such as cell and frame discarding and dynamically adjusted processing. ATM provides for a fairly complete suite of management tools, including those for flow control, path management, state management, proactive response to problems, for example, for detection and response to impending congestion, and measurement tools for traffic data statistics collection, diagnostics, analysis, and assessment.

Traffic Management in ATM 4.0

As experience with traffic management grew, so did the ATM Forum's related specifications (ATM 1996b). Available bit rate may be used to carry IP traffic although some feel that UBR with *early packet discard* (EPD) and MCR may be better for traditional TCP/IP applications. ABR uses a closed-loop rate-based flow control protocol. *Resource management* (RM) cells are transmitted into the network from the ATM attached device at regular intervals. Basically, the idea is that RM cells are used as probes to find congestion. They are transmitted from source to destination and, once at the destination, make a U-turn and return to the originating host. If congestion occurs, the cells can be used to signal it.

In operation, when the ATM switches detect congestion, they set a special bit, *explicit forward congestion indication* (EFCI), in the RM cell. The destinations, or other downstream ATM switches, react to this by setting the congestion indication bit (CI) in the returning RM cell. Once the cell is received by the originator of the traffic, it reacts by slowing down. The UPC algorithm supports PCR and MCR parameters for ABR, implying that a minimum cell rate is guaranteed if the source appropriately shapes the traffic. Sources and destinations must be suitably equipped to support this behavior.

As an extension to the basic behavior described previously, some ATM switches can immediately react to EFCI tagged cells and quickly return them to the destination. They do this so that transmitters can quickly be notified of congestion. This is called *virtual source/virtual destination* (VS/VD); it helps at the edge of the network by acting on behalf of the real source/destination. ABR allows switch developers to minimize the amount of buffering required in high-speed links with high-speed sources (for example, 155 or 622 Mbps) and high source/trunk speed mismatch (for example, 622 Mbps sources and OC3 trunks).

Early use of ATM networks for TCP/IP traffic showed very poor performance when congested. This condition results from packet shredding when a switch output port is dropping cells from several converging virtual circuits. The end effect is that all of the packets become corrupted, and TCP/IP performance is consequently unacceptable. A useful feature supported in some ATM switches that can mange this condition is frame discard. This feature is usually referred to as *early packet discard-Partial packet discard, a separate but related technique can also be used.* With EPD, network elements can discard all cells of an AAL 5 packet (complete AAL 5 frames not merely cells) when congestion develops. Random cell discard would potentially result in many partial packets, which have to be thrown away by the destination after incurring the effort of network delivery. Frame discard, therefore, provides higher network efficiency and better *goodput.* Improved goodput means that it cuts down TCP retransmits and removes the requirement for extremely low cell loss for data applications. Early packet discard is particularly useful in UBR: it is simple to engineer and is insensitive to traffic parameters, just like TCP/IP. (See Figure 8.3.)

Experience with data applications using UBR and ABR shows that these services suffer from the same behavior as data in best-effort IP networks, particularly when run over ATM switches with limited buffering. These switches have shallow queue depths and were designed to anticipate only CBR traffic. ATM switches built from 1990 to 1996 tend to fall into this category. Modern

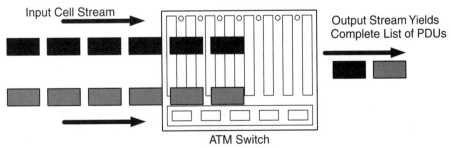

Figure 8.3   Packet shredding in congestion.

switches have queue depths that support 64,000 cells per port and interact well with TCP's congestion avoidance mechanism, *slow start*.

ATM offers flexible service based on five categories, including bandwidth-on-demand services with QoS guarantees. The CAC allocates resources in the switch to "guarantee" QoS to conforming traffic. Policing ensures, for example, that the only traffic exiting a router is traffic conforming to the UPC contract/function. Efficient queuing (for example, WFQ) enables the network to achieve QoS requirements with optimal resource allocation. ABR offers increased control of traffic entering the network, while discard can provide optimized management of congestion for AAL 5 streams.

LAN Communication: ATMF and IETF Approaches

This discussion has addressed signaling, models, and transport protocols that permit applications to request different *classes of service* (CoS). In this section we will shift the focus away from high-level protocols to application of protocols in ATM LAN networks. First, this section discusses protocols in use today to help utilize ATM as the physical communication media in a local area network without necessarily utilizing QoS features. This information is critical for network managers and designers because the technology described in this chapter provides the foundation of multiprotocol networks. After the discussion of these LAN protocols, this section will diverge into a discussion of technologies that function to expose ATM's QoS support and how these technologies are used in network design.

Scope of the Local Area ATM Networking Problem

The network manager faces several problems when migrating legacy networks to ATM, regardless of whether the transition is to a simple network or to a complex system. Several of these problems are associated with joining a connection-oriented ATM network with a connectionless LAN, like Ethernet. When joining these different technologies, the problems encountered can be subdivided into two categories:

Address resolution. Final determination of where the destination resides.

QoS requesting and mapping. Configuration and creation of a communication path between the source and destination.

The ATM Forum and the IETF have devised several approaches for building ATM networks that coexist well with legacy LANs. When selecting a migration path from existing LAN infrastructures to QoS-capable, ATM-based internetworks, network engineers need to consider the strengths and weaknesses of each approach. To best illustrate the components used when migrating legacy networks to ATM, this information is divided into sections that address standards developed by different bodies.

Prior to LAN Emulation (LANE), early implementers of ATM encountered significant difficulty, which was due to the connection-oriented nature of ATM. This occurred because most network protocols, such as Ethernet or token ring, were designed as connectionless networks. On connectionless networks, any host can communicate with any other host simply by placing a packet onto the network. The packet is then transmitted to all hosts attached to the local network without any further intervention by the originating host. If the packet is destined for a computer that is a member of the local network, then the packet will be seen by that machine and read directly from the LAN. If the packet is destined for a host outside the local network, then it is the responsibility of the local *router* to forward the data to the correct destination. This type of communication is possible on connectionless networks because all the hosts share the same physical media.

Connection-oriented networks are much like circuit-switched networks in that they require an established connection prior to communication. Additional complexities are associated with connection-oriented networks because of their difficulty with broadcast messages. In addition, because virtual circuits provide for one-to-one communication, a host broadcasting to a set of other hosts, as would be the case in a multicast video conference, must be aware of any addition or deletion to the receiving set. That is, when any new device joins or leaves the multicast group, a change of virtual circuits must be made. This problem has been a difficult one to solve with connection-oriented networks, such as ATM, and will continue to be an area of active research for some time.

The constraints imposed by ATM's connection-oriented methodology, coupled with a lack of destination-address-resolving switched-virtual-circuit software, such as LANE, resulted in ATM networks first using only PVCs. As these networks grew, PVCs became cumbersome to create for each pair of communicating hosts. Even though this could be tolerated for networks with dozens of interconnected computers or routers, it quickly became problematic in a network of hundreds of hosts where any host could communicate with any other host. To improve the ability to *plug and play* and increase scalability, the ATM Forum formed the Local Area Network Emulation Over ATM working group, chartered to develop protocols that allow quick and easy use of ATM. The requirements set forth by the ATM Forum LANE group were that the solution be based on the User Network Interface Specification version 3.0, provide high performance, and be capable of protocol-independent switching across logical LANs, as well as be capable of seamless interworking with legacy

LANs via bridges and capable of supporting PVCs, SVCs, or any combination (ISO 1993).

One of the chief benefits of LANE is the ability of all devices attached to a LAN emulation network to function in a plug-and-play fashion, requiring minimal configuration. This ease of use is primarily due to the fact that application programs use the network services via standard device driver *application program interfaces* (API). That is, by emulating the API of a standard Ethernet network interface to the higher-layer applications, the LANE software can allow these applications to run unmodified on ATM networks.

The longer term viability of LANE is questionable. One of the major highlights of LANE is that by hiding ATM, hosts are not required to understand all of the potential complexities of operating on a connection-oriented network supporting multiple levels of QoS. On the other hand, hiding ATM does not allow applications to utilize the technology to its fullest or make use of QoS because there are no provisions for communicating QoS requests. Ironically, this capability is one of the fundamental strengths that the developers of the ATM protocol envisioned. Also, with the wide deployment of low-cost efficient, switched Ethernet LANs at 10, 100, and 1000 Mbps, much of the motivation for LANE is disappearing.

Another key issue in developing a network based on LANE will be its performance capabilities related to scalability and reliability. In terms of scale, LANE, by design, is intended to emulate the operation of a legacy LAN segment. As bridged LANs grow, the number of broadcasts generated by Address Resolution Protocol (ARP) can become overwhelming (RFC 1577). An additional problem is posed when the network is used to carry broadcast/multicast traffic. For example, if a LAN network was used for video distribution, it is conceivable that the broadcast servers could quickly become overloaded. Both of these conditions have the potential to overload LAN emulation servers. With no QoS capabilities, severely restricted scalability, and problematic reliability, the future of LANE is uncertain.

Synchronous Optical Network

The majority of large-scale ATM networks and current, advanced IP networks are deployed as IP over ATM over SONET/SDH (Synchronous Optical Network; internationally, the equivalent is the Synchronous Digital Hierarchy, SDH, formulated by the ITU-T). The SONET standard was developed by the Exchange Carriers Standards Association (ECSA) for the American National Standards Institute (ANSI). SONET/SDH, as well as optical layers, is traditionally regarded as core transport layers. SONET is an electrical transmission standard (derived from voice transmission technology, essentially allowing the substitution of fiber for copper on trunk lines for telephony) that provides functionality for optical networks.

A basic function is multiplexing and signal conversion for fiber transmission, converting electrical signals to optical signals and the reverse. The SONET standard defines electrically equivalent *synchronous transport signals* (STS) for fiber-based transmission. SONET was developed in part to allow for using fiber for long-distance transmission while maintaining an ability to interconnect with existing copper infrastructure. Virtually any type of major communications service can be supported by SONET through available service adapters. Add-drop multiplexers allow for easily provisioning circuits within a SONET environment.

SONET Frames

Data is transmitted within SONET frames. SONET utilizes a basic unit of STS-1, which has a bit rate of 51.84 Mbps. Higher rates of speed are multiples of STS-1. The SONET frame format is divided into transport overhead and the *synchronous payload envelope* (SPE). The SPE comprises the STS path overhead and the data. The SONET/STS-1 frame is usually depicted as a matrix of 9 rows, each with 90 bytes. One frame is transmitted in 125 microseconds.

SONET is hierarchical (upgrades to higher speeds require significant investments for new equipment). SONET defines specifications for transmission, such as bandwidth transmission rates over fiber-optic cables. *Optical carrier* (OC) levels are based on multiples of Optical carrier 1 (OC1 or 51.84 Mbps), for example, OC3 (155.52 Mbps), OC12 (622.08 Mbps), OC48 (2488.32 Mbps), OC192 (9.95328 Gbps), and OC768 (39.81312 Gbps). An OC3c designation indicates that the link is implemented as a single concatenated channel, not merely multiplexed STS-1.

SONET Reliability and Management

Another strength of SONET is its reliability, especially its self-healing properties. Although linear systems are common in some wide area deployments, SONET is frequently configured as a ring, for example, with dual fiber paths, each transmitting in a different direction (*bidirectional line switched ring*). If one link is cut, the majority of the ring continues to function. SONET also has a wide range of powerful infrastructure and traffic tools. Sophisticated detectors within a SONET environment continually monitor for loss of signal, loss of data, transmission errors, and other fault conditions. SONET also provides for recovery measures as a response to those conditions.

SONET provides for management and operations through its defined capabilities for *operations, administration, maintenance,* and *provisioning* (OAM&P) suite of services. An OAM&P architecture has been formulated that provides for bandwidth and management functionality as part of the overhead structure. OAM&P data communication channels allow for internode and individual node signaling as part of an extensive system of infrastructure management services. There is an opinion that overall SONET architecture may have been designed with too many functions and features, for example, many fields are not used. A number of groups are discussing the concept of a lightweight SONET.

The Foundation Layer: Fiber Optics

ATM can be used over many different types of media, but it is usually implemented over optical fiber cables. Optical fiber will be the basic foundation layer for advanced digital communications for the foreseeable future, and it is being rapidly developed everywhere that is economically justifiable regionally, nationally, and internationally. This technology communicates information by sending light through thin glass cables. Fiber has many advantages: It is small, lightweight, flexible, nonelectrical, capable of error-free signaling over extremely long distances, and increasingly able to carry very large amounts of data. For various reasons, some areas, such as remote locations, are better served with broadband wireless technologies.

There are two basic types of fiber, single-mode and multimode. Single-mode fiber has a smaller core and, therefore, is less susceptible to dispersion of its light signal, requiring fewer amplifiers along a path. It is more difficult to terminate, however, so for local use and where termination is otherwise an issue, multimode fiber is used.

Over the past few years, optical fiber technology has undergone multiple transformations through successive innovations. Extremely large amounts of digital communications traffic can be transmitted over fiber worldwide in microseconds, assisted by optical amplifiers, transmitters and receivers. More recent fiber-optic signaling techniques, such as those based on dense wave division multiplexing (DWDM), are extending existing capability with continuous improvements in efficiency and performance. Later chapters describe some current developments in DWDM.

Conclusion

Currently, ATM is an important support protocol for the Internet. IP over ATM has become a powerful combination for high-performance networks worldwide. This type of implementation is expected to continue to be prominent for the near term. Longer-term directions are key issues being widely debated.

Some have predicted the ATM layer will vanish sooner rather than later and that IP will be transmitted directly over SONET or lightwave (topics covered later in this book). On the other hand, others note the rich function and feature set of ATM, presented in this chapter, and suggest that the power of the IP protocol can be extended by a system that would provide mappings to those capabilities. A number of development efforts exist to accomplish this goal. More IP-over-ATM issues are explained in the next chapter.

References

ATM Forum Technical Committee. 1993. *ATM User-Network Interface Specification: Version 3.0.* Upper Saddle River, NJ: Prentice-Hall.

ATM Forum Technical Committee. 1995. *ATM User-Network Interface Version 3.1.* Upper Saddle River, NJ: Prentice-Hall.

ATM Forum Technical Committee. 1996a. *ATM User-Network Interface Version 4.0.* Upper Saddle River, NJ: Prentice-Hall.

ATM Forum Technical Committee. 1996b. *Traffic Management Specification Version 4.0* (af-tm-0056.000). Mountain View, CA: ATM Forum. ftp.atmforum.com/pub.

ISO/IEC 10038: ANSI/IEEE Standard 802.1D. 1993. *Media Access Control Bridges.*

Minoli, D. and G. Dobrowski. 1994. *Principles of Signaling for Cell Relay and Frame Relay.* Norwood, MA: Artech House.

Minoli, D. and A. Schmidt. 1998. *Network Layer Switched Services.* New York: John Wiley & Sons.

Minoli, D. and A. Schmidt. 1999. *Internet Architectures.* New York: John Wiley & Sons.

RFC 1577. 1994. M. Laubach. *Classical IP and ARP over ATM.* ftp://ftp.isi.edu/in-notes/rfc1577.txt (proposed standard, rendered obsolete by RFC2225).

Schmidt, A. and D. Minoli. 1998. *Multiprotocol over ATM: Building State of the Art ATM Intranets Utilizing RSVP, NHRP, LANE, Flow Switching, and WWW Technology.* Upper Saddle River, NJ: Prentice-Hall.

Spohn, D. L. 1997. *Data Network Design.* New York: McGraw-Hill.

CHAPTER 9

Classical IP over ATM

Classical IP over ATM Overview

In Chapter 8, the problem of running LAN traffic over ATM was addressed with the LAN Emulation suite of protocols. In this chapter[1] an alternate technique, called classical IP over ATM, will be discussed. Classical IP and ARP over ATM (CIP) predates LANE slightly and is the method of running LAN traffic over ATM developed by the Internet Engineering Task Force (IETF). The IETF's specification is defined to provide native IP support over ATM and is documented in the following requests for comments (RFCs): (ATM Forum 1993), (RFC 1483), (RFC 1577), (RFC 1755), and (RFC 2022):

RFC 1483, Multiprotocol Encapsulation over ATM Adaptation Layer 5

RFC 1577, Classical IP and ARP over ATM

RFC 1755, ATM Signaling Support for IP over ATM

RFC 2022, Multicast Address Resolution (MARS) Protocol

These protocols are designed to treat ATM as virtual "wire" with the special property of being connection-oriented and, therefore, as with LANE, requiring a unique means for address resolution and broadcast support. In the classical-IP-over-ATM model, the ATM fabric interconnecting a group of hosts is considered a network, called Non Broadcast Multiple Access (NBMA) (RFC 2332). A NBMA network is made up of a switched service like ATM or frame relay with a large number of endstations that cannot directly broadcast messages to each other. On the NBMA network, there may be one OSI Layer 2 network, but it is subdivided into several logical IP subnetworks (LIS) (RFC 2205) that can be traversed only via routers.

One of the principal philosophies behind classical IP over ATM is that network administrators will build networks using the same techniques that are used today, that is, dividing hosts into physical groups called subnetworks, according to administrative workgroup domains. Then the subnetworks are interconnected to other subnetworks via IP routers. An LIS in classical IP over ATM is made up of a collection of ATM-attached hosts and ATM-attached IP routers that are part of a common IP subnetwork. Policy administration (such as security, access controls, routing, and filtering) will still remain a function of routers because the ATM network is just "smart" wire.

In classical IP over ATM, the functionality of ARP is provided with the help of special-purpose server processes that are typically co-located. Each classical IP over ATM LIS has an ARP server that maintains IP-address-to-ATM-address mappings (see Figure 9.1). All members of the LIS register with the ARP server, and subsequently all ARP requests from members of the LIS are handled by the ARP server. This mechanism is a little more straightforward than LANE version 1 since, for ARP, there is only one server and this server maintains direct IP to ATM address mappings.

In the CIP model, IP ARP requests are forwarded from hosts directly to the LIS ARP server using MAC/ATM address mappings that are acquired at CIP registration. The ARP server, which may be running on an ATM-attached router, replies with an ATM address. When the ARP request originator receives the reply with the ATM address, it can then issue a call setup message and directly establish communications with the desired destination.

Communication between LISs must be made via ATM-attached routers that are members of more that one LIS. One physical ATM network can logically be considered several logical IP subnetworks; but the interconnection, from the host perspective, is accomplished via another router. Using an ATM-attached router as the path between subnetworks prevents ATM-attached endstations in different subnetworks from creating direct virtual circuits between one another. OC12 ATM router ports can be wire-speed, negating, or at least minimalizing, any SA-induced latency.

CIP provides multicast support via the multicast address resolution server (MARS) (RFC 2022). The MARS model is similar to a client/server design because it operates by requiring a multicast server (MCS) to keep membership lists of multicast clients that have joined a multicast group. A network administrator assigns a client to a multicast server at configuration time. In the MARS model, a MARS system, along with its associated clients, is called

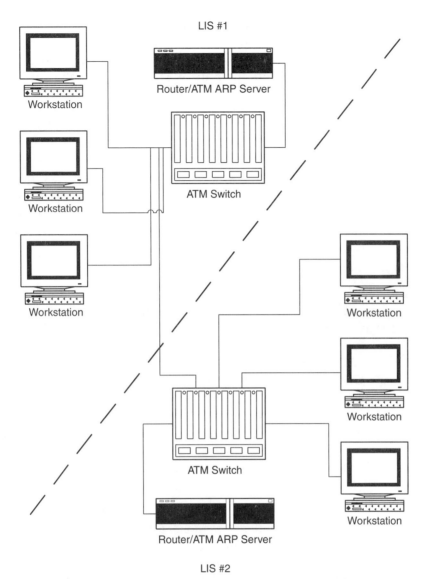

Figure 9.1 Classical IP over ATM LIS.

a cluster. The MARS approach uses an address resolution server to map an IP multicast address from the cluster onto a set of ATM endpoint addresses of the multicast group members.

The MARS model is based on a hierarchy of devices. The three primary components of a MARS-based IP-over-ATM network are top-level server(s) called the MARS, zero or more multicast servers that provide second-level multicast distribution, and clients that utilize IP multicast by building point-to-multipoint paths based on information learned by MARS.

Every MARS has at least one client and server contained within a classical IP over ATM logical IP subnetwork. To operate the system, clients use the MARS as a means of determining what other hosts are members of a multicast group. In a MARS network there are two modes of operation, full mesh or multicast server. In the full mesh, client queries are sent to the server to identify which hosts have registered as members of a multicast group. Next, the client establishes a point-to-multipoint virtual circuit to those leafs. In the second mode, the MCS acts as the focal point of all multicast packets originated anywhere in the multicast tree. In this case, in order to simulate IP multicast over an ATM network, the MCS simply retransmits, over the ATM multicast connections, all packets sent to the IP multicast group by the clients. Because the set of hosts in a multicast group is constantly changing, the MARS is also responsible for dynamically updating the set of clients with new membership information as changes occur, along with adding and removing clients from the active members.

When running multicast over an ATM network, selecting between these two modes of operation is left to the discretion of the network designer. Adding multiple layers of hierarchy to the distribution tree can make an additional design determination with MARS. For example, multicast clusters may contain the second level of the hierarchy by elevating a client to the role of a multicast server. One of the trade-offs conceded to gain the simplicity that MARS offers is the required "out of band" control messages used to maintain multicast group membership. In order for clients and multicast servers to send and receive control and membership information, the MARS protocol specifies the setup of a partial mesh of virtual circuits. The MARS maintains its own point-to-multipoint circuits, called the ClusterControlVC, for the members within the cluster.

The ClusterControlVC carries leaf node update information to the clients as members leave and join the multicast session. Each client in a multicast cluster maintains a point-to-point virtual circuit to the MARS, which is used to initialize itself and to receive path-group change messages. Finally, the MARS manages the MCSs through point-to-point virtual circuits between each MCS and the MARS, and point-to-multipoint circuits, called ServerControlVC, from the MARS to the MCSs. These circuits are used, like the ClusterControlVC, to pass information from the MARS to keep the cluster membership updated.

In the classical IP model, data transfer is done by creating a virtual circuit between hosts, then using LLC/SNAP encapsulation of data that has been segmented by AAL 5. Mapping IP packets onto ATM cells using LLC/SNAP is specified in RFC 1483, Multiprotocol Encapsulation over ATM. RFC 1483 specifies how data is formatted prior to segmentation. The RFC documents several different methods; however, the vast majority of host/router implementations use the LLC/SNAP encapsulation. LLC/SNMP specifies that each datagram is prefaced with a bit pattern that the receiver can use to determine the protocol type of the source.

The advantages provided by the encapsulation method specified in RFC 1483 are that it treats ATM as a Data Link layer that supports a large maximum transfer unit (MTU) and that it can operate in either a bridge or a multiplexed mode. Because the network is not emulating an Ethernet or token ring, like LANE, the MTU has been specified to be as large as 9180 bytes. The large MTU can improve performance of hosts attached directly to the ATM network.

RFC 1577 specifies two major modifications to traditional connectionless ARP. The first modification is the creation of the ATMARP message used to request addresses. The second modification is to the InATMARP message for inverse address registration. When a client wishes to initialize itself on an LIS, it establishes a switched virtual circuit to the CIP ARP server. Once the circuit has been established, the server contains the ATM address extracted from the client's call-setup-message calling-party field. The server can now transmit an InATMARP request in an attempt to determine the IP address of the client that has just created the virtual circuit. The clients respond to InATMARP requests with IP addresses, and then the server uses this information to build an ATMARP table cache.

Multiprotocol ATM Networks

Throughout the previous sections, the groundwork has been laid for protocols used by data communications to build networks supporting legacy protocols over ATM and, ultimately, QoS. Building on this information, this section examines the work done in the ATM Forum on the Multiprotocol over ATM (MPOA) (Schmidt 1998) (Minoli 1997) protocol suite. MPOA is considered a protocol suite because its primary goal is not to develop new technology, but rather to draw on the work of several different standards bodies, synthesizing them into a "big picture" document that describes how all these protocols interact.

MPOA provides a means for seamlessly internetworking a triad of protocols. On one side are ATM's legacy protocols, such as classical IP and LAN Emulation, which allow hosts to discover each other on a local logical subnetwork and form the basis for intra-LAN communication. On the second branch are protocols developed in the IEFT that allow hosts to establish direct communication paths across an ATM network traversing subnetwork boundaries without a router. The final leg of the triad is provided by a set of Integrated Services protocols, such as RSVP and other protocols such as RTP/RTCP/RTSP, which provide a means to specify QoS and then help realize and monitor network performance. The first major distinction between MPOA and its predecessors is the ability to support the Next Hop Resolution Protocol (NHRP) (RFC 2332) on the multiprotocol servers.

MPOA can be viewed as a superset protocol that brings together many underlying technologies. It is also one that is responsible for solving the problems of establishing connections between pairs of hosts across administrative domains, and it enables applications to make use of a network's ability to provide guaranteed QoS. Some of the key advantages of MPOA are these:

- Edge devices, which can establish direct connections between themselves without using routers

- Lower latency communication between devices after ARP due to route elimination

- Reduced or restricted amounts of broadcast traffic

- Flexibility in selection of maximum transfer unit size to optimize performance

- Fabrication of multiple virtual LANs on one ATM network

In the multiprotocol-over-ATM model, a virtual LAN is similar to virtual subnetworks or virtual network although intervirtual LAN connections are not necessarily mediated by routers. With MPOA, hosts are capable of directly communicating with each other, even in the case where the path is between different logical IP subnetworks. The path of the data can be determined based on decisions made by the edge device. The traffic can be forwarded along the default path established between routers on the subnetworks, in the same manner as in LANE or classical IP. Or a new virtual circuit can be created that interconnects the two different subnetworks and passes the flow. This type of connection is called a cut-through or short-cut path. The important distinctions between these points are the decisions made by the edge devices and the measurement of flows.

The MPOA model operates by relying on multiprotocol route servers to maintain knowledge of the location of either the devices or the ATM network egress device closest to the ultimate destination. When the location is found, the ATM network can then place a call directly between hosts, thus relying on the low-latency ATM network and eliminating the potentially high delay introduced when routing individual IP packets. An MPOA server model is likened to using directory assistance on a voice network. The directory assistance agent is asked for the phone number of a destination and returns the value. With the phone number, a call can be placed to the desired destination. With MPOA, however, there will be no restriction on local versus long-distance directory assistance, and the phone call may be placed using differing degrees of QoS. The QoS determination is left to the discretion of the endsystem.

MPOA uses LANE as the core building block for intra-LAN address resolution. LANE emulation's strength is that it enables network designers to treat ATM as a bridged technology for legacy intra-LAN communication, whereas classical IP over ATM treats ATM as a point-to-point link between hosts or routers, much the same as a WAN circuit.

The benefits of an MPOA network are that it provides the connectivity of a fully routed environment with few route servers and empowers the attached devices to utilize large topographic databases. It thus separates routing and switching from routers and edge media converters taking advantage of ATM. (Participation of devices in the utilization of the protocols necessary to maintain topological databases is an important related issue.) Direct interdomain connection for best-effort traffic (and in some cases QoS) provides a unified approach to Layer 3 protocols over ATM via default forwarding followed by segregation post-flow detection. Also, multiple standards bodies have been standardizing this new paradigm and separating routing decisions from data forwarding for several years. Only recently have these efforts come together to develop a common set of protocols. This work is focused with the IETF's Internetworking Over NBMA (ION) working group and the Integrated Services (Int-Serv) working group. Their efforts have yielded the Next Hop Resolution Protocol (NHRP), and the MPOA document that may form the basis of advanced service provision for the next-generation Internet. Also, separately, the important Resource Reservation Protocol (RSVP) continues to be developed.

Next Hop Resolution Protocol

Classical IP over ATM and LAN emulation suffer from the limitation that hosts in different logical subnetworks (but attached to the same physical ATM network) must communicate using intermediate routers. This traditional model of routing is shown in Figure 9.2. In order to provide for additional flexibility for such a system, a new paradigm is needed that allows the hosts to communicate directly. Directly establishing communication between hosts in different subnetworks, without using a router, may be desirable because of potential improvements in performance. For example if a large amount of traffic moves between two organizational units in relation to all other traffic on the network. As noted, this technique is referred to as cut-through or short-cut routing because it bypasses routers and cuts a path through the ATM, or any nonbroadcast multiple access network.

When a router or endsystem has data to transmit, short-cut routing allows the host to find the ATM layer address of the ultimate IP destination or the router closest to the destination. Cut-through routing is also designed to work even if the destination is in a different administrative domain or subnetwork. Once the ATM address has been found, the idea is to circumvent the intermediate routers

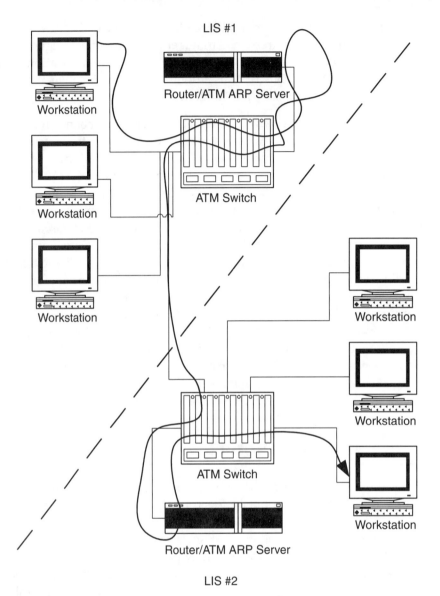

Figure 9.2 First-generation inter-ATM LAN networking.

and establish a direct-communication virtual circuit to that destination. Cut-through routing uses a device called a next hop route server (NHS) to acquire information about the host on the network, but it then relies on Layer 2 technology, like ATM or frame relay, to communicate with the remote host. The NHSs play the critical role of maintaining address information for the network in much the same way as the directory assistance operator described earlier.

NHRP's designers consider the technology to be one that is restricted to the topological boundaries of an enterprise network. That is, it is not envisioned as something that will cross administrative boundaries. NHRP is restricted to topological boundaries because the processes provided by the directory assistance do not scale well across boundaries.

NHRP is an excellent technology for creating short-cut paths across an ATM campus network interconnecting routers. Because of its scope, the roll-out of this service into next-generation networks may flow from the campus networks, next possibly to include a few ISP networks, and finally allowing cut-through of international networks (see Figure 9.3).

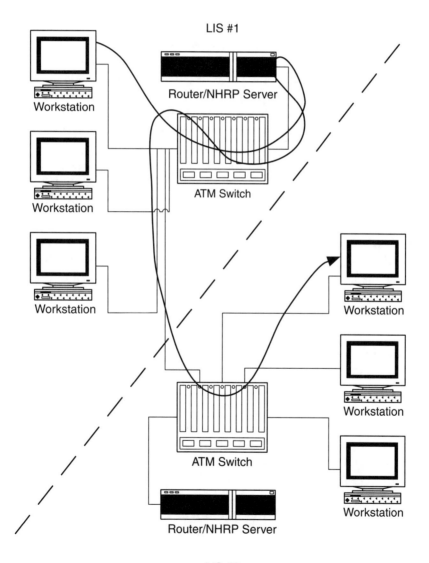

Figure 9.3 Cut-through routing.

Establishing a direct virtual circuit that crosses multiple administrative domains is a very complex problem, one that is sometimes referred to as the "Large Cloud Problem" (RFC 2332). One can appreciate this problem by considering conventional routing protocols. Typically, routing protocols operate by summarizing or aggregating information to build their routing tables. When information is summarized, details about the Layer 2 technology are either lost or hidden by the routing protocol. For applications to establish direct communication across an ATM network, they need the details of exact locations of destinations, not just summarization.

MPOA/NHRP, in performing cut-through routing, also needs these details (such as ATM addresses) to set up virtual circuits between hosts. To cope with this problem, MPOA/NHRP has an associated query protocol used as a probe to follow the routed path to the destination. This protocol is capable of removing the aggregation of the route prefix and distilling the actual Layer 2 address of the destination. Each query is generated by an edge device or host and then passed along the default path toward the target. The query is passed, hop by hop, between the route servers until a server is reached that contains the mapping of the IP address to the ATM address. When the query protocol reaches this final route server, it asks for the Layer 2 address of the destination computer. When the ATM address is returned to the query generation host/edge device, the source can use it to establish an ATM switch virtual circuit that cuts through the ATM cloud.

NHRP is designed to allow endstations to locate each other via an "extended" ARP on networks, such as frame relay or ATM. In a network supporting virtual circuits, devices attached to the same network must establish paths or calls to exchange data but, unlike LANs, lack the ability to easily broadcast a message to all hosts. In the NHRP model, these networks are called nonbroadcast, multi-access (NBMA) (RFC 2332).

The NBMA Next Hop Resolution Protocol allows a host or router to determine the internetworking layer addresses and NBMA addresses of the suitable "NBMA next hop" to a destination station. This address, in effect, will be that of the true destination or a device relatively close to the destination that will act as a data proxy. A subnetwork can be nonbroadcast and therefore benefit from the short-cut routing, either because it technically does not support broadcast (as is the case with frame relay and ATM) or because broadcasting may not be feasible (as is the case with large SMDS networks). If the destination is connected to the NBMA subnetwork, then the NBMA next hop becomes the destination station. Otherwise, the NBMA next hop is the egress router from the NBMA subnetwork "nearest" to the destination station.

NHRP describes a next-hop resolution method that relaxes the forwarding restrictions of the LIS model. For example, when the internetwork layer address is IP and the NBMA next hop has been resolved, the source may immediately start sending IP packets to the destination, or, in the case of ATM, it may first establish a connection to the destination with the desired bandwidth and QoS characteristics, if the hosts are connected to a connection-oriented network. A next hop server (NHS) provides support when MPOA employs NHRP for short-cut resolution of the NHRP function of holding client addresses and responding to inquiries.

The function of generating queries and establishing direct virtual circuits is the responsibility of the next hop client (NHC) residing in the ATM host or ATM edge device. The NHS maintains a cache containing the mapping of IP addresses to ATM addresses. The cache is built either by having end nodes register at initialization time or by propagating the cache with values learned from the operation of NHRP over time. There is also a cache of address mappings on the client that are learned from the operation of NHRP Resolution Reply messages or manual configuration.

Before the NHRP process can begin, the NHCs and NHSs must be initialized with the ATM address of the next hop server and its IP address. The NHS is configured with its own ATM address at startup, and it may be configured with the IP address prefixes that the NHC serves.

When hosts use NHRP, there are three distinct phases: configuration, registration, and address resolution. NHRP clients and servers transition through the phases by following a protocol of exchanging messages. In the configuration stage, the client must be configured with the ATM address of the NHS that is serving its domain; typically this information is provided manually. The servers are configured with their own IP and ATM address. In addition, the server is configured to know what IP addresses are within its domain, that is, which addresses it takes responsibility for when NHRP queries arrive.

After configuration, a client registers with the NHRP server and provides an ATM address and an IP address. When the clients have registered themselves with the server(s), the process of address resolution can begin. The process of resolving queries, from a high level of abstraction, is straightforward. The NHSs receive queries along the default IP route. If they do not maintain the domain, then the query is forwarded along the default path toward the NBMA destination, where the NHSs continue the process of address checking.

NHRP Message Types

NHRP supports two basic message types: query and reply. In creating the short cuts, clients first register and then the next hop servers synchronize their information. At this point the clients can issue queries. From the two basic message types, the complete set of operations can be further expanded into the following:

NHRP Registration Request. This is used to explicitly register an NHC's NBMA information with an NHS.

NHRP Registration Reply. This is the reply issued by the NHS on successfully registering a client.

NHRP Resolution Request. As described later, this message type requests the Network-layer-to-ATM-address mapping that provided the necessary information prior to establishing the short-cut VC.

NHRP Resolution Reply. The NHS that has responsibility for the target and contains the NBMA address returns this message type.

NHRP Purge Request. This explicitly requests the deletion of a NHC cache entry.

NHRP Purge Reply. This acknowledges the deletion of the NHC's address from the NHS's cache.

NHRP Error Indication. This signals an error condition, for example, unrecognized extension, protocol error, or invalid reply received.

NHRP Operation

NHRP's operation is initiated by the edge device and proceeds in a client/server-like manner. This can be caused by flow detection in the edge device or an explicit short-cut creation generated by the ATM host. The first step in NHRP is the creation of an NHRP Resolution Request packet that is transmitted toward the destination along the default routed path. The Resolution Request contains the source's Network layer and ATM address along with the destination's Network layer address. If the source has additional data to immediately transmit to the destination, as may be likely with an edge device, it can continue to transmit the packets along the default path until the short-cut response is returned and the short-cut VC is created. The second phase of NHRP is the work done by the NHSs to find the ATM address belonging to the target. As each NHS receives the Resolution Request packets, it checks to determine if it is responsible for the target's IP-ATM mapping. If it does not serve the destination, it forwards the packet to the downstream NHS. (See Figure 9.4.)

An important detail critical to the protocol's operation is that the downstream NHRP servers must not generate NHRP Resolution Requests for data they receive over their ATM interfaces. If they did, it would cause each downstream router to generate an NHRP request for the data flow. Therefore, every router along the default path would request a virtual circuit to the destination. This is called a domino effect and is clearly undesirable.

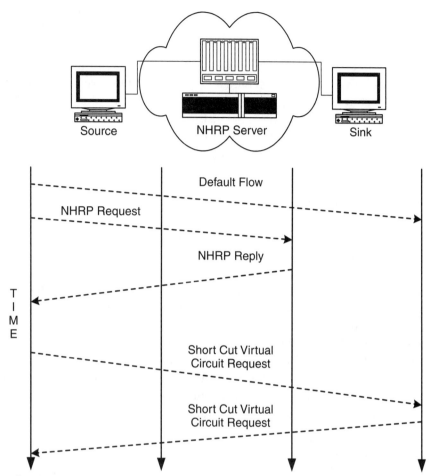

Figure 9.4 NHRP messages.

As the NHRP Resolution Request traverses the network, the NHSs run Network layer address cache checks. If the present NHS does maintain the target's LIS, then it replies to the source with the target's ATM address. Also, if the path to the target is through a router or bridge placed at the egress of the ATM network, then that device's address is returned in the NHRP reply. If no NHS on the ATM network possesses an IP-to-ATM address mapping that matches the NHRP request, then a negative (NAK) NHRP Resolution Reply is returned.

The NHRP reply can contain a single IP-ATM mapping or an aggregate mapping of several IP addresses to one ATM address. The latter would be useful in cases where the egress to the ATM network is a bridge. In this case, the bridge would generate an NHRP reply containing the target's address information, a prefix length that would (in essence) specify the amount, and the portion of the IP address space accessible via the egress router.

As the NHRP reply is passed along the default path back to the source, the NHSs along the path have the ability to read the response and locally cache the result. When the result is cached, the local server can reply to subsequent NHRP requests for a known destination. If this behavior is undesirable or untrustworthy, then two mechanisms can be used to turn this feature off. First, the source can request an "authoritative" reply, which means that only the NHS that truly maintains the address mapping can reply. Second, the cache entries can be systematically purged, which will force the NHRP request to travel to the destination's NHS.

Distributed Routing

Distributed routing is the realization of separating the higher-level functions of route determination from the lower-level functions of switching data before, or while, the time data passes through a network. A distributed router consists of a central route server that controls multiple edge devices, as shown in Figure 9.5. In the distributed router model, the edge devices do most, if not all, of the Data Link layer switching. Together, the route server and edge devices are used to build a Layer 3 protocol independent of distributed architectures and physical implementations. Routing servers in this model run traditional legacy routing protocols along with ATM routing protocols (that is, PNNI) and supply routes to the edge devices. By isolating the route server function, in some cases, it is possible to maximize the use of the routing engine.

Route servers can be constructed with a very-high-performance, computationally powerful machine that can serve an entire campus. In this model, MPOA edge devices are seen as simple bridges detecting flows, generating

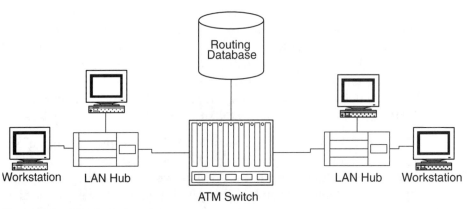

Figure 9.5 Distributed routing.

NHRP messages, then establishing direct virtual circuits. As will be shown, this distributed router is an excellent way of conceptualizing MPOA. In MPOA, functions are defined and the actual implementation of these functions is distributed throughout the cloud.

Multiprotocol over ATM

The ATM Forum established the goals of MPOA in close cooperation with the Internet Engineering Task Force. The original intent was to generate a document that resolved all of the problems of short-cut path selection, QoS routing, multiprotocol operation, and more. It was determined in late 1996, however, that achieving the original goal would not be possible if the specification was to be completed by the end of the year. Therefore, the phases were accepted, with short-cut and legacy interaction being the scope of the initial requirement set. That is, NHRP and integration with LANE were chosen, and the focus was on critical problems that needed to be solved quickly and were of utmost importance to end users. Two of the principal goals of MPOA's first phase are to allow different administrative domains to concurrently exist on one physical ATM network and to support communication between any two devices running Layer 3 protocols.

MPOA leverages much of the knowledge gained by the ION working group and extends the model to allow multiple protocols and distributed routing architectures. This goal will be accomplished in the realm of lower-cost edge devices that are Network layer intelligent, due to extracting route-server functions.

The remainder of this chapter focuses on the MPOA model. Using QoS in the first phase of MPOA is then relegated to RSVP over ATM. When the protocol development is divided into different phases, MPOA's critical Phase 1 requirement can be further described as the following:

- Allowing MPOA devices to establish direct ATM connections using NHRP
- Integrating with LAN emulation in the edge device and allowing the MPOA server (MPS) to support LANE's servers
- Providing support for firewalls and protocol filtering by allowing the network administrator to create virtual LANs on the Layer 2 fabric
- Supplying support for broadcast traffic
- Providing support for automatic configuration of ATM hosts via an initialization protocol
- Clearly illustrating of the concepts of separating switching and routing concerns

Multicasting within the Subnetwork

The completed specification reduces limitations found in previous network models and allows customers to work in a multivendor environment. In addition, it provides a higher-performance and more scalable solution for multiprotocol LAN internetworking over ATM that will enable next-generation intranets and extranets.

Multiprotocol Operation

An MPOA network consists of several Network-layer-aware components that can be subdivided into router servers, edge connection devices, LANE servers, next hop servers, and ATM-attached hosts. In the MPOA model, the ATM fabric is considered one physical network capable of supporting many virtual LANs, and each network, although separate, is reachable using short cuts. In a sense, the ATM network can be considered as an emulated multiprotocol bridge/router (that is, ATM with MPOA yields a "virtual router"). The network is called a virtual router because, with MPOA, the process of routing is separated from switching. (See Figure 9.6.)

An MPOA network is built from special-purpose address resolution servers, edge-bridging devices, and new software on ATM-attached devices like hosts that allow them to communicate with the server. The actual protocol documented in the MPOA specification describes what pieces are used to build the network, along with the information flows between these components. The low-level details of implementation and separation of actual processes running on devices is left to the manufacturer or network designer.

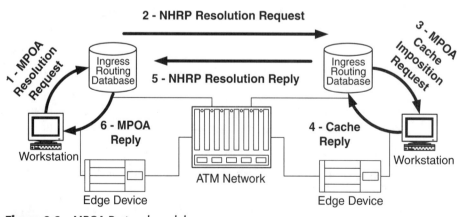

Figure 9.6 MPOA Protocol model.

The MPOA model defines only logical components, message flows, and suggested behavior, not product. The key architectural components are these:

Edge connection devices used to physically attach legacy networks to an MPOA system (that is, an Ethernet-to-ATM converter). These are similar to LANE bridges. An MPOA client is responsible only for maintaining a listing of Layer 2 addresses to Layer 3 for the host(s) with which it is communicating.

Route servers having topological information gained by running routing protocols and distributing state among themselves. These are network components that support MPS functions along with LANE and NHRP. An MPOA server maintains knowledge of Layer 3 protocols and topologies for the areas served.

Information flows comprising the protocol descriptions for exchanges for MPOA client (MPC) to MPOA server (MPS) and MPC-to-MPC and MPS-to-MPS exchanges.

An MPOA system utilizes several information flows among the two major hardware groups listed previously. The information flows describe how the components exchange MPOA state information and resolve target addresses and state. The MPOA system works by allocating tasks to groups, then defining the protocol's operation by specifying information flows among the groups. In defining the information flows between functional groups, the ATM Forum has broken the problem into specific cases that correspond to different states of the protocol.

From a high level of granularity, MPOA's logical components can be divided into clients and servers such that the implementation of the protocol follows several distinct steps:

Configuration. Used to retrieve configuration information and register themselves in the network.

Discovery. The phase where the MPOA devices learn their topological relationships.

Address Resolution. Used after configuration to query the MPOA servers, then inform servers of state change on the client side. It is also an informational flow between MPOA servers containing routing information.

Data Transfer. The actual transmission of information between hosts using an MPOA system.

These protocol phases can then be further subdivided into information subflows that perform the detailed operations. For example, client members of an MPOA system pass information to the following:

- Their route server to obtain address resolution information
- Their LANE LES for destination resolution of intra-LAN traffic
- Their LANE BUS, to forward broadcast data in the absence of a direct point-to-point virtual circuit

MPOA servers pass information used to do the following:

- Establish peering conversation with other MPSs
- Communicate with edge devices to communicate topology reachability information

Before the MPC and MPS can begin using the MPOA system, they must be registered and configured. The configuration process is accomplished manually by a network administrator, or the MPC/MPS can make use of a LANE configuration server. As in LANE, devices in an MPOA network usually contact the configuration server at boot time. The configuration server knows which clients and servers are associated within which virtual networks, and the configuration server notifies the client and servers of their respective MCS/MPS ATM addresses. When route servers are initialized, they pass a TLV identifying themselves to the LECS specifying a configuration request. They are given the identity of the subnetwork(s) they control along with the Layer 3 protocol type(s) used. In addition, the route server is a member of the subnetwork(s), so it also acquires a Layer 3 address.

The MPCs then register with the LECS by sending a configuration request containing a TLV identifying the MPC. When MPCs and ATM-attached hosts are initialized on an MPOA network via the LECS, they are given information about what policies should be followed for short-cut setup, when to time out and delete idle virtual circuits, and which protocol (for example, IP) should be using short cuts. In addition, the ATM address of the MPS can be forwarded; however, this information could be inferred to be the default router's IP address. The mapping from Network layer address to ATM address on the default router would be learned via LANE.

The discovery phase occurs after initialization and concerns the set of information exchanges used to inform each MPOA device of their existence, capabilities, and domains. The term *discovery*, when related to MPCs, describes their ability to determine the location of the NHS in their domain. As with the configuration phase, the mapping from Network layer address to ATM address is learned via LANE LE_ARP. Once the discovery phase is complete, the MPOA components within a domain can pass NHRP/LANE messages, and they can now begin to allow MPCs to communicate among themselves across subnetwork boundaries.

Once a host has been configured and has registered itself on the network, it can begin to communicate with other hosts. In order to communicate, the mapping of Layer 2 to Layer 3 addresses must be resolved via the MPS. Data flow between computers on an MPOA system can be one of three types:

- Intra-subnetwork via the LANE (or classical IP) servers
- Inter-subnetwork via default forwarding
- Inter-subnetwork via short-cut routing

Intra-subnetwork communication takes place primarily using the mechanisms of LANE, but in some cases it can be accomplished via classical IP. The choice between the two is based on the expected internetwork layer protocols used on the network. When the MPC that is connected to non-NBMA receives a flow of packets, it attempts to determine, by examining the internetwork address, if the flow should "short cut" via NHRP.

The multiprotocol servers along the path will generate and process NHRP messages in the manner described previously. Each NHRP message is forwarded, hop by hop, until it reaches the egress MPS. At the egress MPS, a message is passed from the server to the MPC to determine the ATM parameters for encapsulation, as described in RFC 1483. The MPC serving the legacy-attached host replies with addressing information to the MPS so that it can successfully generate an NHRP reply. Before the MPC replies to the MPS it must, however, ensure that it has sufficient resources to accept a new virtual circuit. At that point the egress MPS can generate an NHRP reply and return it along the path the resolution message took.

When an MPC has successfully received a response to its NHRP query, it can now establish a direct virtual circuit and begin transferring user data. The parameters, such as PCR/SCR/MBR, used during creation of the ATM virtual circuits between MPC-to-MPC or MPC-to-ATM endstations are to a great degree left to the discretion of the end user or the network administrator. Several base rules have been specified to help ensure smooth default operation. For example, MPOA specifies that, as a baseline, the parameters documented in RFC 1755 covering signaling parameters for classical IP over ATM should be used for user data communication.

When selecting a service category, the default choice is unspecified bit rate (UBR). If an MPC desires to create a virtual circuit with another MPC that is a service category other than UBR, then it can signal this desire via an NHRP extension. If the receiving MPC is able to support the source's QoS request, it can signal this fact to the source MPC by returning the NHRP extension. QoS is left as an option for the end devices and should be negotiated with the RSVP protocol.

Virtual circuits used for data communication or to pass control messages can be deleted when their usefulness is no longer apparent. Most likely the deletion will be done by the edge device that has created the circuit after an idle period has been exceeded. For example, control circuits by default are deleted after 20 minutes of idleness. Virtual circuits between MPCs are deleted shortly after the traffic flow has stopped.

Conclusion

This chapter has presented the ATM protocol as developed primarily by the ATM Forum with contributions from the IETF. Understanding the subtle interworkings of ATM helps network engineers understand if ATM is an applicable solution for next-generation networks. Important to network engineers are the services supported, the overbooking percentage, the peak and sustainable cell rates, whether PVCs and PVPs will be supported, and whether SVC will also be supported.

Many of the components required to build ATM systems are based on architectures already in place in networks that support LANE or classical IP over ATM. The key technologies involved in building a first-generation MPOA network are the Next Hop Resolution Protocol and LAN Emulation. Baseline MPOA systems can be built with edge devices and traditional IP routers, and these networks can take advantage of ATM's higher speeds and lower latencies.

The protocol is currently being used to build products and has been deployed successfully. By allowing the standards bodies to develop protocols such as RSVP the ATM standards group's work has become one of documenting protocol interactions and, when necessary, extending previous work to support ATM's special requirements and features. The current state of the protocol has yielded a completed document that has been used by vendors to construct compliant hardware and network designs based on the new hardware.

End Note

[1]Portions of this chapter are based on a treatment in *Internet Architectures*, by Dan Minoli and Andrew Schmidt (1999, John Wiley & Sons).

References

ATM Forum Technical Committee. 1993. *ATM User-Network Interface Version 3.0*. Upper Saddle River, NJ: Prentice-Hall.

Minoli, D. and A. Alles. 1996. *LAN, ATM, and LAN Emulation Technologies*. Norwood, MA: Artech House.

Minoli, D. and J. Amoss. 1998. *Broadband and ATM Switching Technology*. New York: McGraw-Hill.

RFC 1483. 1993. J. Heinanen. *Multiprotocol Encapsulation over ATM Adaptation Layer 5*. ftp://ftp.isi.edu/in-notes/rfc1483.txt (proposed standard).

RFC 1577. 1994. *Classical IP and ARP over ATM*. ftp://ftp.isi.edu/in-notes/ rfc1577.txt (proposed standard, rendered obsolete by RFC 2225).

RFC 1755. 1995. M. Perez, F. Liaw, D. Grossman, A. Mankin, E. Hoffman, and A. Malis. *ATM Signalling Support for IP over ATM*. ftp://ftp.isi.edu/in-notes/rfc1755.txt (proposed standard).

RFC 2022. 1996. G. Armitage. *Support for Multicast over UNI 3.0/3.1 based ATM Networks*. ftp://ftp.isi.edu/in-notes/rfc2022.txt (proposed standard).

RFC 2205. 1997. R. Braden, ed., L. Zhang, S. Berson, S. Herzog, and S. Jamin. *Resource ReSerVation Protocol (RSVP)—Version Functional Specification*. ftp://ftp.isi.edu/in-notes/rfc2205.txt. (proposed standard).

RFC 2332. 1998. *NBMA Next Hop Resolution Protocol (NHRP)*. ftp://ftp.isi.edu/in-notes/rfc2332.txt. (proposed standard).

Schmidt, A. and D. Minoli. 1998. *Multiprotocol over ATM: Building State of the Art ATM Intranets Utilizing RSVP, NHRP, LANE, Flow Switching, and WWW Technology*. Upper Saddle River, NJ: Prentice-Hall.

CHAPTER 10

Development and Implementation of New Advanced National Infrastructures, New Advanced Regional Networks, and GigaPOPs

Introduction

Chapter 3 presented a framework for a general, advanced, digital-communications architecture, including core components that addressed basic functional requirements. Subsequent chapters have presented formulations of responses to these requirements. Those chapters described a number of initiatives established to develop second-generation Internets, and they also examined some of the basic technologies used for implementations of those networks. As noted, most of the earliest efforts to address these issues emerged in the early 1990s from the same research communities that developed the first Internet.

This chapter and the next present three case studies that describe three fundamental building blocks of next-generation advanced Internets. In part, these examples demonstrate how next-generation Internet applications, engineering, and other technical requirements were translated into a set of network designs used to develop early implementations of advanced networks. These examples also describe how the technologies covered earlier in this book were actually implemented in production networks. The two case studies presented in this chapter and the one presented in the next describe the first major next-generation Internet national backbone network, the first major next-generation regional network, the concept of a GigaPOP, and they introduce a related facility, a network access point (NAP). NAPs are evolving to become particularly significant facilities for next-generation Internets, and Chapter 11 describes them in greater detail. Also growing in importance are private interconnects, where a substantial amount of IP traffic is exchanged.

It is important to note that these implementations are not final models, but rather that they represent particularly interesting initial steps in the evolution of a next-generation Internet. For example, early implementations have been based on the IP-over-ATM-over-SONET model, a number of more recent implementations have been based on IP over SONET, and two major national Internet projects have implemented IP over lightwave. These topics are discussed in later chapters.

The first case study describes the National Science Foundation's very-high-speed Backbone Network Service (vBNS), a specialized national connectivity initiative. The vBNS was created as a significantly improved national data path for advanced research applications, requiring high performance and high speed. When the vBNS was established, with an OC12 backbone, it was 100 times faster than the commodity Internet; plans are being implemented to quadruple that speed. However, it is notable that OC48 commercial backbones now exist and that all of the tier-1 ISPs have multiple OC12cs between POPs.

This chapter also describes the activities of two related organizations that provide important functionality required to support such an advanced national infrastructure. One is the National Laboratory for Applied Networking Research (NLANR), established in 1995 to provide technical and engineering support for the vBNS. The other is CAIDA, the Consortium for Advanced Internet Data Analysis, which works closely with NLANR on many projects.

The second case study in this chapter presents one of the earliest implementations of a specialized regional second-generation Internet—the Metropolitan Research and Education Network (MREN), which interconnects many of the advanced research organizations in the upper Midwest and which comprises multiple networks throughout seven states. Finally, within this regional context, this chapter also describes a new concept in regional, advanced, network aggregation called a GigaPOP, a gigabit per second point of presence, a concept derived from the MREN model.

The National Science Foundation and a New National Advanced Network for Advanced Research

Beginning in the early 1990s, as the commodity Internet became increasingly congested, the National Science Foundation (NSF) initiated a plan to provide an improved national backbone network for those in the research community requiring high-performance connectivity. In 1994, the NSF allocated funding to provide, initially, for direct access from remote sites to national supercomputing centers for scientists with meritorious applications. Another goal of this project was to ensure the continuous development of advanced Internet technologies, especially those requiring longer-term research.

The program to develop this networking resource was developed by the NSF's Directorate for Computer and Information Science and Engineering (CISE), which funded the very-high-speed Backbone Network Service or vBNS. As noted in Chapter 4, CISE was established to support research in computing, information sciences, and advanced networking. Through these and other activities the NSF supports the goals of the Science and Technology Council Committee on Information and Communications (CIC) (NSTC 1995).

Very-High-Speed Backbone Network Service

Just as the first Internet developed as a three-tiered hierarchical structure, the second also developed as such a hierarchy, although not initially in all areas. NSFnet, the first interorganizational national Internet backbone, provided for interconnections to supercomputing centers, regional networks (providing interconnectivity among university campus networks and other, related local research networks), and often widely dispersed campus networks.

Similarly, the second-generation Internet began as a means of interconnecting supercomputing centers through the new NSF-sponsored network, the vBNS. Originally, the vBNS was developed to enable researchers with meritorious applications to have remote access to the five existing national supercomputing centers. It was designed to interconnect these five supercomputing centers and four national interchange points, called National Access Points, or NAPs.

A later program, the High-Performance Connections Program, however, allowed other researchers with meritorious advanced-network-based applications to connect to the vBNS. This program provided access to resources that would not have been otherwise available because such services were not being provided commercially. The vBNS, therefore, became a means for researchers nationwide to access supercomputing centers, interconnecting new, advanced regional networks, which were interconnected to campuses, other research and education institutions, and national interchange points. Much of the new connectivity was funded by the NSF's High Performance Connections Program, although the vBNS allowed for substantial additional leveraging through institutional investments, especially by universities.

Unlike the period during which NSFnet was being developed—when there was no existing related infrastructure—the vBNS was planned while multiple, national, commercial backbones were being rapidly expanded. Consequently, the new model could assume the existence of the numerous interconnected commercial Internet providers. As the original NSFnet was decommissioned, provision was made for interconnecting commercial Internets at major network access points, which were initially set up by the NSF. The design and development of the NSF-sponsored NAPs is discussed in the next chapter.

The vBNS, therefore, was developed to interconnect supercomputing centers, advanced regional networks, research and education institutions, and national interchange points, NAPs. As this network developed, it was also interlinked to another type of specialized interconnection point-of-presence, which was named a GigaPOP by George Strawn of the NSF, for Gigabit point of presence. These specialized POPs were established to serve as regional aggregation points and value-added points for new, advanced regional research networks. The first one was established in Chicago by the first next-generation regional network, the Metropolitan Research and Education Network.

Implementation of the vBNS

In 1994, the five-year cooperative agreement for the development of the very-High-Speed Backbone Service (vBNS) was awarded to MCI (then MCI Telecommunications Corp., now MCI WorldCom). The vBNS was implemented as an IP-over-ATM network, with tests beginning in 1994 and production implementation on a completed initial network topology on April 1, 1995. The original contract provided for a national OC3c backbone, although later the network was upgraded to OC12c. The development of the vBNS created a significantly improved national network for advanced research organizations. As noted at the time, the vBNS was 100 times faster than the commodity Internet.

The vBNS backbone connects 12 advanced POPs within MCI facilities and the National Center for Supercomputing Applications (NCSA, now the National Computational Science Alliance), the National Center for Atmospheric Research (NCAR), the San Diego Supercomputing Center (SDSC), and the Pittsburgh Supercomputing Center (PSC). By early 1999, the vBNS connected, at various speeds, more than 75 organizations and another 25 were planned. The vBNS may soon interconnect more than 100 organizations, and it peers with many national and international research networks (see Figure 10.1).

The vBNS provides access to remote instrumentation nationwide, not just to supercomputers, but also synchrotrons, telescopes, and scanning electron microscopes, and through interconnections with other research networks developed by federal agencies to various national laboratories and research centers, such as Brookhaven National Laboratory, Sandia National Laboratory, Lawrence Livermore National Laboratory, the national supercomputing centers, and the Goddard Space Flight Center. These research networks

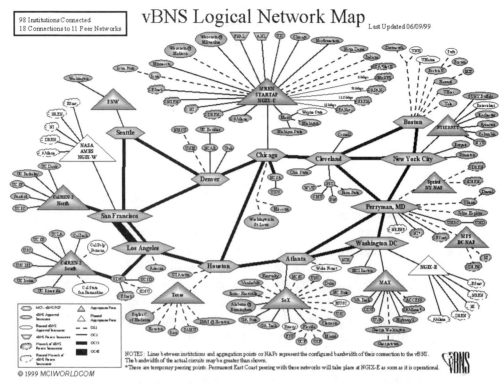

Figure 10.1 vBNS Logical Network Map as of June 1999. (courtesy of MCIWorldCom).

include ESnet, NASA's NREN, DoD's DREN; the vBNS also peers with various international research networks at the STAR TAP (these networks and STAR TAP are described in earlier chapters).

Part of the National Science Foundation's mission is to ensure the continuous development of advanced Internet technologies. Consequently, although the vBNS is a production network, it also enables advanced network research.

The vBNS also allows researchers in academia, industry, and the government to cooperate on advanced network development. A number of projects related to the vBNS initiative are directed at developing the state of the art for advanced networking.

Hyperstream

The vBNS is based on the MCI Hyperstream network, which provides general commercial ATM services. Within the POP's core support is provided by ATM switches with user network interface (UNI) ports and routers. Additional services, such as native ATM and frame-based connections, are also available. The vBNS ATM network provisioned through the Hyper-stream ATM network has a topology consisting of a full mesh of PVPs among all 16 nodes. These PVPs provide an unspecified bit rate (UBR) service, rely-ing primarily on capacity for performance and traffic engineering rather than specific guarantees. SVCs are also provided for organizations that would like to provide signaling directly to vBNS ATM switches, bypassing routers. A set of net VBR VPs is also available to the vBNS for QoS development.

IPv4 Services

The vBNS implements high-performance, best-effort IPv4 services on a full mesh of ATM PVCs, using core switches and 25 IP routers, with two basic rout-ing protocols implemented. These are the Border Gateway Protocol (BGP) for external routing among research centers, universities, and peer networks and for policy services; the internal Border Gateway Protocol (iBGP), which is used by the vBNS routers to exchange routes; and the Open Shortest Path First Proto-col (OSPF), which is used to exchange routes with networks to which the vBNS is directly connected. The vBNS is directly connected to networks via the high-performance parallel interface (HIPPI), ATM, and fiber-distributed data inter-face (FDDI) networks at the supercomputer centers.

Because of the current topology, there is a maximum of two router hops on the backbone. The network is generally uncongested, spiking at times for special events, such as a supercomputing demo or a research experiment. High-end advanced routers provide for high-volume packet switching and data flows of up to 120 Mbps over national distances. Two OC48c routers are in production at the San Francisco and Los Angeles vBNS POPs, which can sustain flows of over 2 Gbps and forward nearly 40 packets per second.

vBNS IP Multicast

The vBNS provides both a unicast and a native IP multicast service, which is used for video, video-conferencing, Web casting, and performance monitor-ing. The vBNS provides for BGP4 peering between a specified vBNS router and a specified peer router for unicast route exchange under bilateral peering agreements. Multipoint routing for media was a service that the vBNS first initiated in 1993 using a dense mode configuration (PIM-DM), but soon migrated to PIM-SM. The vBNS also supports the Mbone (multicast back-bone), and is using state-of-the art multicast routing.

ATM Services: PVCs and SVC Logical IP Subnet

If specific applications require direct native ATM services, the vBNS provides PVCs, authorized through a special review process. In general, however, the vBNS meets ATM requirements by providing an SVC service for ATM-linked vBNS-authorized organizations. This SVC logical IP subnet (LIS) can provide for high rates of transmission by enabling an IP node on the LIS to signal for the setup of an ATM connection to another node on the LIS and thereby avoid using the IP routers. The signals to establish the connection are transmitted via user network interfaces (UNI) to an ATM switch at a vBNS-authorized organization. The vBNS uses PNNI, an ATM routing protocol to route SVCs in its LIS.

The LIS ATM addresses are International Code Designator (ICD) format prefixes. The Address Resolution Protocol (ARP) server that translates IP addresses into ATM addresses is an ATM switch at the vBNS Chicago POP. All vBNS backbone routers are members of the LIS, and LIS-attached hosts can communicate with nonattached hosts through these routers.

IPv6 Services

An emerging technology is IPv6, the next-generation Internet protocol, discussed in Chapter 12. The vBNS has capabilities for provisioning for native IPv6, not tunneled IPv6, in its core backbone service. Dedicated IPv6 routers (ATM-attached at OC3c) have been implemented on the East Coast, West Coast, and at the vBNS Chicago POP. When needed, vBNS-authorized sites can establish a PVC to the closest IPv6 router. These routers also provide end-node services for IPv6-in-IPv4 tunnels for non-IPv6 sites and 6bone sites. (The 6bone is a research implementation of IPv6, based on tunnels.) The vBNS also provides for MBGP peering between a specified vBNS IPv6 router and a peer IPv6 router.

Performance Measurement and Analysis on the vBNS

The vBNS provides for high-quality performance measurement and analysis, and the program has established a number of efforts to continually enhance existing tools and to add new tools. Two primary tools for information gathering are SNMP and OCXmon (OC monitoring), primarily OC12mon (described later).

Every few minutes, SNMP collects detailed data (packet, octet, cell counts) on ingress and egress flows from all interfaces on the network switches and routers. Measurements are also taken of error and discard levels. These statistics are formulated into periodic reports on utilization, total counts, average rates, peak rates, and other aggregations. Reports for specific sites are provided.

OC12mon is an IP over ATM over OC12c monitoring device based on a PC, running DOS, with two OC12c interfaces connected with a passive optical splitter to the transmit and receive fibers, one for send flows and one for receive flows. Using IP header information, packets are categorized in accordance with data flows designated by protocol port number, source address, destination address, and a time-out indicator. The collected information is stored in a database and analyzed with various software tools.

The vBNS also uses UNIX workstations with OC12c ATM interfaces to conduct performance tests and to collect other data, particularly measures of throughput. Scripts are used to manage a set of measurement tools. Four core tools used are ping (timing both ways between two points), mping (which uses the User Datagram Protocol, UDP, and the Internet Control Message Protocol, ICMP), treno (which also uses UDP, to model congestion patterns), and ttcp (which measures flows for individual connections).

vBNS+

MCI WorldCom is developing a new service, originally called NGNet, then vBNS+, which will allow vBNS-equivalent services to special constituencies that cannot currently use the vBNS because of policy restrictions. Through this service, NGNet will provide vBNS-type capabilities to organizations that may not qualify for vBNS services but have aggressive applications requirements for advanced networking services.

The National Laboratory for Applied Network Research (NLANR)

National advanced Internets are dynamic infrastructures and require the ongoing support of specialized facilities, instrumentation, and expertise. To provide support for users of the vBNS, the NSF-funded the National Laboratory for Advanced Network Research (NLANR). NLANR was established in 1995 to provide technical and engineering support for vBNS connections to the original five supercomputing sites and to provide general coordination for the development of the vBNS with MCI WorldCom. Subsequently, as the vBNS mission expanded, the NLANR mission was also widened to include technical, engineering and traffic analysis support for the NSF High Performance Connections sites. NLANR now supports connectivity to more than 100 sites connected to the vBNS, and it also supports individual projects utilizing that network and other related National Science Foundation-funded high-performance communications initiatives. NLANR's mission is now "to provide application, engineering, and traffic analysis support for the NSF High Performance Connections sites and wider vBNS community." NLANR is conducting innovative research across a broad spectrum of applied networking application areas.

NLANR has a distributed organization. It consists of three entities, each with a focus on a specific area of advanced networking activity. The Distributed Applications and Support Team (DAST) is a distributed applications support center with a primary home at the National Computational Science Alliance at the University of Illinois Champaign-Urbana (UIUC/NCSA). This group is a team of engineers and software experts that support distributed applications through direct contact with the developers of those applications. This group also supports the development of prototypes of advanced applications that may require special techniques or methods to effectively utilize the NSF-funded high-performance infrastructure.

The National Center for Network Engineering (NCNE), an engineering services group at Pittsburgh Supercomputing Center, Carnegie Mellon University, provides in-depth technical information and direct network engineering support for research sites connected to the NSF-funded high-performance network infrastructure. In addition to providing technical and operational support, this group facilitates the migration of leading-edge technologies from research to production in order to continually provide newer enabling technologies for advanced applications. This group is experimenting with new routing technologies, QoS techniques, IPv6, multicast, and network management tools.

The Measurements and Operations Analysis Team (MOAT) (a measurement, analysis, and optimization group, which is located at the San Diego Supercomputing Center, University of California at San Diego) gathers, measures, and analyzes vBNS data traffic. This group also develops and deploys related software tools that lead to a more in-depth understanding of the behavior of traffic on high-performance networks. Through these efforts, NLANR is attempting to develop an advanced networking-analysis infrastructure that will enable managers of advanced networks to identify and resolve problems, optimize network designs and use, and create optimal future network technologies.

NLANR developed and currently maintains a technology that assists in reducing commodity-Internet congestion, the Web Cache Hierarchy, which provides for specialized storage of frequently retrieved Web information. Currently, Web traffic accounts for over one-half of all Internet traffic, and the growth rate of its traffic share is increasing. If frequently requested Web items can be stored in locations close to users through proxy sites, instead of at remote locations, traffic on the Internet can be reduced. NLANR's IRCACHE Web Caching project, which is researching advanced caching techniques, manages nine advanced Web caches, connected to more than 400 others nationally and over 1,000 worldwide.

The OC12mon flow-monitoring technology mentioned in an earlier section was developed by two researchers at the NLANR, Hans-Werner Braun and Kimberly Claffy. This innovative technology allows for passive monitoring of extremely high-speed data streams.

Cooperative Association for Internet Data Analysis

Another important type of capability required by advanced Internets, as well as by the general Internet, is a set of mechanisms for monitoring and measuring traffic performance. The Cooperative Association for Internet Data Analysis (CAIDA) is a collaborative initiative established to promote enhanced cooperation in engineering and maintaining a reliable, scalable, global infrastructure. This initiative was originally formulated at the University of San Diego and established as a project under the auspices of NLANR in 1997. It is currently a neutral forum—an independent organization that coordinates the efforts of academic researchers, industry experts, and government agencies in the area of advanced metrics and analysis.

CAIDA undertakes projects that address complex challenges arising from the need to effectively measure and analyze Internet traffic, particularly those issues that would benefit from interorganizational communication and cooperation. Analysis of Internet traffic presents a number of interesting problems because of its high rate of growth and variable characteristics, and because it transits across multiple domains, provider services, and specialized facilities.

CAIDA's stated goals are to encourage creation of common metrics, create a collaborative research and analytic environment, and develop advanced technologies related to measurements, analysis, and related tools. The development of metrics is undertaken in cooperation with related efforts within the IETF IP Providers Metrics (IPPM) subgroup of the Bench Marking Working Group (BMWG), which develops standard metrics and procedures that can be used to evaluate ISPs and other organizations. Individual projects include efforts related to traffic performance and flow characterization (for example, developing baseline standards against which performance can be measured), traffic visualizations, simulations, and analysis; Web caching protocols and hierarchies; QoS and related bandwidth reservation techniques; BGP instability diagnosis; multicast and Mbone; and emerging protocols such as IPv6.

A Case Study: An Advanced Regional Network—Metropolitan Research and Education Network

The Metropolitan Research and Education Network (MREN) provides another interesting case study for examining high-performance digital-communications networks. MREN is a regional, multistate network, based primarily on dedicated OC3c (155 Mbps) links. MREN was developed by a consortium of universities and research laboratories in the upper Midwest, which created a strategic plan for advanced networking to meet the needs of leading-edge research and educational applications, primarily those of research scientists. Initial partners included Northwestern University, University of Illinois at Chicago, Argonne National Laboratory, Fermi National Accelerator Laboratory, the National Center for Supercomputing Applications, and the University of Chicago. The MREN model that was developed was a departure from the traditional approach to broadband regional networking in a number of ways. MREN has been recognized as a prototype for the development and promotion of existing and future Internet services utilizing high bandwidth. It has introduced a number of innovative concepts, processes, and facilities, including a GigaPOP. Currently, a number of MREN-related regional, national, and international projects exist, ranging from aggressive bandwidth-utilizing applications to research and development. Many of these research and development projects center on advanced network architecture, methods, experimentation, and tools.

MREN was established on the premise that the core foundation and enabling technology for most research and education activities will be high-performance, broadband digital networks. The MREN consortium was also convinced that its research community would continue to drive advanced networking technologies for the foreseeable future and that those technologies would shape the ones deployed for other, more general applications. In part, MREN's design was motivated by the unique research and development challenges of the many technology and infrastructure management components of the project and by its complex engineering issues. When the project began, designing and implementing regional broadband networks based on new technologies were particularly complex tasks.

Requirements Analysis

MREN began as a strategic planning project. In the 1992–1993 period, a strategic network planning analysis was undertaken by Chicago-area networking specialists and research scientists from many different disciplines. This project examined currently available and emerging technologies and trends in digital-communications convergence, in advanced digital communications technology, and in advanced application requirements.

MREN's initial technical design was based on extensive analysis of multiple requirements of a number of leading-edge applications. Special attention was paid to advanced applications of the future—those that would most likely be critical to a wide range of advanced science initiatives that were planned for initiation at Midwest research institutions during the mid-to-late 1990s.

Next-Generation Applications

This extensive analysis of multiple advanced-application requirements produced results that were similar to those described in Chapter 3, especially those driven by major interorganizational scientific research projects. MREN was developed to support a wide range of such advanced applications, requiring high performance and high bandwidth. Many of these applications require instantaneous communication of extremely large amounts of data (zero tolerance for latency).

MREN currently supports some of the world's most aggressive research applications, including the following:

- Supercomputing
- High-performance distributed computing
- Advanced digital video
- Advanced medical imaging
- Computer-aided diagnostics
- Computational biology and chemistry
- Astronomy and astrophysics
- Advanced networking research
- Advanced synchrotron experimentation (especially for the Advanced Photon Source APS, a 7 GeV synchrotron at Argonne National Laboratory)
- High-energy physics (for example, collider detectors and high-energy physics computers at Fermi National Accelerator Lab)
- Scientific visualization
- Extremely high-resolution imaging (especially for medical applications)
- Multimodal medical imaging
- Physical structure prototyping
- Computer-aided medical diagnostics
- Remote management of research instrumentation
- Terabyte storage systems
- The advanced virtual-reality environments based on CAVE technology developed at UIC (described in Chapter 3)

Networking Design

During the period from 1993 to 1994, MREN members undertook an extensive review of currently available and emerging technologies. After an extensive analysis of current and anticipated communications requirements, advanced applications, and existing and emerging technologies, the project team concluded that a new type of Internet would be required to meet future needs. They determined that the technologies of the existing Internet would fall far below requirement needs and that a new type of network design was required. Balancing the needs of scientific researchers against implementation economics, and after separating immediate technical requirements from future requirements and highly desirable features, they specified a set of requirements for a new type of Internet and translated those requirements into a design for a new type of advanced, high-performance regional network for advanced applications. The following section describes the model that was implemented.

Network Architecture

MREN became operational for testing in 1994 and for production in May 1995, allowing for real-time, state-of-the-art applications to actively use multi-site advanced networking technologies. The MREN project specified a layered solution, based on IP-over-ATM on a SONET metropolitan fabric connected to regional sites with fiber links. This solution addressed a wide range of considerations. The MREN project specified that its communications services would require an infrastructure that would incorporate the following characteristics: a) standards-based, b) high performance, c) high reliability, d) modularity, e) scalability, f) expandability, g) manageability at all technical layers, h) reasonable security, and i) operational in the near term. These MREN design specifications are detailed in an earlier chapter.

High-Performance IP Best-Effort Service

MREN's basic service provided for high-performance, highly reliable, best-effort delivery of IPv4 datagrams. Best-effort services on the general Internet are sometimes defined as a point on the opposite end of the scale from high performance. In 1994, best-effort over an uncongested DS-3 link provided a significant performance gain over T-1. Currently, MREN is essentially an OC3c-based network with only one hop per route among member organizations; high performance is ensured with current traffic volume. OC12 is available as an expansion option. Of course, high performance is a measure not just of throughput speed but also of quality of service.

The scalability of IP and its manageability are well proven. Expandability is straightforward because of the ubiquity of IP. Additional security mechanisms are being investigated in conjunction with experiments with IPv6. The IP layer infrastructure for MREN was primarily implemented with IP routers, with BGP as the external routing protocol, over a full mesh of ATM permanent virtual circuits among member institutions.

SMDS and ATM

MREN is primarily built on commercial infrastructure, including that of multiple commercial fiber networks throughout seven states in the upper Midwest. The core of MREN in Chicago is built on a commercial local-loop infrastructure—the Ameritech Public Data Network (APDN), provided by Ameritech Advanced Data Services (AADS). This principle of utilized leased fiber allowed MREN network development to proceed quickly.

MREN was initially established as a switched IP (IPv4) over Switched Multimegabit Data Service (SMDS) network. In 1994 SMDS seemed to be a reasonable transport service. Developed by Bellcore, it provides for high-speed, connectionless, packet-based, switched services; it can operate at multiple speeds; and it can service wide areas. SMDS uses a global addressing specification defined by ITU-T (Recommendation E.164). The interface is a subset of the IEEE 802.6 standard for Metropolitan Area Networks. After a short initial SMDS trial that did not meet performance expectations, however, the MREN network was upgraded to asynchronous transfer mode (ATM).

MREN, GigaPOPs, and NAPs

The Metropolitan Research and Education Network (MREN) in the Chicago area established the world's first GigaPOP. Interconnections among new, advanced regional Internets required local aggregation centers. A GigaPOP is a Gigabit-per-second POP, the function of which is to provide reliable, high-performance, regional aggregation services to local communities, as well as to allow for additional access to other networks. The GigaPOP's combination of a large, multilink, regional network and a powerful central switch provided for a significant gain in network performance.

Shortly after MREN was established, the NSF began privatizing NSFnet, which required the creation of large-scale ISP exchange points. The success of the initial MREN project helped prove the viability of the NAP concept. To provide for high-performance interchange among its member organizations, MREN was based on a "carrier class" ATM switch (a Lucent ATM GlobeView2000), which scales well and has highly redundant components. This core MREN ATM switch eventually became the same physical switch that supported the Chicago National Access Point (NAP), first established by the NSF as part of the transition from NSFnet. As part of the commercialization of NSFnet, the NSF sponsored the NAPs as high-performance ISP peering exchange points.

The Chicago NAP is managed by Ameritech Advanced Data Services (AADS), which also provides mechanisms for customers to develop multi-lateral peering and transit agreements to allow for mutual exchange of routes. Other specialized agreements for establishing connectivity have also been possible, for example, those related to noncommercial, specialized research related to advanced networking for advanced applications, such as MREN. Policies also allow for transit agreements with national carriers (AT&T, MCI, etc.) to establish specialized intra-LATA service communications.

Using the NAP switch allows switched IP traffic to be provided through a full mesh of PVCs and BGP peers among MREN member organizations. Independently, members are able to establish additional peering agreements in accordance with their requirements, including those with national carriers. Also, the sites are connected to other national research networks, such as the vBNS (1996) and, more recently, Abilene (1999, described in a previous chapter). Most MREN organizations are also connected to agency and international networks at the NAP, such as ESnet, NREN and DREN and international advanced research networks.

Peering is also arranged between MREN members and ISPs at the NAP for commodity Internet services. ATM peering is implemented through point-to-point virtual circuits (PVCs), interconnecting IP routers at member sites. No central router is used. A single "one-armed" router was recently implemented to serve international connectivity route policies, but it is not part of the core facility. The service on this PVC mesh is UBR, which is useful for Internet traffic because it is bursty, mixing different types of patterns, including large spikes of heavy traffic.

The PVC mesh established by MREN has been extremely reliable. Setting up PVCs is a manual process. Although ATM does provide for dynamic provisioning of circuits through switched virtual circuits (SVCs) established by means of a signaling mechanism, few regional networks depend on them currently because of issues related to reliability. For example, if there is an SVC failure, it is difficult not to lose packets because of buffer limitations, especially for high-speed traffic. In the expectation that these issues will be resolved, MREN plans to migrate to SVC at a future date.

PVCs can be rate-limited to different specified parameters within the allocation of the permanent virtual path (PVP, described in a previous chapter). For example, one PVP can be limited to 4 Mbps while another can be limited to 12 Mbps—up to the total allocation for the PVP. Routers at the edges (which have more buffer capacity relative to switches) are given the burden of buffering and packet discard when PVCs are congested. This also spares processor load on the switches. The ATM switch undertakes early packet discard to manage bandwidth and maintain the specified allocations, for example, to manage a specified 16 Mbps for a PVP distributed between one PVC with 12 Mbps and another with 4 Mbps.

Throughout the initial phases of the development of next-generation Internets, quality of service has been maintained primarily through provision of sufficient bandwidth, for example, MREN's utilization of OC3c (155 Mbps). Specific service guarantees are not necessary for bursty data traffic within a highly provisioned (capacity-rich) broadband network—UBR services suffice as long as the network is not congested. The performance penalty incurred by extra processing required by communicating IP over ATM is minimal within the frame of overall performance.

As noted, however, bandwidth allocation alone is not sufficient for high-performance, much less quality of service. Eventually, traffic demand and efficiency requirements will result in the implementation of a reservation service for network resources. The next phase of the development of the Internet requires implementing such services, such as those that would be provided under some form of DiffServ model. This topic is discussed further in later chapters.

High Reliability

Over the past five years, uptime on the core facilities for the MREN network has been 99.999 percent. This high reliability depends on many different elements in its core infrastructure and basic network services. The key to maintaining reliability in the future will be continuing improvements in each of the network's core components, especially by implementing new techniques. The next section provides one such example.

Manageability at All Technical Layers

Too often the importance of network performance measurement and analysis is not sufficiently recognized, but it is crucial to understanding the state of the network, to problem detection and resolution, and to plans for future provisioning. For general network management, as well as use of specialized techniques (for example, flow control, controlling IP routing, and more) the Simple Network Management Protocol (SNMP) is still popular as a common and easy-to-use tool. Priority queuing techniques allow for special, extremely high-bandwidth experiments and provide SNMP-based information for optional management of specialized network configurations. General performance measurements and statistical analysis are utilized, as well as special techniques. For example, some MREN members use OCXmon and data visualization methods.

Expandability with High Performance through SONET

The MREN SONET infrastructure was provided by the Ameritech Public Data Network (APDN). By providing a fiber infrastructure as a foundation, MREN addressed major interorganizational requirements for regional, high-performance networking. Because this fiber infrastructure is shared among the member institutions, it allows for the easy, cost-effective addition of other institutions. One strength of the design of the MREN network is that additional sites can easily be linked simply by connecting a local-loop fiber link, allowing immediate switching capability and high-speed connectivity among all connected sites. Currently, it is possible to accomplish this goal with a high performance router with multiple OCX interfaces, which was not an option in 1995.

The original design provided for full-cell switching connectivity among the sites regardless of location. This design allowed for extremely high performance among relatively distant Midwestern cities, for example, between the University of Minnesota at Minneapolis and Northwestern University, just north of Chicago. The single delay encountered among the sites is the central ATM network switch. The expected high-quality IP traffic performance has been reliably and consistently achieved. Another advantage of fiber is that a variety of different services are available through the same communication infrastructure; not all participants are required to implement the same service level.

GigaPOPs

Through its GigaPOP facilities, MREN mitigates problems of communication and geographical distance by providing a high-performance networking infrastructure extending from the desktop, to campus networks, to regional networks, national networks, and international networks. The function of a GigaPOP (Gigabit-per-second POP) is primarily to provide reliable, high-performance, regional aggregation services to local communities, as well as to allow for additional access to other networks. Although the GigaPOPs provide for Layer 2 connectivity (and some are L3 -IP as well), it is clear that they also have a significant potential for higher-layer, value-added services. Consequently, another function is to provide value-added services beyond connectivity, such as provision for IPv6 services.

Also a GigaPOP can provide for universal, not just local, high-performance communications services. MREN was designed and implemented to allow for access paths to many other different types of networks and to remote instrumentation, such as those at national research labs, for example, advanced experimental facilities and support infrastructure, such as advanced synchrotrons, particle accelerators, observatories, advanced control systems, high-performance computers, mass storage systems, specialized application technologies, and advanced instrumentation controls systems. MREN connectivity allowed its community to be among the first to connect to the vBNS, to Abilene (described in a previous chapter), and to federal-agency networks. MREN also provides its members with connectivity to advanced international networks through the STAR TAP, which enables MREN members to access distant technical resources worldwide. Recently, two additional GigaPOPs have been established in the MREN community, one by MERIT and one by Indiana University. Several others are planned.

Next Generation Internet Exchange

MREN provides for high-performance IPv4 interconnectivity with a number of federal agency networks, including the Department of Defense Research and Engineering Network (DREN), the National Aeronautics and Space Administration Research and Education Network (NASA's NREN), and the Department of Energy's Energy Science's Network (ESnet), most of which are members of MREN. MREN is also assisting in formulating a federal agency, Next Generation Internet interchange (NGIX) in Chicago.

The NGIX would provide not only for peering among advanced agency networks, but also for peering with higher-education advanced networks and advanced international networks.

Conclusion

This chapter presented three case studies describing three fundamental building blocks of next-generation advanced Internets, advanced national Internet infrastructure, advanced regional Internet infrastructure, and GigaPOPs. These case studies provide examples of how next-generation Internet application, engineering, and other technical requirements were translated into a set of network designs that were the basis of early implementations of advanced Internets. They also demonstrate that the actual implementation of in-production networks does not always follow the intentions of technical designers, in part because the real world often imposes unexpected conditions or new requirements that must be addressed. This chapter also noted that actual implementations also give rise to new opportunities for technical facilities and services, such as a GigaPOP. This chapter introduced GigaPOP and a related facility, a network access point (NAP). NAPs are continuing to evolve and may become a particularly important type of facility for next-generation Internets. The next chapter describes them in greater detail.

References

NSTC (National Science and Technology Council). 1995. "Strategic Implementation Plan." *America in the Age of Information: A Forum.* Co-chaired by John Toole (ARPA) and Paul Young (NSF). (March 10). Bethesda, MD: National Coordination Office for HPCC: www.hpcc.gov

URLs

Cooperative Association for Internet Data Analysis (CAIDA): www.caida.org

Metropolitan Research and Education Network: www.mren.org

NGI: www.ngi.gov

National Laboratory for Applied Network Research: www.nlanr.net

Science, Technology, and Research Transit Access Point: www.startap.org

Very-High-Speed Broadband Network Service: www.vbns.net

Example Advanced Regional Networks and GigaPOPs

Corporation for Educational Institutions in California: www.cenic.org

Great Plains Network: www.greatplains.net

Merit: www.merit.edu

Metropolitan Research and Education Network: www.mren.org

NYSERnet: www.nysernet.org

North Carolina: www.ncgia.net, www.ncren.net

Oregon GigaPOP: www.ogig.net

OARnet: www.oar.net

Southern Crossroads: www.sox.net

CHAPTER 11

NAPs and GigaPOPs

Introduction

Previous chapters noted that as the Internet continues to grow in size, number of customers, traffic volume, complexity, and innovative applications, new components are required to provide for continuous, reliable services. Chapter 10 provided some examples of early implementations of emerging infrastructure required for next-generation Internets, a new type of national advanced infrastructure, an advanced regional network with GigaPOP sites, and network access points (NAPs).

NAPs are the focus of this chapter. Since the mid-1990s, the NAPs have been a fundamental infrastructure component of the Internet; they are major access points where significant volumes of inter-ISP and other traffic can be exchanged. The Internet continues to expand, with increasing numbers of private commercial networks, private research networks, federal Internet eXchanges (FIXes), and others. A substantial amount of tier-1 traffic is exchanged through private interconnections. As the individual networks that make up the larger Internet continue to grow and to exchange increasingly large amounts of traffic, NAPs may become ever more critically important Internet components, as they develop and implement additional services. This chapter explains the basic concept that led to the NAPs, provides an overview of the initial development of the NAPs, presents a case study based on the Chicago NAP, and indicates some future potential directions for NAP services and technologies.

As noted in the last chapter, in 1994, before the NAPs were formally established, MREN, a regional, next-generation, high-performance network, worked with Ameritech to establish a major high-performance exchange point to provide for traffic interchange among its member organizations and support for advanced applications. Independently, members were able to establish additional peering agreements in accordance with their requirements, including with national carriers. To illustrate the design and operation of a NAP, in this chapter the Chicago NAP will be closely examined. It makes an interesting case study because it is one of the largest Internet exchange points in the world, contending for first place with MAE-E (depending on traffic volume for particular periods). Traffic at the Chicago NAP doubled in less than 12 months to more than 6 terabytes a day in early 1999. The Chicago NAP is utilized significantly by ISPs, and also it is used by major universities and national laboratories as a regional *GigaPOP* (the world's first, established at the Chicago NAP by MREN, as explained in Chapter 10). The success of this project demonstrated the viability of the NAP model.

The NAP Concept: High-Performance Traffic Exchange

The basic premise of a NAP exchange point is that an ISP, corporation, research center, or consortium can purchase a connection to the exchange point infrastructure and gain the ability to pass traffic to the other members at the exchange point. Many different types of physical topologies are used at exchange points; however, the same, basic function is that of providing paths among enterprises. In addition, because of the topology choices, some variation may exist in the exchange point's ability to provide peering (see Figure 11.1).

An analogy to this model is a major airport hub served by several different airlines. At an airport, the airlines exchange passengers between flights. At a NAP, the connected community exchanges IP packets among different corporations or other types of enterprises. The NAP serves a role similar to that of an airport in that it provides a well-known point at which many different carriers can direct their traffic, confident that other providers will also be members of the hub. NAPs benefit the Internet because they provide the function of traffic exchange. Some also allow individual organizations to connect in order to gain direct access to ISPs, and others allow for specialized private interconnections among consortia and for specialized advanced services.

As central focal points, NAPs also have the capability to provide advanced features such as monitoring traffic flow, establishing settlement, and facilitating provisioning agreements. To help with monitoring, some exchanges can gather statistics on the traffic and report this information to the attached users. These reports are usually maintained on the WWW, but sometimes they are distributed via e-mail. Some exchanges also are involved with interprovider settle-

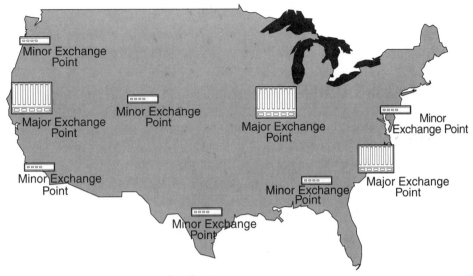

Figure 11.1 Exchange point distribution.

ments. In this role, the exchange point can expand on its traffic-monitoring responsibilities and act as a trusted third party to determine how much traffic is flowing between Internet service providers. This information is one of the key metrics used to determine peering policy on the commodity Internet.

Finally, some high-end exchange points built on ATM technology allow users to create or delete virtual circuits via a WWW interface. This service allows the exchange point to have more control over the service and consequently to have better control over traffic that arrives over the exchange point interface. The following sections describe the initial stages of establishing a NAP, including system facilities.

Development of the NAP Model

In the mid-1990s, the NAP model was developed to provide for large-scale Internet peering. In 1995, the NSFnet backbone was decommissioned, and in anticipation of this move, most regional networks became commercial enterprises. To support this transition, the NSF, along with commercial communications providers, established three network access points (NAPs) as major peering points for various Internets. One was established on the East Coast by Sprint (referred to as the New York NAP although physically located in Pennsauken, New Jersey), one on the West Coast by PacBell in the San Francisco Bay area, and one in Chicago by Ameritech, in the central city area. In addition, MFS (Metropolitan Fiber Systems, now MCI WorldCom) established the Metropolitan Area Ethernet East (MAE-East) near Washington, D.C., in

McLean, Virginia (now at a WorldCom facility in Vienna, Virginia), and, much later, Metropolitan Area Ethernet West (MAE-West) in Palo Alto, California (now at an MCI facility in San Jose).

Direct Interconnections

Beginning with the NSFnet's transition from a private network to a public system of ISP and exchange points in 1994, the major U.S. ISPs established peering via the original four NAPs. In the period from 1994 to 1997, as the number of connected ISPs and aggregate traffic grew from 1994 to 1997, most of the NAPs became congested. Further, traffic carried on each ISP backbone, and traffic exchanged between the major ISPs, grew exponentially. This development led to a need for large ISPs to make use of all available bandwidth for transmitting traffic to other ISPs. NAP circuit utilization grew to nearly 100 percent, to the point where the shift of traffic caused by a failure of one NAP or corresponding hardware would cause a corresponding congestion collapse of another part of an ISP backbone.

In order to address these problems, large ISPs began establishing what are called *private peering* circuits. The majority of Internet traffic is exchange from one ISP to another through these private interconnects. These circuits are direct connections between two ISP routers without the use of an intermediate NAP. Private peering connections costs are shared by the ISPs, and their implementation is based on the desire to move large traffic flows around NAPs. The earliest report of a major private interconnect was by ANS and Sprint in early 1995 (www.ans.net/WhatsNew/PressReleases/Press/Sprint-ANS-AOL.html). In June 1995, ANS, Sprint, and MCI reported adding private interconnects (www.ans.net/WhatsNew/PressReleases/Press/ANS-MCI-Sprint.html). There is evidence that all of the larger providers established interconnects about this same time, though the ISPs typically consider this information proprietary.

It is estimated that large ISPs may maintain approximately 50 direct peering arrangements. Often, these connections are made at public exchange points by running dedicated fiber between the two ISPs. In the case of non-NAP direct connection where facilities costs are involved, the cost of the connection is shared between the two ISPs or the ISPs will take turns purchasing connectivity into each other's networks. The ISP that purchases the connection is responsible for trouble isolation during an outage.

Chicago Network Access Point and the Routing Arbiter

The Chicago NAP is managed by Ameritech Advanced Data Services (AADS). From its inception in 1995, AADS provided a forum at the NAP for customers to begin developing multilateral peering and transit agreements (MLPA) to allow for mutual exchange of routes. Other specialized agreements for establishing connectivity were also possible, for example, bilateral peering agreements and those related to noncommercial, specialized research related to advanced networking for advanced applications.

Initially, in setting up the NAPs, there was much discussion about the implementation of the primary mechanism for providing stable, global routing, the Routing Arbiter. A mechanism was needed to replace the functions based on the system used by MERIT for the NSFnet, the Policy Routing Database (PRDB). A plan was developed that specified the development of several components that would interact but remain distinct.

First, a new database was to be established in which any NAP customer could record the routing policies that it wished to establish. The database was implemented using a routing IP exchange standard (RIPE-181), and it was set up so that it would be synchronized with other RIPE-181 databases. Route servers at NAPs act as central repositories or databases for Internet routing information. The route servers (RS) (www.rs.org) are Unix workstations attached to the exchange point that run routing software developed by the Routing Arbiter project. These computers perform routing exchange and processing functions for ISP-attached routers and potentially eliminate corrupt inter-ISP routing information. The RS is typically funded by the NAP owner but operated by the Routing Arbiter project.

The route server facilitates routing exchange among the NAP-attached ISPs by gathering routing information from participating ISPs' routers on the NAP, processing the information based on the ISPs' routing policy requirements and policies, and then passing the routing information to each ISP router. Through the MLPAs, NAP customers agreed to ensure the integrity of the data in the databases. Analysis software was provided to support policy development and management. This analysis software uses the information in the database to determine and report back to network managers the viability of policy selections. When particular policies are selected, they are stored in the database, and configuration files are automatically generated for the distributed route servers. Route servers can present synthesized policies to peers—specific views based on the policies that are registered in the Routing Arbiter database.

The RS uses BGP4 as the interdomain routing protocol to exchange routing information with NAP-attached ISP routers. Another advantage of this system is that these views allow customers to examine the global view of a peer without the inconvenience of having to continually activate multiple BGP sessions with numerous different peers. The route server also provided proxy aggregation to minimize the number of routes transmitted to peers. The route server does not forward packets among the NAP-attached ISPs; all inter-ISP traffic is passed across the actual NAP. Instead, it uses BGP's third-party routing information capabilities to pass routing information from one ISP to another, with the next hop pointing to the ISP router that advertises the route to the RS. Traffic is therefore exchanged directly among the ISP routers on the NAP, even though the route server provides the routing information.

One key use of the route servers is to reduce the number of BGP peering sessions ISP routers will need to maintain when peering across the NAP. The reduction in load occurs because each ISP at the exchange point maintains a peering session with the RS rather than multiple individual peering sessions. At the larger NAPs this service is critical because the number of individual BGP peering sessions supported by today's router typically is no greater than 60.

An additional use of the RS is to sanitize the routing information being exchanged by ISPs. Because the RS provides a very sophisticated tool set for managing the inter-ISP routing updates, the data can be filtered for invalid conditions, or routing policy can be applied by the RS on behalf of the ISP's prestated desires.   ·

To ensure stability and reliability, the servers were production-hardened, such as through redundancy, so they would be reliable and available 7 days a week, 24 hours a day. Also, to ensure ongoing enhancement to meet upward demand, a plan was developed to create new routing methods, techniques, and protocols. Customers desired flexibility with regard to routing services; for example, database entries registered as confidential or limited should not appear in displayed forwarding tables. It is notable that the RA is not popular among tier-1 ISPs, who prefer not to provide their BGP configurations to a third party.

Initial Chicago NAP Facilities

Some early non-NAP exchange points were established with protocols that did not scale well. AADS, on the other hand, was the first to select a high-end ATM switch as its core component, which scaled particularly well. To support the NSFnet transition, at its switching facility in downtown Chicago, AADS purchased and installed a high-performance Lucent GlobeView2000 ATM switch (at the time AT&T GCNS-2000) and routers (Cisco 7010s) for major ISPs, such as ANS, MCI, and Sprint. These and other organizations began peering and exchanging production traffic. To support traffic exchange, a Routing Arbiter route server was attached to an FDDI ring. Connections to the switch were almost all implemented as DS-3 ATM. The interface was provided initially by Kentrox ATM and later exchanged for a Cisco DS-3 AIP to allow for better traffic management, for example, through rate shaping. AADS set up a program of ongoing testing of router, DSU, and switch performance at its interoperability lab in Hoffman Estates, Illinois.

Pacific Bell NAP

On the West Coast in 1995 (in the San Francisco Bay area, or LATA 1), the Pacific Bell NAP was also established with ATM technology, basically two Newbridge 36150 ATM switches (16 by 16), both able to provide for as many as 12 DS-3s. Both switches were configured with two ports dedicated to trucking between switches and two for timing. Rate of growth in traffic, management needs, and buffering requirements, especially for the type of TCP flows that characterized NAP traffic, however, led to the establishing of a switch architecture evaluation project to investigate ATM products for the longer term. Also, Cisco AIP rate-controlled interfaces were added after initial implementation to allow for improved traffic flow. It was clear that OC3c would have to be supported in the near term. Management and monitoring for the ATM services, 7 by 24, were provided by Pacific Bell's Network Data Products Service Center (NDPSC).

Initial problems with cell loss for volumes in the range of 20–30 Mbps led to a reconfiguration that allowed for some traffic to pass through an FDDI ring before interconnecting to the ATM switch. This two-domain configuration allowed for better traffic management through segmentation. It was considered a temporary configuration, though, one that would be too limiting for anticipated future traffic flows. The FDDI part of the NAP service was managed by the Pacific Bell LAN Management Center.

A series of tests were conducted by a project group composed of engineers from the Network Data Products Services Center, Pacific Bell's Broadband Labs Governance, and LAN Management Center. For example, some early tests were developed to evaluate the maximum throughput possible for multiple, simultaneous inflows and outflows. The test program used was ttcp, and tests were run with multiple TCP window sizes. Various tests were conducted of multiple combinations of FDDI and Ethernet source and destinations flows. A single DS-3 Newbridge ATM was set up as an output port as the convergence point for five source DS-3 traffic flows through the Newbridge ATM ports.

Currently, the Pacific Bell NAP is comprised of a fully meshed network of nine high performance Cisco Stratacom ATM switches, and supports public and private peering through multilateral and bilateral agreements. It uses the Merit Networks Routing Arbiter and provides for an additional level of monitoring thorough the Merit NOC.

Current NAP Technologies

Most exchange points today are built with switched Ethernet, switched FDDI, or ATM as a core. Ethernet exchanges are common because they are relatively inexpensive to build and the connection speed is a good match for most applications. The next most common exchanges are built from FDDI switches. These are popular because they support high-speed traffic flows between providers and they are also relatively inexpensive.

FDDI exchange points gained their greatest popularity on the East and West Coasts of America when they were used for the MAEs in the mid 1990s (MAE-East, www.mfst.com/MAE/east.stats.html and MAE-West, www.mfst.com/MAE/west.stat.html). These large FDDI hubs were built with Compaq Corp.'s (nee Digital) Giga-switches. Each switch has the ability to support 24 FDDI ports, and the exchange can grow above 24 users by interconnecting multiple switches. The FDDI exchange points work well but have scale limitations when the total number of users exceeds approximately 100. Another limitation of FDDI or Ethernet exchange points is that users can connect at only one speed (10 or 100 Mbps); therefore, they do not support connection speeds that match well to a wide-area circuit speed. In order to build larger exchange points, a different technology is necessary. MAE-E now has implemented ATM, in addition to FDDI, using Stratacom switches.

NAPs and ATM

Currently, the most popular technology by number of ports at the major exchange points is ATM. ATM provides for an exceptional technological base for several reasons. First, ATM has the ability to scale its port speeds over a wide spectrum. For example, at a single exchange point it is possible to support DS-1, DS-3, OC3c, and OC12 connected users. In addition, ATM switches are very scalable as to the number of ports supported on a single device. As opposed to FDDI switches, for example, ATM switches can be built with many more than 24 ports, and some architectures are in production with hundreds of ports on a single switch, although at lower speeds. Finally, ATM has been shown to facilitate superior exchange points because, unlike Ethernet or FDDI, ATM is not a local-area network technology. This feature means that there are few geographical topological constraints on the exchange point's architecture; and it is possible to build a NAP, with routers, all co-located within a single room, or within a major city, or globally interconnected on wide-area ATM links. In general, the scalability of ATM allows for straightforward procedures for continual upgrades.

In all of these cases, the configuration of the routers would be identical and the operation of the exchange would also be identical except, of course, for transit delay. ATM has proven to be an important technology for the Internet, but NAPs are clearly a type of facility for which ATM currently is unsurpassed (see Figure 11.2).

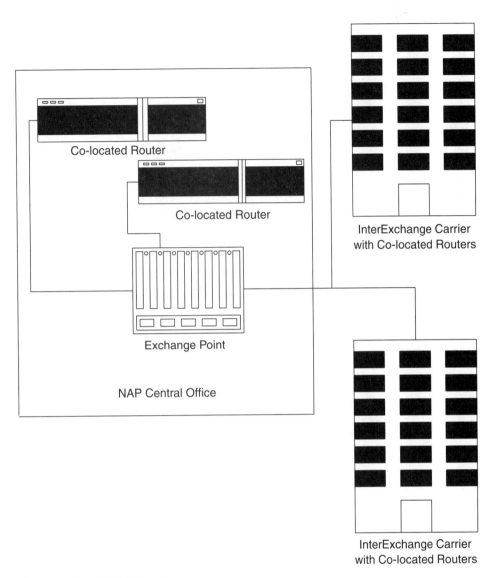

Figure 11.2 ATM NAP options.

Continuous Growth of the Chicago NAP

The Chicago NAP is now constructed around a cluster of ATM switches (Ascend) that route traffic to a single, large, central switch that supports speeds ranging from DS-3 to OC12c. OC48c is being planned. (See Figure 11.3).

The Chicago NAP has been successful for several reasons. First, it was designed to provide services for a large, diverse set of constituencies, includ-

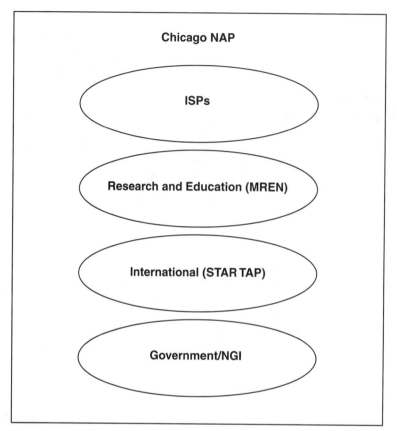

Figure 11.3 Chicago NAP user community.

ing research universities and labs with the most aggressive applications in the world. The NAP has successfully built communities of interest that comprise different types of constituencies, including ISPs, universities, federal laboratories and international sites, and U.S. government agencies.

The NAP began as an exchange point that was focused on providing high-performance connectivity among MREN members, but it soon expanded to include ISPs. Shortly after MREN was established and began the development of its prototype GigaPOP, the NSF privatization of the Internet went into effect, and the NAP became a major ISP exchange point. Soon after that, the MREN GigaPOP became a major access point for the vBNS (www.vbns.net). Based on the exceptional success of the Chicago NAP as the MREN and ISP hub, the site was chosen as the primary exchange for international research and education sites connecting to American research backbones, such as the vBNS, and, in 1999, Abilene (www.ucaid.edu). This international program, the Science Technology and Research Transit Access Point (STAR TAP, described in a previous chapter), further established Chicago's importance in 1998.

Finally, the Chicago NAP began to be utilized as a Next Generation Internet Exchange (www.ngi.gov) in 1998. In this capacity, the NAP served as a point where U.S. government agencies could connect their networks and exchange traffic with other agencies.

Most recently, as part of its evolution, the Chicago NAP has added a role as a business exchange point, similar to the Automotive Network eXchange (ANX). This capability means that the NAP is now used to connect major corporations to each other and to provide connectivity between corporations and ISPs and/or universities and national research labs (see Figure 11.4). This application is unique in the exchange-point industry and reflects the flexibility that the Chicago NAP has always provided.

It is interesting to note the total amount of traffic that flows through a major Internet exchange like Chicago's. If one considers that a typical written page contains approximately 30,000 bits of information, then the Chicago NAP carries the equivalent of an average of 60,000 full pages of text every second—over 7 terabytes each day.

The traffic volume at the Chicago NAP has at least doubled every year (see Figure 11.5). At some points, because load is affected by new users being added, the load can double in as little as three months.

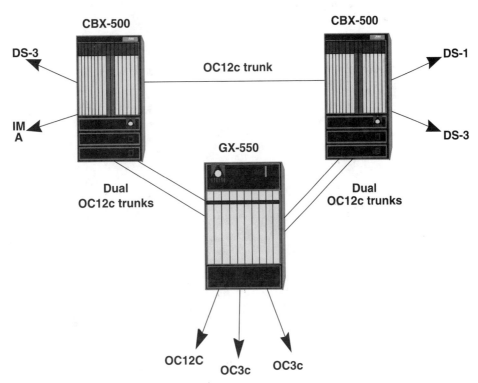

Figure 11.4 Chicago NAP architecture.

Chicago NAP Description

This section and the next few sections present the Chicago NAP from a service perspective. The AADS NAP provides core facilities that comprise an Internet exchange point where ISPs can meet to exchange traffic with other attached ISPs. At this time, the NAP is a Layer 2 switched service that is not directly involved with routing IP datagrams, only forwarding asynchronous transfer mode (ATM) cells between ISPs. The NAP is a Layer 2 service because it does not restrict internetworking protocol or routing policy selection.

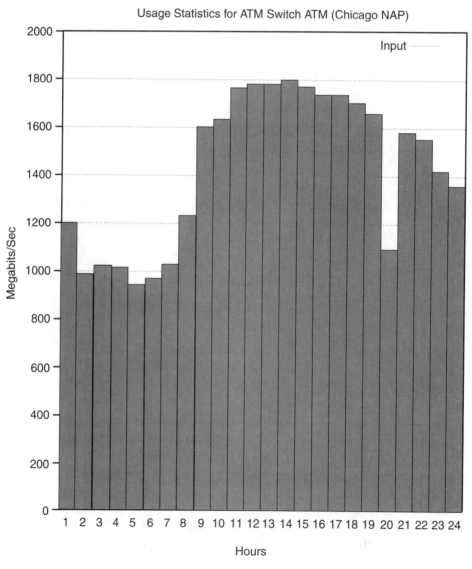

Figure 11.5 Chicago NAP traffic (Tuesday 30 Mar 99).

The fabric of the Chicago NAP is an ATM switch providing both high speeds and a high degree of scalability. Interface speed currently supported include these:

- DS-3 (45 Mbps) ATM
- OC3c (155 Mbps) ATM
- OC12c (622 Mbps) ATM

Higher speed services are being planned.

VPI/VCI Assignment

The information in this and the next few sections is a paraphrase of Ameritech's standard agreements.

Customers of the NAP service use ATM permanent virtual circuits (PVCs) to exchange traffic among routers. A full mesh PVC configuration among NAP customers is included in the NAP access fee. By default the NAP operator will create a full mesh of PVCs between connecting ISPs. At any time ISPs may request that any of the PVCs be deleted to prohibit communication to other selected ISPs.

Each PVC endpoint has an associated unique virtual path identifier and virtual circuit identifier (VPI/VCI) pair. All NAP customers are assigned a VPI/VCI pair that is unique to their ATM port. When PVCs are built interconnecting two ISPs, the VPI/VCI used at each endpoint is associated with the customer on the opposite end of that PVC. AADS project managers provide their customers with the VPI/VCI assignments.

Address Assignment

The AADS NAP address space administration is handled by MERIT. To obtain an IP address, customers use the form located at www.merit.edu. To see a list of current IP address assignments, check the NAP home page or obtain the IN-ADDR.ARPA zone file for the AADS NAP space from ns.merit.edu.

Peering: Multi-Lateral Peering Agreement and Bilateral Agreements

Customers who use the NAP generally intend to form bilateral or multilateral agreements with other NAP-attached networks and participate on the Chicago-NAP mailing list. A physical connection to a NAP should not be considered as an "Internet connection." Peering arrangements between ISPs should be made before connecting.

There are two ways to arrange peering:

1. Join the Multi-Lateral Peering Agreement (MLPA).
2. Form bilateral agreements.

Many NAP customers participate in a Multi-Lateral Peering Agreement, which facilitates peering for exchange of traffic. The text of the MLPA can be found at nap.aads.net/MLPA.html. A link on that page also contains a list of current MLPA members.

As noted, the MLPA is a document that has been developed to facilitate peering among customers connected to an Internet exchange point. When an ISP agrees to the terms of the MLPA, it agrees to form and support peering agreements with all other MLPA participants at the NAP. It generally also peers with the route server.

When an organization has joined the MLPA, AADS builds PVCs interconnecting all existing, and future, MLPA members and provides a list of VPI/VCI assignments. ISP contact information is added to the MLPA contact Web page. Because not all NAP customers are MLPA members, some form bilateral peering agreements. Once the agreement has been made and both parties have been notified, AADS builds the appropriate PVC.

Route Server Basics

The route servers are workstations running routing software developed by the RA project that performs the routing exchange and processing function described in detail later in this chapter (the Routing Arbiter Project is a joint undertaking of Merit Network, Inc. and the University of Southern California Information Sciences Institute (www.isi.edu).

The route server facilitates routing exchange among the NAP-attached ISPs by gathering routing information from participating ISP routers on the NAP, processing the information based on the ISP's routing policy, and passing the processed routing information to each ISP router. The RS uses BGP4 as the inter-domain routing protocol to exchange routing information with NAP-attached ISP routers.

The route server does not forward packets among the NAP-attached ISPs. Instead, it uses BGP's third-party routing information capabilities to pass routing information from one ISP to another, with the next hop pointing to the ISP router that advertises the route to the RS. Traffic is therefore exchanged directly among the ISP routers on the NAP, even though the route server provides the routing information.

One key use of the route server is to reduce the number of Border Gateway Protocol peering sessions router(s) will need to maintain at the NAP. As an MLPA member, it may become beneficial to make extensive use of the route servers located at the NAP.

The two most common routers used for NAP connections are those made by Cisco Systems and Bay Networks. In this section information will be provided covering sample configurations for the former because Bay Networks routers use a GUI for configurations.

Using a Cisco router, the possible interfaces for NAP connections are these:

1. HSSI (with an ATM DSU)
2. AIP for DS-3
3. AIP for OC3c
4. VIPZ with ATM PAs

When configuring the router, it is important to note the type of AAL 5 encapsulation because it must match peers in order to communicate with them. The two types of encapsulation are NLPID (RFC 1490) and LLC/SNAP (RFC 1483). NLPID is compatible with frame relay and is more prevalent. If the default is preferred, this should be the selection.

Below are examples of how to configure an ATM interface (DS-3 or OC3) and an HSSI interface for use with an ATM DSU.

This is a sample ATM interface configuration:

```
interface ATM3/0
ip address 192.168.1.1 255.255.255.0
atm pvc 1 0 50 aal5nlpid
atm pvc 2 0 51 aal5nlpid
atm pvc 3 0 52 aal5snap
map-group aads_nap
!
!
map-list aads_nap
ip 192.168.1.2 atm-vc 1
ip 192.168.1.3 atm-vc 2
ip 192.168.1.4 atm-vc 3
```

This is the corresponding HSSI interface configuration:

interface Hssi1/0

ip address 192.168.1.1 255.255.255.0

encapsulation atm-dxi

dxi pvc 0 50 nlpid

dxi pvc 0 51 nlpid

dxi pvc 0 52 snap

dxi map ip 192.168.1.2 0 50

dxi map ip 192.168.1.3 0 51

dxi map ip 192.168.1.4 0 52

After an NAP circuit has been tested and turned over to the entity that requested it, the circuit should be immediately tested for connectivity with its peers. The three main problems encountered with new turn-ups are as follows:

1. **Problem:** VPI/VCI to IP mapping incorrect or nonexistent at one side.

   Solution: Do not assume a peer has the new site configured on its router. Get explicit confirmation that this work has been done and that it has been rechecked from a technical contact on the peer's side. Do the same for the new router.

2. **Problem:** Mismatched AAL 5 encapsulation.

   Solution: Find out what the peer is using. The encapsulation type should match exactly. If the peer is using frame relay behind an ATM DSU, AAL 5-NLPID should be used.

3. **Problem:** PVC provisioned incorrectly by AADS.

   Solution: If 1 and 2 have been checked and the problem still exists, AADS operations should be contacted and the switch checked for provisioning errors.

Future Exchange Point Roles

The future direction of exchange points, beyond just the service provided by first-generation NAPs, is focused on enhanced services that allow the exchange point to facilitate member communication. Examples of the types of services being implemented are these:

Real-time allocation and provisioning of interconnecting fabric. This allows the GigaPOP's members to control the creation of virtual circuits or packet filters that can be used to control traffic flow on their interface. The user interface to control provisioning is usually based on HTML.

Real-time reporting of traffic flows between GigaPOP members. This feature allows GigaPOP users better access to information about how much, or what type, of traffic is flowing across their interface. It can be very useful for performance monitoring for regional network members or for enforcement of settlements ISPs.

Better control over traffic flowing within the exchange. Scaling is a major challenge facing large exchange points and operators of large networks. To alleviate this problem, new protocols, such as Multiprotocol Label Switching (MPLS), are being developed. These protocols address scaling by allowing the members to acquire reachability information from the exchange and then use this information to route traffic. This can have the benefit of reducing the number of routing adjacencies.

Switched Virtual Circuits (SVC) are another new feature that can enhance exchange points: SVCs allow members to dynamically establish connections across the exchange fabric very quickly without human intervention. SVCs can be used to reduce router adjacencies or to facilitate experimentation.

Implementation of different levels of quality of service (QoS) can also be seen as an improvement to next-generation exchanges. These features can be used in two ways. First, inter-ISP virtual circuits can be sized differently and given different priority based on ISP settlements. Second, next-generation applications, such as streaming video, can make use of higher priority so that the packet stream will not be interrupted during time of congestion.

As previously mentioned, at large exchange points there is always concern over scalability. In particular, because the NAPs are made up of one logical IP subnetwork, the number of router adjacencies can be large, equal to the number of routers connected to the NAP. Therefore, it is beneficial for the exchange point to support a one-arm router that acts as a single peering arbiter. This router would offer high performance and would be connected over one or more very high-speed links into the NAP. Because of the diversity of routing policies, it would also need to support policy-based routing. In practice this router would establish peering with all NAP members and would eliminate or reduce the need for interprovider peering sessions. It is notable also that other approaches are also possible, for example, NAPs need not be comprised of a single logical subnet.

In order to improve general performance of Internet applications, it is often beneficial to host services directly at the exchange point. Two common applications utilizing servers are WWW caching and content hosting. WWW caching can take several forms, from NAP-based proxy caches to satellite distribution systems. Each provides the exchange the ability to quickly distribute WWW content, but each can raise complicated legal issues. Original content based at exchange points can also provide value. This takes the form of content based on large computers that are part of the NAP subnetwork and accessible to the attachment members. Content on these machines can be quickly transmitted across the NAP and can be efficiently shared.

Much of this work is being realized first at *GigaPOPs*—the next-generation Internet exchange points—thereby allowing participants to share advanced services traffic with other next-generation Internet participants.

A number of next-generation Internet initiatives have been established, and a primary goal of these projects is cooperatively to develop the next generation of computer network applications and the underlying broadband infrastructure to facilitate advanced research development. For example, in order to yield the best results, the outcomes of these efforts are shared by all participant groups, often at national advanced networking workshops. Universities and national laboratories are driving these projects because they have the unique ability both to demand cutting-edge applications and to help develop the working implementations.

Differences between GigaPOPs and NAPs

The primary differences between the GigaPOPs and the NAPS are these:

A NAP is a neutral, Layer 2 meet point for ISPs to exchange routes and traffic. The NAP is not usually involved with higher-layer protocols and processes; therefore, it is not involved with routing.

A GigaPOP is a value-added, Layer 2/3 meet point where the attached users can communicate with other sites and service providers.

Researchers connected to next-generation Internets coordinate efforts in advanced networking services, technologies, and related applications with those with similar interests at universities, at other nonprofit organizations, at national government laboratories and agencies and at corporations.

As part of this effort and other various next-generation Internet initiatives, leading research organizations, such as MREN, are conceptualizing new types of GigaPOPs, which will support leading-edge applications such as teleimmersion, digital libraries, and virtual laboratories. These projects will simultaneously push the leading edge of multimedia broadband networking and help meet the growing production requirements of member universities.

Currently, this type of research is focused on broadband network design, network management, and QoS applications. Network engineering will be developed as needed to enable these applications. The primary goal of the first phase for network engineering is design of high-performance GigaPOPs.

The basic GigaPOP provides a peering point for advanced technology networks and serves as the regional aggregation point for many advanced Internet services and capabilities. One characteristic that differentiates the GigaPOP from traditional NAPs is that these next-generation peering points offer connecting sites a variety of services from one central location. For example, a GigaPOP provides specialized architecture and interconnection that allows the consolidation of traffic from various organizational networks into a regional meet point(s) similar to a NAP, but with more features and services. Second, it provides support for the physical interconnection among other regional GigaPOPs so that high-speed, QoS-aware, inter-GigaPOP communications can take place. As they are evolving today, there are several types of GigaPOPs. Some are fairly simple, routing traffic through one or two connections, while others are more complex, serving both GigaPOP members and other networks to which those members need access. Some support a rich set of connections to other GigaPOPs and therefore must provide mechanisms to route traffic correctly and to prevent unauthorized or improper use of connectivity. These GigaPOPs, like MREN's at the Chicago NAP, have connections to ISPs and national research networks, like the vBNS and Abilene.

GigaPOP Services

By providing several services from the GigaPOP's one location, the task of procuring networking features and functionality is facilitated. From the set of advanced and evolving services described previously, the following categories are considered core:

Commodity Internet services. Traditional Internet connectivity—typically the connecting organization establishes access at speeds much higher than conventional connections. Most GigaPOPs are capable of support commodity connections of hundreds of megabits per seconds.

Research network services. High-end value services such as ATM Switched Virtual Circuits, IPv6 routing, enhanced PPP over SONET, and new protocols for multicast IP routing.

Information servers. Servers such as those for access to terabyte disk arrays for temporary data storage, WWW cache servers, and Stratum 1 Network Clocks.

ISPs, corporations, and research institutions connected to a GigaPOP are able to pick and choose from the menu of available services. Institutions are attracted to the prospect of being able to obtain various types of services from one physical connection that should be lower in cost compared to procuring multiple individual circuits and services. Therefore, by connecting to a GigaPOP the members are able to aggregate research and commodity traffic onto a single high-bandwidth link. The single link offers higher capacity and supports QoS. Because the link offers higher capacity, the cost per bit is lower.

Consolidation of traffic enables GigaPOP members to reduce expenditures on local loops, back-haul, equipment, and support costs, thus allowing the institution to step up to a higher aggregate level of service, such as higher-speed access, than would be possible otherwise. This philosophy also has the potential to create economies of scale for commodity Internet services because the GigaPOP can be used as a wholesale distribution point serving a large number of customers (see Figure 11.6).

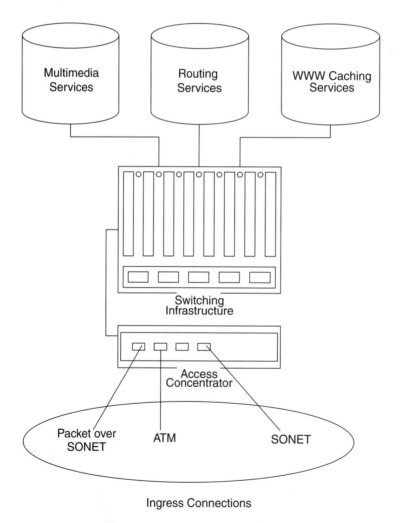

Figure 11.6 GigaPOP architecture.

There is currently some debate over what services must be implemented by GigaPOP service providers. It is generally believed, however, that the services a premier GigaPOP must offer include the following:

Access ranging from OC12 (622 Mbps) to OC48 (2.4 Gbps). This access can be provided over a circuit-switched technology such as ATM or over a clear channel technology such as packet over SONET. The most common GigaPOP initial connections have been built on ATM; however, much current development is also directed at IP over SONET. High performance L3 switches can function as effective large scale cross connects, using MPLS. In addition, some researchers will demand PPP over SONET to reduce overhead. It is likely that in the long run GigaPOPs over 2.4 Gbps will support only SONET because of difficulty in segmenting packets into ATM cells at that speed.

Switched Layer 2 and 3 connectivity options. Both ATM switching and IP routing will be required at the GigaPOP.

Connectivity to research partners and other organizations with which GigaPOP members wish to communicate. This connectivity will be provided via the vBNS, Abilene, or possibly NGNet (vBNS+) networks.

Connectivity to other high-performance wide area networks, which may be implemented for their own missions and research, such as the government agencies: Department of Defense, Department of Energy, NASA, and others.

Connectivity to other metropolitan area or community networks to provide for fast access to regional, digital, subscriber-line technology.

Network services provided by commodity Internet service providers. This connectivity will be easy to achieve for existing NAPs that wish to augment their product to encompass a GigaPOP role.

GigaPOP Operations

As opposed to the major NAPs that are operated by telecommunications carriers, operational management of a GigaPOP is a joint effort involving the advanced Internet institutions and the carrier operators. This relationship is necessary because operation of a GigaPOP involves protocols and processes that are leading edge and that are not part of mainstream products. Operational procedures include collecting network utilization and performance data, and making necessary data available to schedule, monitor, troubleshoot, and account for network service in a manner acceptable to network managers.

To facilitate implementation of the GigaPOP, operational support is provided by a small number of regional advanced networking technical committees, such as the MREN Technical Committee, and next-generation Network Operations Centers (NOCs). For example, the Abilene network received substantial early support from Indiana University. These NOCs offer high-level coordination, troubleshooting, expertise, and driver applications. Few end-user support services are available; therefore, the GigaPOP operator is expected to cooperate on end-user support, with the bulk being offered at the institutional level.

GigaPOP Quality of Service

GigaPOPs must supply the aggregate bandwidth demands of participants while serving a number of customers with special quality of service (QoS) requirements. It is expected that the IETF DiffServ initiative will result in capabilities that will support multiple levels of QoS requests among next-generation Internet entities; however, these criteria are likely to change as concrete applications are developed. The work in specifying QoS will utilize MPLS and RSVP, coupled with focused research on mapping RSVP to underlying transport systems. The following are examples of how QoS can be supported on GigaPOPs.

Transmission speed. This is the minimum available effective data rate and a sustainable maximum limit. For example, a user might request a connection whose sustainable data rate never falls below 10 Mbps and agrees not to expect transmission faster than 20 Mbps. On the other hand, the application may request an average data rate along with the minimum acceptable rate that can be tolerated.

Bounded delay and delay variance. These parameters specify the maximum effective lag and/or delay variability allowed specifically for video and other signals that carry real-time information. For example, the user may specify, via an ATM signaling message, that the delay between packets should not be long enough to interrupt or freeze live video.

Throughput. The amount of data transmitted in a designated time period. For example, a user may indicate that a gigabit of data is to be moved between two hosts in no more than one minute.

Schedule. The starting and ending times for the requested service. For example, a user may wish that the requested connectivity be available at some exact time in the future for some specified period.

Loss rate. This parameter is the maximum acceptable bit error rate over a specified time interval that results in corrupted data that must be discarded by the destination.

GigaPOP and Other Internet Components

GigaPOPs provide an opportunity to introduce new and enhanced components to the Internet infrastructure. In the progress toward developing enhanced Internets, designs are being developed to enhance virtually all components that are part of the layer picture of next-generation Internet.

Virtual Private Networks

One method for allowing for the Internet to substitute for leased lines while implementing provisions for certain types of traffic guarantees is through virtual private networks (VPNs). Currently, the Internet Engineering Task Force is investigating options for the management of VPNs across multiple domains, such as through various ISP networks. There are a variety of options for implementing VPNs, each with a particular set of trade-offs.

In order to make VPN traffic more identifiable, one proposal suggests the implementation of VPN identifiers, which would classify traffic through unique data bits within a VPN IP packet header. An additional layer, between OSI Layer 3 and Layer 4, would provide for dynamic routing based on requirements at a given time. Two options for implementation are through BGP, which would require routing protocol translation, and through Multiprotocol Label Switching (MPLS), which would not require that translation.

Virtual Router Redundancy Protocol

In routing traffic across domains, default gateways are sometimes determined through dynamic route-discovery protocols, such as Open Shortest Path First (OSPF) and Routing Information Protocols (RIP). Occasionally it is useful to optimize processor utilization by implementing statically configured default gateways. For such configurations, router loss is extremely problematic. Consequently, the Internet Engineering Task Force is developing a standard to resolve problems caused by loss of routers through a Virtual Router Redundancy Protocol (VRRP) method that allows for "failover" to an alternative router. VRRP allows for the definition of logically defined clusters of routers keyed to a central router.

IP packets are forwarded by relating their addresses to the physical identification of a device, its media access control (MAC) address (at OSI Layer 2). Through VRRP, the central (or master) router is provided with a virtual MAC address that can be transferred to a second router. With VRRP implemented, failure of any given router enables automatic continuous service provision by another router. Through VRRP, two routers can provide redundancy for each other. Status is continually checked (for example, each second) through communication to the backup of a VRRP packet called an "advertisement." Disruption of the signal triggers a brief diagnostic event that, upon failure detection, leads to the second router's assumption of the functions of the first.

NAPs and the International Community

The NAP model has now been established worldwide. One of the first developed outside of the United States was developed in Canada in partnership with CANARIE. One of the largest is the London Internet Exchange (LINX). In the Netherlands, the Amsterdam Internet Exchange (AMS-IX) will soon have the potential to be well connected internationally through the national Giga-Port project. Japan also has one of the most internationally connected NAPs, the Japan Internet Exchange Company (JPIX), which was established by a consortium of ISPs, networking equipment companies, and carriers, including Kokusai Denshin Denwa (KDD), which hosts the NAP at its building in the Otemachi district of Tokyo.

Conclusion

To support ever-increasing levels of Internet traffic, many new exchanges have been deployed, and growth in use of existing exchanges is constantly increasing. Despite some years of uncertainty, the future role of these exchange points in supporting the growth of the Internet is expected to continue for the foreseeable future. The NAP model seems to directly support the growth of the local and regional ISP industry, allowing local traffic exchange, providing a platform for advanced services, and multiple opportunities for traffic exchange. Also, the model allows for regional customization as exemplified by MREN (described in Chapter 10). Much advanced research and development centers on components with a potential for a large gain in performance-optimization, for example, innovative designs in routers and switches. In addition, however, other important research focuses on more basic improvements to core components, such as enhanced reliability. These topics are much too extensive to be covered in this book, but it may be useful to provide two examples. One is the rapidly developing area of virtual private networks. Another is directed at increased network reliability in enhanced network router redundancy.

Finally, with this type of flexible model, regional advanced networking organizations can freely innovate to develop breakthrough next-generation Internet technology, services, and applications. Some MREN developers are designing a next-generation GigaPOP, a MetaPOP, which should have a wide range of functions and features.

References

Ameritech Data Services. Web site [Available May 1999]. www.nap.aads.net

Pacific Bell, "Network Access Points." [Available May 1999]. www.pacbell.com/products/business/fastrak/networking/nap/index.html

RFC 1483. 1993. J. Heinanen. *Multiprotocol Encapsulation over ATM Adaptation Layer 5*. ftp://ftp.isi.edu/in-notes/rfc1483.txt (proposed standard).

RFC 1490. 1993. T. Bradley, C. Brown, and A. Malis. *Multiprotocol Interconnect over Frame Relay*. ftp://ftp.isi.edu/in-notes/rfc1490.txt (draft standard, rendered obsolete by RFC 2427, STD0055).

URLs

Ameritech: www.ameritech.com

Information Sciences Institute: www.isi.edu

MCI WorldCom's Advanced Network Systems: www.wcom.net

University Corporation for Advanced Internet Development: www.ucaid.edu

Very-High-Speed-Broadband Network Services: www.vbns.net

MAEs

MAE-East: www.mfst.com/MAE/east.stats.html

MAE-West: www.mfst.com/MAE/west.stat.html

Next-Generation IP: IPv6

IPv6 Services

All technologies require ongoing renewal and enhancement to remain viable in an environment of dynamically changing requirements. The Internet must respond to explosive growth, the high volumes of information, the expansion of e-commerce across a range of new applications, the development of integration capabilities (including video and voice), new requirements for ensured quality of services, the proliferation of networked resources worldwide, and the need for secure transmissions.

In response to these needs and others, the IETF has been developing the next-generation Internet Protocol, IP version 6, which for a time was referenced as IPng. IPv6 has been proposed as a replacement for IPv4. The development of IPv6 is taking place under the aegis of IETF design and development efforts (RFC 1883), as well as projects that provide early implementation experience, for example, via the 6bone testbed.

This chapter describes the characteristics that IPv6 introduces to enhance functionality. For example, it provides for a major increase in address space and options for the implementation of security mechanisms. It also allows for enhancement of routing mechanisms and automatic procedures for configurations, as covered in detail later in this book.

The next-generation Internet must be scalable—to billions of devices given the growth of the Internet. This goal is problematic with IPv4 because of its limited 32-bit address space. IPv6 is a major enhancement over IPv4, in part because it allows for a significant expansion of IP addresses—it expands the 32 bits provided by IPv4 for addressing to 128-bit addresses, allowing for 2 to the 128th addresses.

IPv6 allows for a 24-bit flow label field, thus providing the ability to distinguish among flows to help ensure quality of service by allowing for different classes of services. Different flows then can be monitored to ensure that they conform to policy rules and that they receive the services required to provide the performance they have been guaranteed.

IPv6 also provides for enhanced security. For example, the Internet Engineering Task Force's IPv6 initiative has developed concepts for IP-level encryption and for new techniques for address authentication. Some efforts have been made to specify BGP4, Open Shortest Path First (OSPF), and Routing Information Protocol (RIP) for IPv6; all currently are at least IETF drafts. The 6TAP project is an international early deployment IPv6 testbed currently being implemented.

IPv6: Scalable Addressing and MAE

Although the 32-bit address mechanism in IPv4 can handle more than 4 billion devices on about 16.7 million networks, the usable address space is more limited, particularly given the historical address classification into Class A, B, and C. For example, an organization might have received a Class B address but may not make full use of it. Any time the administrator decides to subnet, a price must be paid in available devices. The total number of devices under subnets is always less than the number of devices without subnetting. That circumstance is the trade-off required for the ability to manage the network more easily. The lost addresses for each subnet consist of all 0s and all 1s, and all the 1s and all the 0s values for the subnet field itself are also lost. As one can see, the price of subnetting varies with the numbers of subnet bits and the class of network used.[1]

The IETF started to look at this problem in 1991. Part of its 1992 recommendation was to look at "bigger Internet addresses." IPv6 has a 128-bit address. What is now called IPv6 originated from work known as Simple Internet Protocol Plus (SIPP). The group working on the protocol, also known at times as the SIPP Group, included the "working" IPv4 functions (though in some different places in the IP header or by different names), and removed (or made optional) infrequently used or "nonworking" functions. As noted, the protocol is described in RFC 1883; additional information on transition mechanisms can be found in RFC 1993.

The IPv4 address space problem is just one of the motivations to adopt IPv6, although it is the most important (and an argument has been made that it is the only reason). Some contend that today's IPv4 host implementations lack such features as autoconfiguration, network layer security, and others. IPv6 is intended to address most of the inadequacies in the existing IPv4 implementations. These inadequacies require the introduction of a new network layer header. IPv6 removes the Header field and the IP Header checksum and changes the Time-To-Live field to become a Hop Count limit. IPv6 is identified in the Ethertype field in the SNAP/LLC header with the bit pattern "86dd" hex instead of "0800" hex.

Although IPv6 significantly increases the total size of the available IP address space, the challenge is whether this increased space sufficiently enables the continued growth of the Internet. Within the current IP routing and addressing architecture, IP addressing must be unambiguous, but this is not sufficient to guarantee IP-level reachability within an Internet. Within the current architecture, the role of IP addresses is not just to enumerate all the nodes within an Internet, but to provide a capability for routing (IP-level reachability) to all the nodes within the Internet. Therefore, in order to support an uninterrupted growth of the Internet while maintaining the current IP routing and addressing architecture, not only is a larger IP address space needed, but the assignments of addresses must also enable scalable routing (www.cisco.com/warp/public/732/ipv6/ipv6_wp.html).

Specifically, minimizing routing overhead, and thus making the IP address space routable, is one of the fundamental problems in the current Internet. As the Internet grows, this problem is likely to become even more onerous. Without providing an adequate solution to this problem, increasing the total size of the available IP address space (by introducing IPv6) may not be adequate because this would not increase the total amount of the *routable* IP address space and thus would not help to sustain the growth of the Internet. The real limits of a routing table size are not clear; 100k routes exist in some ISP backbones. Fortunately, hierarchical routing is expected to scale, even for the size of the Internet that could be realized with the IPv6 address space. Therefore, for the foreseeable future, the Internet routing system (for both the IPv4 and IPv6 address spaces) will rely on the technique of hierarchical routing (www.cisco.com/warp/public/732/ipv6/ipv6_wp.html).

IPv6 Addressing

IPv6 supports three types of addresses in the target field (Minoli 1999):

1. Unicast
2. Multicast
3. Anycast

Note that the source field must be a unicast address.

A unicast address is unique to the interface/device it names. In IPv6 there is no broadcast IP address. A multicast address identifies a group of interfaces. Each of these interfaces/devices also has a unicast address. The multicast address is utilized to send information to sets of interfaces. One can designate a multicast address for every interface/device in a network or subnetwork, or the group may span multiple networks.

Anycast address is new to IPv6. The network assumes the responsibility of delivering the PDU, with this target address, to anyone in an anycast group or set of addresses, typically the "closest" in the sense of routing protocol metrics. Examples could be the DHCP server, an Internet Relay Chat server, and so on.

IPv4 used the byte-dot-byte or dotted decimal notation. IPv6 uses colons to separate the address into eight 16-bit segments. IPv6 utilizes a hierarchy of bits in the address range (from most significant to least significant). The left-most bits in the address signify a variable-length address prefix; this variable length currently ranges between 3 and 10 bits. Figure 12.1 shows the prefixes that have been assigned (other prefixes have the status of "unassigned").

Some of the reserved addresses have special meaning, as described in Table 12.1.

Currently defined IPv6 address allocation architecture (RFC 1887) is similar, if not identical, to the IPv4 address allocation architecture; both are based on hierarchical routing and specifically, on classless interdomain routing (CIDR) (RFC 1518, RFC 1519). As a result, the IPv6 routing architecture does not offer any significant improvements over the IPv4 routing architecture. Therefore, by combining hierarchical routing and very large IP address space, IPv6 makes it possible to sustain the growth of the Internet for the foreseeable future (http://www.cisco.com/warp/public/732/ipv6/ipv6_wp.html).

Binary	Allocation
0000 0000	Reserved
0000 001	ISO Network Address
0000 0010	Novell Network Addresses
010	Provider based Unicast Addresses
100	Geographic based Unicast Addresses
1111 1110 10	Link Local Addresses
1111 1110 11	Site Local Addresses
11111111	Multicast Address

Figure 12.1 IPv6 assigned prefixes.

Table 12.1 Special IPv6 Addresses

FUNCTION	ADDRESS
Unspecified Address	0:0:0:0:0:0:0:0 Purpose: It can be used when one does not have the true address. Example: A device requests a server for an IP address; while waiting the device can use the Unspecified Address as the source address for any message it must send (the Unspecified Address is not allowed as a target).
Loopback Address	0:0:0:0:0:0:0:1 Purpose: It can be used for diagnostic purposes. The message never leaves the system, but it can be used to test the protocol stack without having to rely on the network (the system sees a message leave and one arrive, but in fact it is the same loopback message).
Subnet-Router Address	Purpose: An anycast address that IPv6 builds by using a nonzero subnet prefix followed by zeros. The prefix identifies a particular subnet.
IPv4 Compatible Address	Example: If IPv4 address is 192.153.185.101 dec. or C0 99 B9 65 hex, then IPv4-Compatible Address is 0000:0000:0000:0000:0000:0000:C099:B965.
IPv4 Mapped Address	Purpose: It can be used to support transition between IPv4 and IPv6. IPv6 devices can communicate with each other over an IPv4 network. The IPv4-Compatible Address system uses routers at the crossover point between the IPv4 and the IPv6 domains. The dual-IP router will convert the IPv4-Compatible Address to a normal IPv4 address to travel over the IPv4 network. At the entry point the remote IPv6 network and another dual-IP router reverse the address substitution process.

Header Format

The header for IPv6 is 40 bytes (without extensions) and the header of IPv4 is 20 bytes. Because the addresses (source and destination) are much longer, the rest of the header has to be simpler so that the protocol is simpler as well. Many of the IPv4 header functions are carried as *extension headers*. The fields are as follows:

Version. This is the version of the protocol, now 6 (4 bits).

Priority. This 4-bit nibble replaces the functions of the Precedence field in IPv4. The lower the priority value, the more willing the source is to have a router discard the PDU.

Flow label. This 3-byte field is used to request special handling of the PDU in the router(s). The designers see this field as important for running TCP/IP over high-speed networks, such as ATM and MPLS. The source IP address and the flow label define a flow. The flow is a sequence of PDUs, for which the source wants special handling (typically in terms of QoS and performance). The routers that recognize the flow label can avoid routing tasks at the network layer (for example, looking up a routing table) by simply following the previous calculations/assignments made in forwarding previous PDUs in this flow. This is the concept of tag switching/netflows/MPLS discussed later in the book.

Typically the flow label is used to reserve resources on the target/destination system. By using the same flow label for all the PDUs during the session, the routers and endsystems reserve network and endsystem resources. By looking up only the flow label (clearly a less complex function for 3 bytes than looking up the entire 16-byte address), the router can decide how to forward the PDU. A system that does not support the flow label function must set this field to 0 for originating PDU, pass/route PDUs without changing the field when forwarding PDUs, and ignore the field when receiving PDUs. All PDUs with the same (nonzero) flow label must have the same destination address, Hop-by-Hop Options header, Routing header, and source address content.

Payload length. This 2-byte unsigned integer field specifies the length (in octets) of the PDU after the IPv6 header (since by specification the IPv6 header is fixed at 40 bytes, the IPv4 Header length field is no longer needed).

Next Header Values. This 1-byte field performs the same function as the IPv4 Protocol field. Protocols shown in parentheses follow the order shown, based on the specification (RFC 1883); all other protocols (those without parentheses) follow that order (the exception is value 59: No Next Header). By following the recommendation's header order, the routers in the path can process the PDU more efficiently.

Hop Limit. This is the maximum number of nodes that may forward the PDU. Being an octet, the integer can be up to 255.

Source/Target Address. This is the 16-octet address of the sender/recipient of the PDU. (If a Routing header is present, it may not be the ultimate destination.)

Host Address Autoconfiguration

The goal of IPv6 address autoconfiguration is to enable an IPv6 host to configure its IPv6 address without human intervention. Specifically, there is a desire to simplify configuration of new hosts and to enable existing hosts to change their addresses (renumber) with the minimum amount of intervention in a minimally disruptive manner (graceful host renumbering).

To minimize the amount of disruption during host renumbering, it is important to take steps that would avoid (or at least minimize) forceful termination of established communications between the host that has to be renumbered and other hosts. Because TCP/IP communications are bound to a particular IP address of a host, one way to minimize the disruption is to avoid binding new communications to an old address, while at the same time allowing the existing communications to use the old address for as long as possible (http://www.cisco.com/warp/public/732/ipv6/ipv6_wp.html). This is the approach adopted by IPv6.

IPv6 requires IPv6 hosts to be able to support multiple IPv6 addresses per interface. Moreover, IPv6 allows for the capacity to identify an IPv6 address assigned to an interface as valid, deprecated, or invalid. A host can use a valid address both for the existing communication and for establishing new communications. In contrast, the host could use a deprecated address only for the existing communications, but it is not allowed to use such an address for new communications. Finally, if a host has an address that is invalid, that address cannot be used for any of the new or existing communications. In the process of renumbering, a host's current IPv6 address would become deprecated, and the host would acquire (through one of the IPv6 address autoconfiguration mechanisms) a new (valid) address. As a result, all the new communications would be bound to the new address.

Transition to IPv6 routing assumes deployment of routers that would be able to support both IPv4 and IPv6 routing protocols and packet forwarding. The routing protocols that are expected to be used with IPv6 (at least initially) are mostly straightforward extensions of the existing IPv4 routing protocols; thus one should not expect significant problems within the IPv6 routing system. To minimize interdependencies, transition to IPv6 routing assumes that there will be noncontiguous IPv6 segments throughout the Internet. These segments could be as large as a collection of many routing domains or as small as a single IP subnetwork or even a single host. Tunneling IPv6 over IPv4 will support IPv6 connectivity among hosts in different segments. IPv6 allows for two types of tunnels: automatic and manually configured. For automatic tunnels to be available, IPv6 addresses of the hosts that are reachable in this manner have to be

IPv4 compatible; IPv4 addresses that are used to form IPv6 addresses of those hosts (IPv4-compatible addresses) have to be routable. In addition, the use of automatic tunnels is currently defined only when the remote endpoint of a tunnel is a host (www.cisco.com/warp/public/732/ipv6/ipv6_wp.html). The transition challenges to IPv6 include the following:

- IPv6 provides a reasonable answer to some, but not all, of the Internet scaling challenges.
- The increase in the available address space provided by IPv6 is fundamental.
- Hierarchical routing supports scaling sufficient for the size of the Internet that could be realized with the IPv6 address space. Therefore, IPv6 adopted hierarchical routing (using the IPv4 routing architecture).
- IPv6 address autoconfiguration is an important step in developing such technologies.
- Currently, defined IPv6 host renumbering attempts to minimize the disruption of applications during renumbering, but it does not guarantee totally nondisruptive behavior.
- It will take some time to develop mature IPv6 host products.
- Supporting IPv6 will have less impact on routers than on hosts and is not expected to pose unforeseen problems.

IPv6 and Specialized Processing

As noted, IP was not developed with a capability for supporting quality of service or resource reservation—it has been a protocol implemented to provide best-effort delivery. Transmission can be characterized by latency, packet loss, and arrival of packets out of order at a destination, resulting in further delay as they are reordered. Real-time applications, such as video and voice, require constant streaming without such delays. Although it provides for a general mechanism for differentiated services, based in part on a potential for marking packets [such as through the type of services (ToS) byte], that mechanism is almost never used.

The IPv6 header contains two key fields, Flow Label and Priority, that allow for packets to be marked for special processing, for example, with IPv6 routers. A flow label is a 24-bit field that can be used to specifically identify a flow through its source address and a flow label. The process by which this labeling takes place is governed by another mechanism—a control protocol, for example, designated with the packets in the flow through the Resource Reservation Protocol discussed in the next section. Priority field is a 4-bit designation that sets the priority of packets relative to others from the same source.

IP Class of Service and Quality of Service

To move toward the goal of allowing for IP quality-of-service provisioning, the Internet Engineering Task Force has developed an Integrated Services architecture (Int-Serv) (RFC 1633) that provides for extensions to allow for differentiating services. It provides mechanisms for classifying packets, scheduling, and flow queue management. This architecture requires state management in the core of the network. A related project, the Differentiated Services (DiffServ) effort, does not require such state management. As this term implies, this architecture is directed at a method for providing differentiated services, as opposed to universal, best-effort service. Such an architecture requires matching the requests of applications (within a policy context) with the network resources needed by those applications.

The Resource-Reservation Protocol (RSVP) (RFC 2205) provides for signaling requests for network resource reservation. RSVP signals bandwidth requirements for specific application flows. Some experiments have been conducted mapping RSVP to ATM signaling. Other techniques are based on methods for classifying packets by flows and packet control using token bucket schemes. Random Early Discard (RED), formalized by Sally Floyd and Van Jacobson, allows for the random discarding of packets from flows. Weighted Random Early Detection (WRED) provides for discarding packets based on differentiated traffic. Weighted Fair Queuing (WFQ) provides for priority based on conformance to a spec, for example, one linked to a particular flow.

These topics are discussed in Chapters 13 and 14.

IP Multicast

If IPv6 is widely implemented, it will enhance the use of multimedia on the Internet. This section provides a kind of overview of IP multicasting (Kosiur 1998). IP multicast services can be used for video, video-conferencing, Web casting, and performance monitoring. Traditional unicast provides for single-node-to-single-node transmission. Multipoint routing for media is an important additional service for next-generation Internets.

IP multicast services provide a capability for an end node to dynamically transmit IP traffic to a number of receiving nodes identified by a group address. The packets are sent to each member of the group. IP multicast also allows end nodes to register to receive different types of multicast traffic, by joining the relevant groups. If this service is native, it does not have to rely on tunneling; in other words, it does not depend on a set of multicast routers.

IP multicast allows computers to register for particular multicast services through an identification by a specific Class D IP address. In general, multicast group registrations are managed through the Internet Group Management Protocol (IGMP) (RFC 1112), which has both host and router modes. IGMP provides for nodes to join and leave multicast sessions dynamically. Nodes can register or unregister with specified groups. Similarly, routers manage these groups dynamically, determining locations of send-receive nodes and building distribution trees that map the paths from sender to receiver. If a router receives a stream from a particular multicast group, the tree built for a given sender is used to direct the traffic.

Protocol-Independent Multicast

The standard protocol for building multicast distribution is Protocol-Independent Multicast (PIM), Dense Mode (PIM-DM) and Sparse Mode (PIM-SM), currently being developed by the IETF. There are other possible implementations for building distribution trees, such as Distance Vector Multicast Routing Protocol (DVMRP) and Multicast Open Shortest Path First (MOSPF). PIM is highly scalable and can be integrated into existing systems that are running any of a number of standard unicast routing protocols, such as Interior Gateway Routing Protocol (IGRP), Enhanced IGRP, Integrated Intermediate System-to-Intermediate System (IS-IS), BGP, OSPF, or RIP.

PIM-DM (PIM Dense Mode), which can be used with MBGP (for Multicast route exchange), was developed for continuous streaming applications that service areas with a high concentration of receiving nodes and relatively large amounts of bandwidth. PIM-DM employs a flood-and-prune scheme, that transmits an incoming stream through all possible interface points except at the stream ingress. If a router is not obligated to carry the stream, it transmits a prune request to the streaming router, which then removes it from its send list. In some instances, such as where ongoing streaming to multiple nodes is not required, this technique can be resource inefficient.

PIM-SM, or PIM Sparse Mode, provides for situations where streaming may be more occasional or may involve few nodes, for example, more teleconferencing than ongoing live streaming. PIM-SM provides for identifying a router as a core point or rendezvous point (RP) where receivers are linked to transmitted streams. Both the sending node and receivers register with the router designated as the rendezvous point. As the sending stream flows from the initiation node to the rendezvous point to the receivers, the various routers involved optimize the paths to eliminate needless hops.

Conclusion

IPv6 issues include those that relate to specifying protocol requirements and appropriate responses to those requirements, such as the actual design specification of IPv6, which is fairly settled at this point, as well as the transition mechanisms required to migrate the Internet from IPv4 to IPv6, a topic of ongoing discussion. This chapter provides an overview of the first set of issues, including issues specifying the need for IPv6 and the protocol attributes required to meet those needs.

The issues related to transitioning from IPv4 to IPv6 are large and complex. The IETF has initiated transition planning efforts and has developed some documents related to those efforts, for example, the early "Simple SIPP Transition" (SST) overview document (RFC 1671) (1994). There have been a number of more recent publications. Another set of considerations includes the impact of that transition on other Internet protocols. Next-generation Internet testbeds provide the best environments for early deployment of IPv6 and for testing techniques, methods, and tools related to implementing the transition to IPv6. Among these efforts are the 6bone testbed project, the vBNS IPv6 service, various international efforts, such as those by APAN and CANARIE, and efforts by advanced regional networks such as MREN.

End Note

[1]Portions of this chapter (pages 238 to 244) are based on a treatment in *Internet Architectures*, by Dan Minoli and Andrew Schmidt (1999, John Wiley & Sons).

References

Cisco Systems. *Internet Protocol, Version 6 (IPv6).* [Available July 1999]. www.cisco.com/warp/public/cc/cisco/mkt/ios/tech/tch/ipv6_wp.htm

Kosiur, Dave. 1998 *IP Multicasting: The Complete Guide to Interactive Corporate Networks.* New York: John Wiley and Sons, Inc. A particularly useful book on IP multicasting.

RFC 1112. 1989. S. E. Deering. *Host extensions for IP Multicasting.* ftp://ftp.isi.edu/in-notes/rfc1112.txt (standard).

RFC 1518. 1993. Y. Rekhter and T. Li. *An Architecture for IP Address Allocation with CIDR.* ftp://ftp.isi.edu/in-notes/rfc1583.txt (proposed standard).

RFC 1519. 1993. V. Fuller, T. Li, J. Yu, and K. Varadhan. *Classless Inter-Domain Routing (CIDR).* ftp://ftp.isi.edu/in-notes/rfc1519.txt (proposed standard).

RFC 1548. 1993. W. Simpson. *The Point-to-Point Protocol (PPP).* ftp://ftp.isi.edu/in-notes/rfc1543.txt (obsoleted by RFC 1993).

RFC 1633. 1994. R. Braden, D. Clark, and S. Shenker. *Integrated Services in the Internet Architecture: An Overview.* ftp://ftp.isi.edu/in-notes/rfc1633.txt.

RFC 1671. 1994. B. Carpenter, Ipng. *White Paper on Transition and Other Considerations.* ftp://ftp.isi.edu/in-notes/rfc1671.txt (informational).

RFC 1833. 1995. R. Srinivasan. *Binding Protocols for ONC RPC Version 2.* ftp://ftp.isi.edu/in-notes/rfc1833.txt (proposed standard).

RFC 1883. 1995. S. Deering and R. Hinden. *Internet Protocol, Version 6 (IPv6) Specification.* ftp://ftp.isi.edu/in-notes/rfc.1883.txt (obsoleted by RFC 2460).

RFC 1887. 1995. Y. Rekhter and T. Li, ed. *An Architecture for IPv6 Unicast Address Allocation.* ftp://ftp.isi.edu/in-notes/rfc1887.txt (informational).

RFC 1993. 1996. A. Barbir, D. Carr Newbridge, W. Simpson. *PPP Gandalf FZA Compression Protocol.* ftp://ftp.isi.edu/in-notes/rfc1993.txt (informational).

RFC 2205. 1997. R. Branden, L. Zhang, S. Berson, S. Herzog, and S. Jamin. *Resource ReSerVation Protocol (RSVP),* ftp://ftp.isi.edu/in-notes/rfc2205.txt.

CHAPTER 13

Quality of Service: Models and Protocols

In today's Internet, each router that is forwarding packets does so based only on the entries in its routing table and does its best to keep up with incoming flows. This service is called "best effort." If the router is overloaded, then packets will be dropped, with no provision made to save higher-priority data that may have traveled a long distance or may have originated from a mission-critical application. The objective of providing different service-level agreements is to realize better service to a subset of the traffic at the expense of the larger community. Quality of service (QoS) generally does not in itself provide guarantees that an individual application will realize that level of service; it attempts only to equip the network with tools to facilitate resource sharing. Even such forms as ATM CBR are not absolute guarantees.

QoS is attractive in the context of next-generation networks for several reasons. First, it allows institutions better control over how their bandwidth is shared by their user community. Second, it allows service providers to create new business-class products that provide "better than best effort" traffic management. With the improvements gained by QoS, potential problems of security and interdomain support arise. Security and authentication are issues because as the service is improved it subsequently may come to have a premium price, and some users will be tempted to steal the service. Interdomain communication becomes a problem because for QoS to become as ubiquitous as the Internet, the end-to-end communication will traverse several network service providers.

This chapter is the starting point for a discussion of what quality of service is, how it has been designed and deployed, and how it can be measured. QoS is important for next-generation networks because it is the technology that allows effective sharing of network resources among dissimilar applications (see Figure 13.1). Different QoS levels can be used to provide premium service for corporate users who are interconnecting their intranet or extranet sites across the public Internet. When ISP-interconnecting corporate intranet sites also carry mainstream Internet traffic, the ISPs can achieve additional returns on their capital investment by sharing the network infrastructure. The ability to have a corporation's traffic carried across the WAN without loss, but also achieving some economy of scale, is a very interesting service; it comes at a premium price and has become important to the business models of most ISPs. When higher priority can be guaranteed via a QoS protocol, and when security is added, the service is usually referred to as a virtual private network (VPN).

Several proposals have come from standards bodies or the research community. The ATM Forum developed some of the earliest work on QoS; ATM is an excellent medium for QoS because it provides strong traffic-management capabilities (ATM Forum 1993, 1995, 1996a, b). In the early 1990s the IETF also began looking at the problem of QoS. Its effort, in the Integrated Services

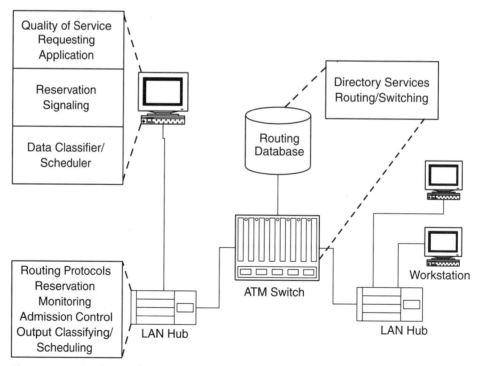

Figure 13.1 End-to-end quality of service system.

working group (RFC 1633), yielded traffic models, real-time transport protocols, and a signaling protocol. Although these two approaches met with some success, there are many who believe that ATM is too cumbersome and that the Integrated Services protocols placed too much overhead on routers. This led to the last set of protocols, called Differentiated Services named by Van Jacobson (when at LBNL—now at Cisco), which attempts to simplify QoS.

This chapter covers this material by first describing the general concepts of QoS, then examining the Integrated Services transport protocols and signaling protocol (RSVP) (RFC 2205), and concluding with an examination of Differentiated Services.

The reasons for TCP's and IP's continued successes are important to consider when developing new protocols and network architecture paradigms. First, consider the reasons for the success of the OSI Transport and Network layer protocols and the benefits realized by subdividing a process into discrete components with clearly defined interfaces:

Delivery of packets. History has shown that the delivery of packets and the development of packet-switched technologies are beneficial, owing to efficient resource sharing and excellent diversity in the range of support applications. The success of packet networks can also be attributed to the physical layer independence that packet switches and datagram delivery pose. As an example of these successes, consider that typical IP applications pass data over Ethernet LAN technology, then over FDDI backbone technology, and finally traverse a WAN over frame relay or SONET before reaching the destination. In all these cases the physical media changes dramatically although the packet format remains a constant. When IP is used in this model, the functionality of packet delivery is delegated to a protocol that supports global addressing but has a problem space limited to datagram transport.

End-to-end model. TCP, on the other hand, has been very successful because of its end-to-end approach to providing connection-oriented behavior across an IP connectionless medium like the Internet. Moving error detection and correction to the endsystems allows the applications that are actually sending to decide what information is really necessary for retransmission, thus building a robust system against network component failure that is not performing undesired error detection and correction. The UDP protocol can be used in the cases where the data is not critical or where retransmission would yield stale data. TCP also frees applications from determining the correct transmission data rate to use because it implements its own adaptive flow protocol that will fairly share resources. The sliding window adapts to varying network delays and allows for the protocol to reduce the offered load when congestion is detected (Romanow 1995).

IP and associated routing protocols provide the means to route packets through the network; however, IP is not involved with the actual delivery to applications and knows nothing about the end application or its requirements. TCP takes care of end application needs and issues; therefore, it isolates the end users from the details of the packet-switched network. To an application, TCP provides an error-free bit pipe between the source and destination.

The work on QoS was started due to the demands that new multimedia or Internet/Intranet applications place on the networking infrastructure, coupled with the desire to augment Internet technology with function-enhancing tools. Examples of applications that are driving this work are these:

Multimedia. Distribution of content-rich data containing video and voice, while requiring high quality of service.

Collaboration and groupware. Data-sharing applications, such as distributed databases, with real-time response.

Distributed simulation. A superset of multimedia applications, which may also employ multiuser data communication for real-time control over computer simulations.

Entertainment. Large-scale distribution of selected entertainment-grade media that can be categorized as high priority.

Multiplayer games. Entertainment applications and enhancement to distributed simulation.

Two key points of the QoS service models are to develop protocols that, in keeping with the Internet's origins, are both flexible and extensible. In addition, as technology progresses, additional applications will emerge that will require the integrated services approach and its tools; and surely this list will continue to grow.

The challenge faced by those wishing to use current IP networks for new applications desiring QoS is how to deal with its single-grade "best-effort" service category provided by the basic Internet fabric. In addition, even if the network understood how to provide higher grades, how can network managers get their applications to negotiate QoS parameters with the network? Due to the work of vendors and standards bodies, routers are now capable of supplying multiple levels of performance or service-level guarantees. As will be shown, there are newly developed means of signaling a desire for QoS; however, this capability is still in its infancy.

TCP and IP are clearly very good protocols for data but do not, in themselves, provide predictable performance on a congested Internet or intranet.

Therefore, unmodified TCP/IP is not appropriate for real-time applications if the end users have tight performance constraints and if new overlay protocols are required to realize next-generation applications. In order to provide multiple controlled qualities of service over this "legacy" Internet, a new architecture has been developed.

Integrated Services Evolution and Components

The key enabler in these models is the ability to divide the traffic within the network into multiple categories and then discard lower-priority commodity Internet traffic during times of congestion. This can be accomplished in several different manners. First-generation networks addressed the quality of service problem solely through bandwidth augmentation. This can be seen in the various phases that NSFnet went through. The network started with very low-speed capacity lines that gradually increased in capacity as the offered load increased. This brute-force method of providing quality of service is effective, provided the offered load does not exceed the network's total capacity.

Second-generation networks may be able to improve their quality of service implementation by utilizing Data Link Layer technologies that could augment the IP router's abilities. This technique can take the form of IP routers interconnected by ATM switches. ATM can be used because it is the only current technology that provides hard guarantees for traffic management (ATM Forum 1996b). ATM switches and virtual circuits can be established between the IP routers so that traffic flowing between the routers can be closely regulated. For example, several IP routers can be interconnected across an ATM switch, and a subset of the routers can utilize virtual circuits with more favorable traffic profiles. The remainder of the IP routers could utilize best-effort virtual circuits. In many cases this type of implementation would be completely transparent to the IP routers because all of the traffic engineering would take place at the ATM layer (see Figure 13.2).

Utilizing ATM as a traffic manager was a good tool for first-generation IP networking engineers, although not for QoS as defined; explicitly routed ATM VCs for traffic engineering is a major benefit for ISP backbones. It also provided the ability to enforce policy because a large set of routers could be physically connected to a network; however, only certain subsets could peer by controlling virtual circuit creation. ATM, however, did come at the cost of reduced or limited scalability. This is due to a routing protocol limitation when multiple routers are interconnected across a "flat" network. As the number of routers interconnected across the ATM network grows, the number of router adjacencies also grows and can become unmanageable.

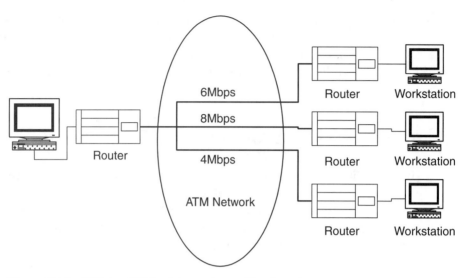

Figure 13.2 Utilizing ATM for interrouter quality of service.

The evolution of the Integrated Services model has been a long, iterative process, underway for several years. In that time, the work completed in the IETF, and heavily augmented at the University of Southern California, CMU, UCLA, and elsewhere has led to the development of the Integrated Services core components:

Framework. Illustrating the scope of work.

Service definition. Describing what benefits a user of the Integrated Services model can expect.

Component requirement. Describing the roles of each device in an Integrated Services network.

The first generation of the Integrated Services working group's specification became available at the end of 1996, with compliant products arriving on the market shortly thereafter. The first generation of products has produced a set of standards that allowed for network designers and managers to implement systems supporting QoS over frame-based IP networks. Granted, the support for QoS was limited to their administrative boundaries because of the reluctance of ISPs to run the protocols except on small pockets in their networks. While these first-phase implementations and specifications were limited by geography, due to lack of ISP support, they were an important proving ground for corporate and campus intranets.

In defining the Integrated Services model, the IETF subdivided the tasks necessary in providing QoS support into categories based on function. The divisions allowed the problem to be better understood by novices to the industry, and it also allowed the systems to follow Internet standard practices; that is, the endsystem can be built from smaller components that are scalable and flexible (see Figure 13.3). The components of the Integrated Services model are these:

Resource Reservation Protocol. Used to set up and control states between endstations.

Admission control. Used to control the total amount of load the network accepts.

Packet classifier. Used to prioritize packets into different qualities.

Packet scheduler. Used to intelligently control the introduction of new traffic into the network.

Integrated Services Model

Network designers and protocol developers have recognized the tremendous success of TCP and acknowledged the reasons why this open standard has become so popular. This knowledge has been applied in philosophy to next-generation protocols for QoS and multiprotocol-over-ATM networks that attempt to continue this success; it is this success that drives the continued use of new protocols and the additional support for new methods of using them in the Integrated Services for the Internet (in the IETF-chartered work). This work is called *integrated services* because it focuses on supporting multimedia

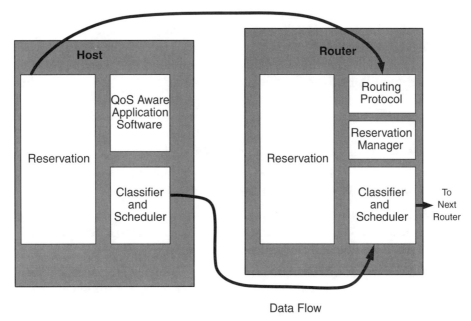

Figure 13.3 Internetworking of Integrated Services components.

applications that place QoS demands on the underlying IP-based network and, in effect, integrate all of today's technology into tomorrow's network.

Over the last several years, the Internet Engineering Task Force has been examining support for QoS over a packet-switched network and has attempted to address several QoS related problems. This work has been focused between two IETF working groups, the Resource Reservation Protocol (RSVP) and the Integrated Services (Int-Serv) group (Braden 1999, RFC 1633). When building a system that supports QoS, the RSVP specification is the mechanism that signals QoS requests, and the Int-Serv specifications concern the capabilities that are available to QoS-aware applications, similar to ATM traffic management.

The goal of the Integrated Services model is to mask the underlying technology from the application while still providing the following features:

Internetwork routing. Allows applications to achieve their desired performance from the network via optimal path section.

Multicast capability. Allows one-to-many or many-to-many communication flows.

QoS facilities. Parameters that describe the desired characteristics that applications can expect from the network and the mechanisms used to request these facilities.

The design of the Integrated Services model that addresses the previous issues was a process that spanned more than three years by the Integrated Services working group of the IETF. The product of this effort is a set of specifications that divide the functionality of providing controlled QoS among several distinct units. In addition, each different aspect of the QoS supporting infrastructure is subdivided into components so that there is clear ownership of responsibility. The specification contains details covering the following:

- End-to-end delivery characteristics seen by an individual application's data as that data traverses a network that contains at least two elements supporting the Integrated Services model.

- Network device behavior realized by applications that utilize nodes conforming to the Integrated Services model.

- Resource reservation dialog rules and languages that are supported by, and used between, nodes on an Integrated Services network for exchange of state and control messages.

- Performance evaluation criteria potentially used for probabilistic measurements and evaluation of Integrated Services components.

In the new service model, the supporting mechanisms are typically software additions made to network hardware (see Figure 13.4). For example, the end

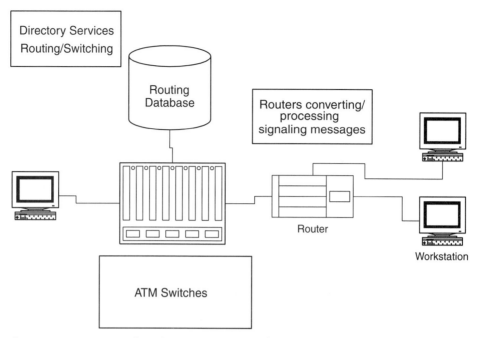

Figure 13.4 Integrated Services supporting mechanisms.

computers will contain new applications capable of generating resource reservation messages, then complying with these reservations while they are transmitting and receiving data (Shenker 1995). The interconnecting routers will have new software allowing them to interpret these messages and segregate traffic into different service classes; they will also need to implement Usage Parameter Control. In some cases, however, lower-end routers may require additional memory in order to maintain state on resource allocation; in other cases, networks, such as shared Ethernet, may have difficulty providing integrated service at all.

It is important to note that the integrated service model is primarily a service description and that the model does not dictate deployment. Because the Internet is made up of heterogeneous parts that are managed by tens of thousands of different organizations, the end-to-end support of the integrated service model will take time to achieve wide-scale deployment. Therefore, the benefits realized are being seen first on progressive research and education networks with restricted administrative boundaries.

At the top level, a Service Model Specification describes behavior of individual elements in an Integrated Services network. In addition to the service specification, the following service categories have been defined to help differentiate what end users can expect to receive from their networks: datagram service, controlled-load service, and guaranteed service. The Integrated Services model contains three different degrees of potentially realized quality of service. These are very similar to the service categories as specified by the ATM Forum. Briefly, these can be divided into the following high level groups.

Datagram Service

The datagram service model is the same service expected from traffic on the first-generation Internet if the routers have not been modified for integrated services. Therefore, they provide partial or no guarantees. Most traditional network protocols, such as IP, supply this best-effort service. In a multiservice network, this type of service will be used for commodity communications.

For example, if a corporation builds a high-quality intranet with connections to the Internet, the datagram service would be used for Internet communication, while one of the higher-grade services would be used for internal mission-critical communication. In addition, this type of response will clearly not be achieved from the Internet for some time, owing to the inevitable delays in deploying Integrated Services technology.

Controlled-Load Service

The first new service model developed by the Integrated Services working group is the Controlled-Load Service (RFC 2211). This service model was designed for applications that were capable of adaptive behavior, for example, a voice-over-IP application that is capable of modifying the data being transmitted by changing the compression ratio or providing high quality voice capabilities.

In the controlled-load service, the network attempts to control the total load of reserved traffic. The network controls the total load by carefully measuring the amount of resources requested and allocated. Any application that wants to reap the benefits of the reserved resources must also be a participant in the resource reservation process. The controlled-load service does not provide any quantitative performance assurance to the traffic that is being carried. There are no guarantees made with respect to maximum delay or congestion that may be experienced. Instead, this service class attempts to impose no substantial requirements on the network elements and simply attempts to accurately predict what the realized QoS will be when the resources are intelligently shared.

The only assurance with controlled-load service is that performance will be as good as an unloaded datagram network. Granted, this performance guarantee, while not stellar, may prove to be more than adequate for the vast majority of applications on the Internet or intranets that desire higher grades of service. This is due to the fact that traditional IP routers and legacy networks provide very good performance when unloaded; therefore many protocol/networking experts in the industry feel that this may be the only protocol necessary in the new Integrated Services model.

A final important point with respect to the controlled-load service is that it is widely believed to be the dominant real-time service in initial deployment of integrated service support. The controlled-load service is a simple protocol from both the ability of programmers to understand and end users to characterize their applications' use of the protocol and subsequent controlled-load service networks. An additional benefit includes the potential for functioning well in networks with only partial deployment because the performance of interconnect links can be predicted with a degree of certainty.

Guaranteed Service

The last model developed by the IETF's Integrated Services working group is the guaranteed service class. This service class is designed to provide applications with the tools to communicate with a network capable of understanding reservation requests, so as to provide a service that supports firm bounds on data throughput and delay along the path between communication endstations.

Guaranteed services provide quality guarantees that can be stated explicitly in a deterministic or statistical representation. Deterministic bounds are specified by a single value, such as average bandwidth or peak required bandwidth. Statistical bounds are determined by a statistical measure, such as the probability of errors, while predictable services are based on past network behavior. QoS parameters for reliable services are estimates of the consistent behavior based on measurements of past behavior.

In order to achieve this highest degree of service-level guarantee, the service class imposes substantial requirements on network elements. Every element along the path must provide delay bounds and maintain conformance to the advertised bounds. In addition, topology changes must force the recompilation of the delay bounds and subsequent new advertisement messages sent to endstations, notifying them that their realized quality may have dramatically changed.

The guaranteed service class is intended to provide the highest achievable service in the current version of the Integrated Services model. This class is believed to provide a mathematically provable delay bound and packet loss for a given path when the reserved resources utilize guaranteed service class definitions. Because this protocol places tight constraints on network components and their ability both to advertise correctly and then supply resource, we will discuss some examples where it may not be usable.

It may be possible that the guaranteed service protocol will not be achievable if the intermediate network systems do not support the class or in cases where data communication traverses a shared media, such as Ethernet. These devices and legacy networks are potentially unacceptable to the guaranteed service Integrated Services model because they can provide a large degree of variance in the QoS realized by endstation applications. These concerns further fuel the belief that the controlled-load model will not be very successful; only practical experience will prove the success of guaranteed service.

Real-Time Protocols

Protocol designers in the IETF and the ATM Forum have expended considerable effort on real-time protocols. These protocols are called real-time because they are used when there are tight constraints on the quality of service that must be delivered from the network. For example, the total transit delay or interpacket arrival time must be bounded. Three primary protocols have been developed to support real-time quality-of-service data over IP; a fourth related protocol is used to stream multimedia content:[1]

The Real-Time Transport (RTP). A real-time "end-to-end" protocol utilizing existing Transport layers for real-time applications (RFC 1889 and RFC 1980) (Speer 1996).

The Real-Time Control Protocol (RTCP). Provides feedback on total performance and the quality of the data transmitted so that modifications can be made.

The Real-Time Streaming Protocol (RTSP). A Transport layer protocol designed specifically for controlling the transmission of audio/video over the Internet.

The Resource Reservation Protocol (RSVP). A multicast-capable resource setup (signaling) protocol primarily designed for IP. RSVP is a general-purpose signaling protocol and can be used to map resource reservations to ATM signaling messages (RFC 2205) (RFC 1755) (RFC 2331).

Real-Time Transport and Control: RTP

The first protocol described in this chapter is the Real-Time Transport Protocol (RTP) as specified in RFC 1889. RTP's primary function is to act as an improved interface between real-time applications and existing Transport layer protocols, but not necessarily those providing the connection-oriented behavior of the Transmission Control Protocol; that is, RTP does not dictate which Transport layer protocol is used. It provides functions that allow transport protocols to work in a real-time environment. One of RTP's chief design goals was to provide a simple, scalable protocol independent from the underlying Transport and Network layers. The desire for good scalability is driven not only by the large scope of the Internet but also by the desire for good interworking with multicast IP.

RTP is designed to provide end-to-end delivery services for temporally sensitive data with support for both unicast and multicast delivery (see Figure 13.5). The underlying network is assumed to be any IP packet-switched network, that is, assuming, in all likelihood but not with certainty, that a packet will arrive at its destination. (See Figure 13.6.) Due to the nature of packet switching, variable delay is to be expected. Additionally, due to packet switching and routing, packets may arrive out of order.

It is important to keep in mind that RTP is only a transport protocol that supplies similar functionality to UDP and, in some cases, can be carried inside of a UDP payload. RTP provides the following features and functions:

- Data source and payload type identification that is used to determine payload contents
- Data packet sequencing used to confirm correct ordering at the receiver
- Timing and synchronization that is used to set timing at the receiver during content playback
- Delivery monitoring that facilitates transmission problem diagnosis or providing feedback to the sending computer on the quality-of-data transmission
- Integration of heterogeneous traffic that is used to merge multiple transmitting sources into a single flow

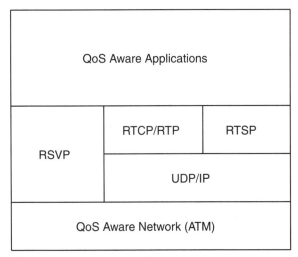

Figure 13.5   RTP protocol interaction.

RTP in itself does not provide any quality-of-service guarantees or deliver data reliably; it is a protocol that monitors and helps control the flow from transmitter to receiver. The functions of quality-of-service guarantees and delivery are the responsiblity of RSVP and the packet-switched network's QoS.

The suite of protocols also contains definitions of which component should perform which specified function. The RTP component carries individual real-time data streams with a source identifier, payload type, time, and sequencing information. The feedback component, which is covered in greater detail in the next section, monitors application performance and conveys information about the session (that is, information about participants).

To help illustrate the interworking between RTP and RTCP, it will be helpful to consider an example of an audio-conference session. The example system is shown in Figure 13.7. The diagram illustrates the playback of an audio-only multimedia system. Packets on the left arrive at the host, where they can be buffered and examined prior to fully decoding the payload and reproducing the sound on the host computer's speakers. As with other RTP applications, receiver feedback and group membership information are provided via RTCP.

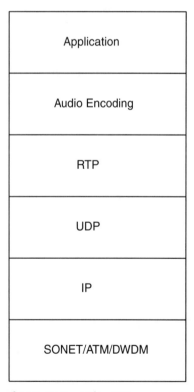

Figure 13.6 Using RTP.

When packets arrive at the destination, each carries a sequence number and timestamp. The sequence number is examined to determine the correct sequencing of data and also to record the percentage of lost frames. The RTP packet's timestamp is used to determine the interpacket gap in the following manner. The timestamp value is set by the source as it encodes the data and transmits the packet into the network. As packets arrive at the destination, the change in the interpacket gap can be examined, and then during playback this information can be used to regenerate the contents at the same rate they were encoded. By utilizing buffering at the receiver, the source can attempt to pace the traffic out independently of the jitter introduced by the packet-switched network.

The concept of source synchronization can be extended to sessions that contain multiple concurrent types of content, for example, a conference with multiple audio and video sessions. In this type of application the recommendation is that each type of content be carried over its own unique RTP session. When the RTP session arrives at the destination, the different sources can have their synchronization source fields compared, in order to synchronize the audio with the video. The RTCP facilitates the synchronization of multiple RTP sessions and reports on their quality (see Figure 13.7). Just how RTCP provides these functions is addressed in the following section.

An additional example of the use of RTP is with HTTP multicast. In this example, the content would possibly be generated from the multicast of WWW server pages (used for proxy updates) or network news distribution.

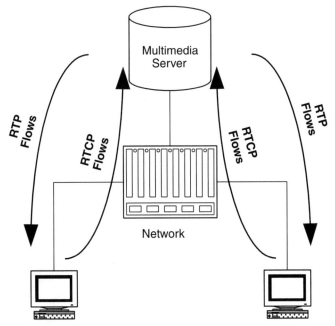

Figure 13.7 Audio and video over RTP.

RTP Packet Format and Terminology

An application using RTP establishes a session to define a pair of destination addresses, a network address and two ports. One port number is assigned to RTP, the other to RTCP (Real Time Control Protocol). The fields and format of an RTP packet are shown in Figure 13.8. Several of the fields are unique to RTP and deserve some explanation in light of the RTP terminology.

The first 12 octets are present in every RTP packet, while the contributing source identifiers (CSRC) list usually will not be present because it is used solely when broadcasting an RTP session. The complete RTP header contains the following fields (see Figure 13.8):

- A version used to identify the release of RTP
- Padding bit that specifies that the payload has additional padding at the end
- A contributor counter for the number of CSRCs contained in fields that follow the fixed header
- A payload type identifier, which specifies the type of data being carried in the RTP packet

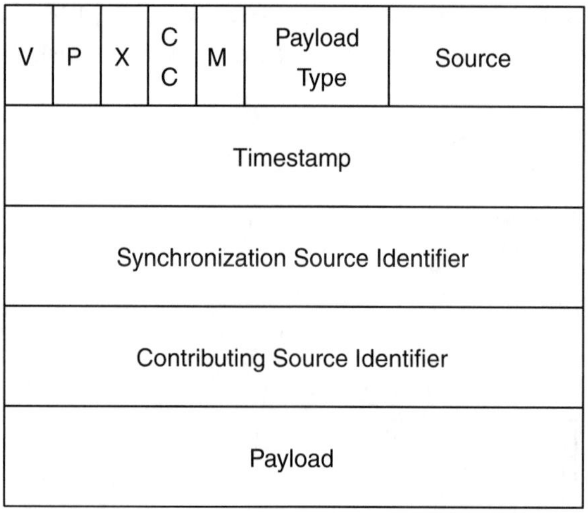

V	P	X	C C	M	Payload Type	Source
Timestamp						
Synchronization Source Identifier						
Contributing Source Identifier						
Payload						

V - Version

P - Padding indicator

X - Extension Indicator

M - Marked Bit

Figure 13.8 RTP header.

- A sequence number that increments to count the number of packets in a stream

- A timestamp that denotes the instant the first octet in the RTP data packet was sampled

- An SSRC field that identifies the synchronization source associated with the data (this identifier is chosen with the intent that no two sources within the same RTP session will have the same value)

- A CSRC field with a list of objects that identifies the contributing sources for the data contained in this packet (the total number of identifiers is given by the third field)

A second possible format for the RTP header is a "compressed" version. The compressed header is used when only one source is contributing to the payload, as would be in the case of a nonmulticast session. The RTP packets are marked as compressed when the first bit of the header, the version bit, is set to 0. When the version is 0, then the header will be modified to contain only the fields up to and including the SSRC.

Real-Time Transport Control Operation

As described in the preceding section, RTP is a simple protocol designed to carry real-time traffic. It provides few additional services that are not present in transport protocols like UDP. With RTP, receivers can utilize the timestamp, along with sequence numbers, to better synchronize sessions and improve playback. To complement RTP, the IETF has designed a protocol, RTCP, which is used to communicate between the sources and destination. This protocol is not used to establish QoS parameters with the network; instead it is oriented toward client/server state exposure.

The design goals of RTCP are to expand this system by providing the following:

- Feedback on the quality of the data distribution
- Persistent transport-level identifier for RTP sources
- Automatic adjustment to control overhead
- Session control information to maintain high-quality sessions

Therefore, RTCP should be considered as primarily a technique in which hosts using RTP can communicate "out of band" to exchange information about their state. The information exchanged would be used to identify the quality of service being delivered by the network. For example, RTCP can illustrate a large degree of packet loss, the value of the round-trip time, or whether the network is providing high jitter values.

In order to achieve these goals, RTCP utilizes the exchange of packets that express End Point State. Two main packet types are exchanged: Sender Reports (SR) and Receiver Reports (RR). Each of these reports is accomplished by generating a packet containing fields that describe the state of the session. In addition, several report packets can be concatenated to form a compound RTCP packet transmitted over the Transport layer as one packet.

Each of the SR and RR packets contains the SSRC of the sender. In the case of an RR, it contains the SSRC of the first source. Perhaps more importantly for maintaining high quality of service, both packet types contain fields that can be analyzed to determine the percent of successfully received data packets. The fields used to help determine the quality of service are the following:

- Fraction lost versus the total number of packets, which provides an instantaneous feel for the percentage of loss
- Cumulative number of packets lost since session began
- Highest sequence number received, which reveals how much of the current data in flight has been received
- Interarrival jitter, which can help specify how much buffering is being used at the destination to faithfully replay the source, related to the jitter value reported at the sending time
- Last SR timestamp received, which reports the time when the last SR was received
- Delay since last SR timestamp

Due to the large amount of information provided by the RTCP packets, these messages can be interpreted in several ways. Throughput can be determined by comparing the number of packets and bytes transmitted since the last report. Round-trip times between the sender and the receiver can be calculated by subtracting the arrival time from the sum of the timestamp of the last report and the delay since the last report. Finally, packet losses are determined by analyzing the fraction lost since the previous SR or RR packet sent or the total number of RTP data packets lost.

In the case of a multicast session, the RTCP packets can be collected and analyzed to determine temporal state. For example, the jitter values can determine transient congestion versus the loss values that provide an indication of persistent congestion. A comparison of loss values can determine the size of the subset of total recipients experiencing congestion and if the problem is global or local. With this information the source can decide if the sender should make any adjustments to maximize available bandwidth.

Additional RTCP packet types support the ability to query the source for descriptive information, indicate the end of a session, or support application-specific functions via the SDES, BYE, and APP packet types, respectively.

Real-Time Streaming Protocol: RTSP

The Real-Time Streaming Protocol, or RTSP, is an OSI Application layer protocol designed to supply a mechanism for making requests about the delivery of real-time content. In a real-time multimedia system, the intent is to use RTP to deliver content and then use RTCP to determine the quality of service being provided. With these two protocols in place, two critical components are still missing: first, a means of notifying the network of the required bandwidth of the upcoming transmission (a topic discussed later) and second, a means for requesting content from a multimedia server.

Content could assume three different formats in the RTSP used to request transmission:

Real-time stored clips. Will include the set of prerecorded multimedia, digitally stored on a server.

Nonreal-time stored clips. Will include content typically transmitted via HTTP or MIME.

Real-time live feeds. Will be fed from radio or televised content digitally converted just before transmission.

In much the same way that traditional client/server systems are built, the RTSP clients generate messages that are transmitted to their multimedia content server. RTSP does not carry data that is actually appreciated or viewed by the end user; it only provides the functionality of a signaling and control protocol random access to content.

The design requirements of RTSP are as follows:

- Supply a means for requesting real-time content
- Have a means for content playback control (that is, pause, start, stop)
- Provide a technique for starting playback at any point in the content (that is, play the second track on an audio CD)
- Secure a means to request information about specifics on the content
- Allow the protocol to specify the Transport layer protocol selection

RTSP uses TCP when exchanging its control message between the client and server. The protocol has been designed to work on both a multicast or unicast environment. When exchanging signaling messages with a server, the client has the option of using the Session Control Protocol (SCP) to improve efficiency. After the multimedia server has received an RTSP request for content, it then transmits the requested data, most likely over RTP, to the client. If the content consists of several components, for example, voice and video, then potentially multiple streams will be created between the server and client. When multiple streams are created, each will be used to carry a portion of the data, for example, one for video and another stream for the audio.

RTSP Operation

The RTSP operates by exchanging signaling messages between the client and the server following a query/response mode. There are three main categories of RTSP messages:

Global control. Used to govern all sessions between the client and server.

Connection control. Used to establish, maintain, and terminate individual content data streams.

Custom control. Used to provide exception messaging beyond the scope of connection control.

From a high level of abstraction, the protocol operates when the client registers itself with the server, which is a global controller. This step is then followed by requests for data streams that are the connection control messages. Therefore, the first messages that must be exchanged before any multimedia data can be transmitted are the global control messages. The possible global control messages are the following:

HELLO. Registration request.

GOODBYE. Global session termination message.

IDENTIFY. A server's requests for authentication.

IDENTIFY REPLY. The client's authentication response.

REDIRECT. Points to other content servers.

OPTIONS. Indicates miscellaneous functionality.

The registration process begins with the client sending a HELLO message to the server. The message contains the client's RTSP version information and may contain the client's host name, machine type, operating system, and more. Upon receiving the HELLO, the server then replies with a similar HELLO message, but the body of the message contains the server's RTSP version number. From that point onward, the client and server can communicate using the lower of the two version numbers.

This communication takes place over TCP; therefore, the exchange of messages is deemed reliable. It is also possible for the server to redirect connection requests by using the REDIRECT message. The REDIRECT message uses a URL that identifies the new location for the client to access content. The next phase of the global initialization process involves the option of authentication. Either the server or the client can generate identification (ID) messages, which request the recipient to prove its identity. The actual technique used for authentication is left to the discretion of the hosts and may range from a simple password check to a challenge/response mechanism. If the response to the ID messages is not acceptable, then the TCP connection is closed immediately. Termination of a global session is accomplished with a GOODBYE message. Clients send these messages only when they are gracefully closing their TCP sessions. The final global message type is the OPTION message. It was designed to provide the ability to incrementally improve the RTSP.

Once the global message exchange has taken place and the client and server have authenticated each other, the next phase, content request, can take place. The process of requesting audio and video is rather straightforward; the client specifies the objects that interest it and the parameters used during transmission. The message types used to request content are these:

FETCH

STREAM HEADER

SET TRANSPORT

SET SPEED

PLAY RANGE

STREAM SYNC

SET BLOCK SIZE

STOP

RESUME

SEND REPORT

RESEND

Even though there are several possible messages, the flow of a request is very predictable. The process starts when a user makes a request to access some content on the server. This request could come, for example, from a user operating a WWW browser who comes across an interesting video clip. The request for the video is carried in the FETCH message. The FETCH contains a pointer to the video clip in the form of a URL. It also contains an estimate, from the perspective of the client, of the bandwidth available for the stream.

If the server accepts the request from the client, it then responds with a STREAM_HEADER message. If a problem was encountered, then an error message is returned. The STREAM_HEADER message specifies the exact bit rate of the stream that will be the result of the bandwidth requested in the FETCH. It also contains much information about the video clip.

When the client has received the STREAM_HEADER message, the server is in a ready state. The client need only notify the server to begin transmitting the stream. Before the client issues the request to begin playing the video clip, it has the option of placing a network resource request. This step is accomplished with the SET_TRANSPORT message that acts as the interface between the application and the RTP protocol. By setting the transport mechanism, the client has the ability to specify a multicast session and the UDP port number for the data stream. The client can also optionally reduce the maximum packet size with the SET_BLOCK_SIZE message.

The next step is to issue a command to actually begin sending the data via the parameters set by the SET_TRANSPORT message. The request to send is done by the PLAY_RANGE message. Its parameters are just the starting and ending points, specified in milliseconds. In response to the PLAY_RANGE message, the server will positively acknowledge and begin sending the request with a STEAM_SYNC message that contains the beginning sequence number and timestamp for the upcoming video.

While the video is in play, the client has the ability to control the data stream in much the same way as playing a movie on a VCR. The data stream can be paused or terminated with a STOP message. It can also be restarted with a RESUME message. A diagram illustrating the flow of the RTSP message exchange is shown in Figure 13.9. In the example, a client is requesting a video file from the server. The client first locates the server with a HELLO and then is asked to authenticate itself. After authentication, the client issues a FETCH containing a URL to request the video clip.

Finally, two diagnostics messages can be exchanged. The server can issue a SEND_REPORT to the client to help identify the quality of the reception. The reply options for a client that has received this message, at a minimum, must include the generation of a PING message directed at the server. If possible, the client can generate and reply with a detailed report containing such items as the number of packets received and internal buffer utilization. The other diagnostics-type message is the UDP_RESEND used by the client to request

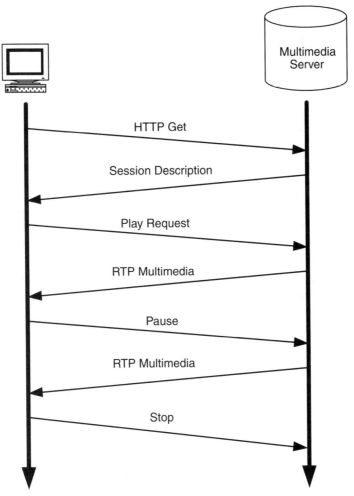

Figure 13.9 RTSP message flows.

the retransmission of data. The message has fields allowing the client to specify exactly what sequence number to begin with and how many subsequent packets need to be retransmitted.

Conclusion

In summary, a large number of components are needed to build networks that support quality-of-service. The next-generation network should provide these type of services. Developing differentiated services/QoS support is critical for the Internet's evolution. There is reluctance to use next-generation applications such as streaming video because there is a lack of quality of service support. One fear is that basic applications will be starved for bandwidth. Another is that the protocols supporting these services will interfere with basic network production services. Lack of QoS is also cited as a key factor for migration from private networks to the Internet because there is the perception that private networks provide better bandwidth guarantees than the commodity QoS-less Internet. By developing QoS support, Internet service providers will be able to offer a product that will allow corporate customers to create virtual private networks, over the commodity Internet backbone, that will provide comparable performance to private networks.

The capabilities that integrated and differentiated services offer are particularly exciting because they allow network managers to take another step toward building a single network infrastructure that supports voice, video, and data. Application developers are also encouraged because the work in the IETF and the next-generation Internet community is focused and generating results. Application developers now have tools that can be used to allocate bandwidth to important applications.

End Note

[1]Portions of this section are based on a treatment in *Internet Architectures*, by Dan Minoli and Andrew Schmidt (1999, John Wiley & Sons).

References

ATM Forum Technical Committee. 1993. *ATM User-Network Interface Version 3.0*. Upper Saddle River, NJ: Prentice-Hall.

ATM Forum Technical Committee. 1995. *ATM User-Network Interface Version 3.1*. Upper Saddle River, NJ: Prentice-Hall.

ATM Forum Technical Committee. 1996a. *ATM User-Network Interface Version 4.0*. Mountain View, CA: ATM Forum. ftp.atmforum.com/pub.

ATM Forum Technical Committee. 1996b. *Traffic Management Specification Version 4.0* (af-tm-0056.000). Mountain View, CA: ATM Forum. ftp.atmforum.com/pub.

Braden, R. et al. 1999. *Internet Resource ReSerVation Protocol (RSVP): Version 1 Functional Specification*. Internet Draft ID: draft-lindell-rsvp-procrules-00.txt (This document is an Internet Draft and is in full conformance with all provisions of Section 10 of RFC 2026).

Ferguson, Paul, and G. Huston. 1998. *Quality of Service: Delivering QoS on the Internet and in Corporate Internets.* New York: John Wiley and Sons. An excellent overview of the issue of Quality of Services.

RFC 1633. 1994. R., Braden, D. Clark, S. Shenker. *Integrated Services in the Internet Architecture: An Overview.* ftp://ftp.isi.edu/in-notes/rfc1633.txt (informational).

RFC 1755. 1995. M. Perez, F. Liaw, D. Grossman, A. Mankin, E. Hoffman, and A. Malis. *ATM Signalling Support for IP over ATM.* ftp://ftp.isi.edu/in-notes/rfc1755.txt (proposed standard).

RFC 1889. 1996. H. Schulzrinne, S. Casner, R. Frederick, V. Jacobson. *RTP: A Transport Protocol for Real-Time Applications.* ftp://ftp.isi.edu/in-notes/rfc1889.txt (proposed standard).

RFC 1890. 1996. H. Schulzrinne. *RTP Profile for Audio and Video Conferences with Minimal Control.* ftp://ftp.isi.edu/in-notes/rfc1890.txt (proposed standard).

RFC 2205. 1996. R. Braden, L. Zhang, S. Berson, S. Herzog and S. Jamin. *Resource ReSerVation Protocol (RSVP): Version 1 Functional Specification.* ftp://ftp.isi.edu/in-notes/rfc2205.txt (proposed standard).

RFC 2211. 1997. J. Wroclawski. *Specification of the Controlled-Load Network Element Service.* ftp://ftp.isi.edu/in-notes/rfc2211.txt (proposed standard).

Romanow, A. and S. Floyd. 1995. *Dynamics of TCP Traffic over ATM Networks. IEEE JSAC,* V. 13 N. 4, (May). p.633-41. Abstract.

Schenker, S. and L. Breslau. 1995. "Two Issues in Reservation Establishment," *Proc. ACM SIGCOMM '95.* Cambridge, MA.

Speer, M. F. and S. McCanne. 1996. *RTP Usage with Layered Multimedia Streams.* draft-speer-avt-layered-video-01.txt. Sun Microsystems, LBNL (June).

CHAPTER 14

Resource Reservation Protocol: RSVP

RSVP Introduction

This chapter focuses on a particularly important protocol, the Resource Reservation Protocol, introduced in earlier chapters. RSVP is a signaling protocol that utilizes traditional IP networks to carry its resource reservation messages from sources to destinations. Along the path between the source to destination, the resource requests are used to gain permission from admission-control software regarding the availability of the desired resources. Then, a resource request reestablishes the Reservation State, essentially, securing the reservation. When the desired request cannot be fulfilled, a request failure message is generated.

Around 1991, RSVP was conceived while the first generation of Internet-based multimedia tools were being deployed at Lawrence Berkeley National Laboratories (LBNL) and Xerox's Palo Alto Research Center (PARC). Researchers at LBNL were working on tools that would permit workstations to transmit voice and video-conferences over IP-routed networks interconnecting their campuses. At the same time, research was underway to develop a scalable solution for IP multicast at PARC. When researchers wanted to test their new applications on the network, they manually provisioned the interconnecting routers and allocated resources via a human operator. These early tests proved difficult to manage and clearly demonstrated the need for automation to ensure the success of large-scale real-time applications.

When designing a suitable resource-reservation protocol for large-scale deployment, the researchers at LBNL and PARC soon realized that they must establish a set of baseline requirements. As with most of their work developing Internet protocols, one of the chief requirements was to have the protocol use Internet resources efficiently and, even more important, scale globally. In addition, it needed to support multicast (that is, one transmitter with multiple receivers) applications in a heterogeneous environment. Finally, the protocol had to adhere to TCP/IP's design principles of being robust enough to handle packet loss and adapting well to changes in network topology.

After the default IP data path is set up by either traditional router or ATM switches, RSVP is used to deliver QoS requests to each switch or router along the path, a key point of RSVP often overlooked. Thus, it is a signaling protocol, not a routing protocol. Each node along the data path processes the QoS request, possibly reserving resources for the connection, then forwards the request to the next internetworking device along the selected path. RSVP is a very robust protocol and is designed to support multicast and unicast data delivery in a heterogeneous network environment; however, it is clearly designed with IP in mind. In addition, the flow of IP datagrams produces a simplex reservation, that is, the endstations are specifying resource reservations for only one direction at a time. Therefore, two reservation requests are needed if bidirectional quality of service is desired.

The protocol uses IP datagrams to carry the signaling messages. This allows the RSVP messages to be transported over any ISP's network. The message can be passed from router to router and processed only by routers that understand RSVP. In the case where the packets cross non-RSVP-capable routers the messages are ignored. Because the RSVP signaling messages are being carried in IP packets there are several methods for placing the RSVP data into the IP payload. The endstations that generate the RSVP messages can transmit the messages in "raw" mode, that is, directly mapped into IP packets or using UDP encapsulation. If transmitted in raw mode, the RSVP message is placed inside the IP payload with a protocol type of 46.

RSVP Philosophy

Coupled with the desire to develop a new protocol and the evolutionary steps required in the Internet, the RSVP suite forces little permanent state on the network devices supporting the protocol. This state is called *soft* because it is believed that handling dynamic routing changes should be a normal procedure, not an exception. Therefore, routers should be constantly updating their reservations when they periodically receive resource requests. This approach is much like the philosophy used by the early Internet architects, in which a design goal or consideration involved datagram-routed networks providing only "soft" routing state; therefore they could be changed at any time. When this idea is applied to RSVP, the product is a protocol that expects routing changes and reacts well to them. It is also a protocol that is independent of the Internet's mature routing protocols.

In order for soft state to work, the system must be periodically refreshed with the desired state. When using RSVP, a signaling system is developed where resource requests are made and then periodically refreshed. The refresh messages are identical to the original resource request messages, only repeated. If the path from source to destination has changed, due possibly to routing change or link failure, then the next refresh message will create a new resource reservation state on the new segments of the path. Or, in the worst case scenario, the new network route returns an error message specifying that the requested resources are not available.

The technique of dynamically changing routes poses some interesting problems to quality of service. If a route from source to destination fails because of a link outage, a soft-state approach with dynamic rerouting supplied by the network will, with some probability, temporarily lose QoS. The length of time will be governed by the time required to determine a new route and process the reservation message. On the other hand, a hard-state protocol, like ATM, will always drop the connection if a route fails and will require a new call setup message.

The next interesting aspect of soft state relates to group reservation support. RSVP is designed to support heterogeneity of bandwidth requirements if there are multiple receivers of a multicast session. Each receiver can get a different QoS either by merging requests or using different QoS layers. An additional benefit of RSVP is that, because it is a receiver-driven protocol, it has the potential to scale to a large number of participants. The large scalability is due to its ability to reduce the number of messages traveling upstream via merging. This has the benefit of possibly requiring less state in routers. Those critics who argue against RSVP believe the scalability claim is grossly overstated because the soft state requires a steady stream of refresh messages that, in their opinion, will not scale.

Assessing which state is optimal depends on one's vantage point. From the standpoint of complexity, the soft-state approach is better if the endstation never realizes the outage because they are always transmitting RESV messages. The hard-state protocol will require the endstation to receive a message from the network specifying that the virtual circuit has been deleted; then the endpoints must reestablish the circuit. If an RSVP reservation is successful, there is no explicit acknowledgment from the network, as there would be with an ATM-switched virtual-circuit call request. This design decision was made to simplify the protocol, but it could pose problems when interworking with ATM. In cases where the reservation messages (RESV) are transmitted but then lost, the endstations may assume their request was accepted. Thus, the source may begin to transmit data to a destination that has no resources reserved for it between the two computers and will likely be dropped between the destination by the routers. In order to allow a host to determine if the RSVP message was a success, there are provisions for the hosts to explicitly query the network for state information. This query-response mechanism must be requested in the RSVP reservation messages and is returned with a positive acknowledgment if the request was successful.

The preceding discussion addresses RSVP's features from a high level, but it is worth noting which functions are clearly not associated with the protocol. RSVP is not a routing protocol. It assumes the prior existence of Layer 3 routing support via protocols like IS-IS, IGRP, and BGP (RFC 1771). RSVP provides only the ability for entities to signal their desired quality of service. It only asks for state, but it does not help provide it. In addition, RSVP is not an admission-control or packet-scheduling application. These functions, while tightly coupled with a network providing guaranteed QoS, are left to the interconnection devices (Shenker 1996a).

Three components are used by hosts to determine and signal QoS in the Integrated Services model. The model is relatively straightforward because tasks are clearly distinguished. Early versions of the protocols have limited functionality. The components are the setup protocol used by hosts or routers to signal QoS into the network. A traffic model or specification called the Flowspec that defines the traffic and QoS characteristics flow data leaving a source. Finally, traffic control or shaping mechanisms measure traffic flows leaving a host or router in order to ensure that flows do not exceed the agreed-upon QoS.

The operation of RSVP centers on the exchange of RSVP messages that contain information objects (see Table 14.1). Reservation messages flow downstream from the senders to notify receivers about the pending content and what would be the associated characteristics required to adequately accept the material. Reservations flow upstream toward the senders, joining multicast distribution trees and placing QoS reservations. The information flows in RSVP can be subdivided into three categories (Schmidt 1998) (Minoli 1999):

RSVP data generated by the content source specifying the characteristics of its traffic (sender TSpec) and the associated QoS parameters (sender RSpec). This information is carried, unmodified, by interconnecting network elements in an RSVP SENDER_TSPEC object to the receiver(s). An RSVP ADSPEC is also generated by the content source and carries information-describing properties of the data path, including availability of specific QoS services.

Table 14.1   RSVP Nomenclature

TERM	DEFINITION
Session	The specific parameters that describe a reservation including unique information used to differentiate the traffic flow associated with the session. Each session is identified by the combination: destination address + protocol + port.
Packet filter	The unique header pattern occurring in packet classification.
Filter spec	Defines the set of data packets that receive the QoS specified by the Flowspec. The session ID, an implicit part of the filter, segregates and schedules in the packet classifier output packet streams according to their source address + port.
Transmission Specification (TSpec)	The characterization of data flow from the standpoint of the packet stream's physical appearance (for example, headers, packets/second, etc.). This information differentiates the QoS requests.
Resource Specification (RSpec)	The characterization of resources reserved to satisfy receivers in terms of what QoS characteristics the packet stream will use. This information evaluates QoS requests.
Advertised Specification (ADSPEC)	A set of network modifiable parameters used to describe the QoS capability (for example, service classes supported) of the path between the source and destination.
Sender Template	The sender's IP address and, optionally, port number.
Flow Specification (Flowspec)	The Flowspec specifies the desired QoS reservation. The Flowspec in a reservation request contains the service class and two sets of numeric parameters: TSpec and RSpec. If the request is successful, the Flowspec sets the packet scheduler.

RSVP data generated by the interconnecting network elements (for example, IP routers and potentially ATM switches and), which is used by receivers to determine what resources are available in the network. The QoS parameters that can be reported help the receivers determine available bandwidth, link delay values, and set operating parameters. As in the sender's RSVP data, an RSVP ADSPEC can be generated by the interconnecting network elements and carries a description of available QoS services. The existence of two objects, an ADSPEC and a SENDER_TSPEC, which describe traffic parameters to downstream receivers, can be confusing. There is a subtle distinction: the SENDER_TSPEC contains information that cannot be modified, while the ADSPEC's content may be updated within the network. An update would most likely be caused by the network element's setting bit patterns to signal lack of QoS support.

RSVP data generated by the receiver specifying the traffic characteristics from both a packet description (receiver TSpec) and a resource perspective (receiver RSpec). This information is placed into an RSVP Flowspec and carried upstream to interconnecting network elements and the content source. Along the path toward the sender, routers, because of reservation merging, may modify the Flowspec.

RSVP is a receiver-oriented protocol, in which receivers send QoS requests upstream toward senders. There are several reasons why protocol designers have receivers control QoS requests. Primary, it is believed that the receiver ultimately is best informed about its local desires for quality. In addition, separating the signaling process from the source will afford better scalability. The argument involves the possibility of the source having thousands of receivers, especially if the requests to receive and the parameters are never seen by the source.

The RSVP protocol is also designed with two reservation styles that assist multi-sender sessions and select a subset of senders identical to the IP multicast model. ATM supplies only point-to-multiunit connections with a single sender (ATM Forum 1996b). The reservation styles supported are Distinct Reservations, which require separate reservations for each sender, and Shared Reservations, which can be shared by multiple senders (see Figure 14.1).

RSVP Reservations

Resource needs vary widely depending on the application. For example, audio- and video-conferencing has a very high likelihood of requiring high quality audio content to be acceptable to the listener. A data transmission

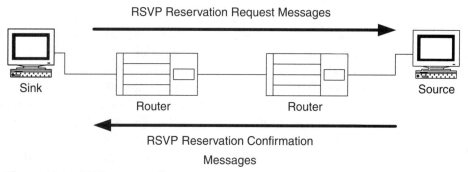

Figure 14.1 RSVP message flows.

more important than the Internet's default best-effort service may require higher quality of service, although it may need to specify only a few parameters and delay may not matter. An example of this would be a virtual private network run over an ISP's backbone network. In order for a corporation to rely on an ISP for intracorporate communication, it must know that the probability of loss due to congestion is low. The ISP can then get a larger return on its infrastructure investment by selling its backbone at both a regular rate and a premium rate for customers using RSVP.

In the RSVP model, applications have the ability to request different reservation styles depending on the type of service requested or economic considerations. Currently, three reservation styles are supported. They are shown in Table 14.2.

The wildcard filter reservation style is designed for sessions in which all sources require similar service guarantees and the sources are able to limit their output, such as is seen in an audio-conference. In a wildcard filter, one reservation is made and shared for all sources. This style would be particularly useful in the case of a multicast session. The final two reservation styles' uses differ from a wildcard filter because they are designed for cases where several different reservations must coexist. The fixed filter reservation uses only one reservation per source and supports applications, like video distribution, that need one data stream per source. With the shared explicit reservation, one reservation is shared by several sources. This type of reservation would be useful if multiple users were concurrently viewing two different video sources, each of which required different service quality.

In developing the RSVP model, the IETF designed a description of the traffic pattern contained in the reservation request sent by the host or router. This description is called the TSpec and is specified by a set of parameters that are very similar to ATM's traffic models. See ATM Forum's UNI 4.1 specification for a detailed discussion of ATM traffic model and cell rate algorithms. The TSpec is communicated to the network to specify the rate of data transmission, then used as a traffic-shaping descriptor. The TSpec is defined as a "token bucket" with a value for the bucket size and the data transmission rate. Data sent by a host or router cannot exceed the value of $rT + b$, where T is a time interval, r is the rate and b the bucket size.

Table 14.2 RSVP Reservation Styles

RESERVATION STYLE	DEFINITION
Wildcard filter	One reservation for all sources
Fixed filter	One reservation per source
Shared explicit	One reservation shared by listed sources

RESV Messages

Implementations of the RSVP protocol[1] are similar to client/server models. The high-level protocol description dictates how messages are exchanged and determines which sequences are supported. The RSVP protocol also defines several data objects, which carry resource reservation information but are not critical to RSVP itself. Five basic message types are used in RSVP (see Table 14.3), and each message type carries several subfields. Each of these message types is used at a particular interval in the establishment of RSVP state.

The protocol operates by the source sending a quasi-periodic PATH message, out of band from the actually reserved quality data session, to the destination address (that is, receivers) along the physical path that joins the computers. (In the case of multicast, receivers must join the multicast group before they can receive PATH messages.) As the PATH datagrams traverse the network, the interconnecting routers consult their normal routing tables to decide where to forward the message. When a router processes a PATH message, it will establish some "PATH state" gleaned from fields in the message. The PATH state records information about the IP address of the sender along with its policy and QoS class descriptions.

Upon reception of the PATH message, the receiver will determine if a connection has been requested and will attempt to determine if, and how, it would like to join the session. The receiver will not join a session by using the PATH sender's IP address but will use the address specified in the SENDER_TSPEC.

Table 14.3   Five RSVP Message Types

MESSAGE TYPES	FUNCTION
PATH	Sent by the source to specify that a resource exists and optionally which parameters should be used when transmitting.
RESV	Transmission of a message in hopes of reserving resources.
CONFIRMATION	Sent by a receiver, this optional message signals successful resource reservation.
TEARDOWN	Deletes an existing reservation.
ERROR	Notifies of an abnormal condition such as a reservation failure.

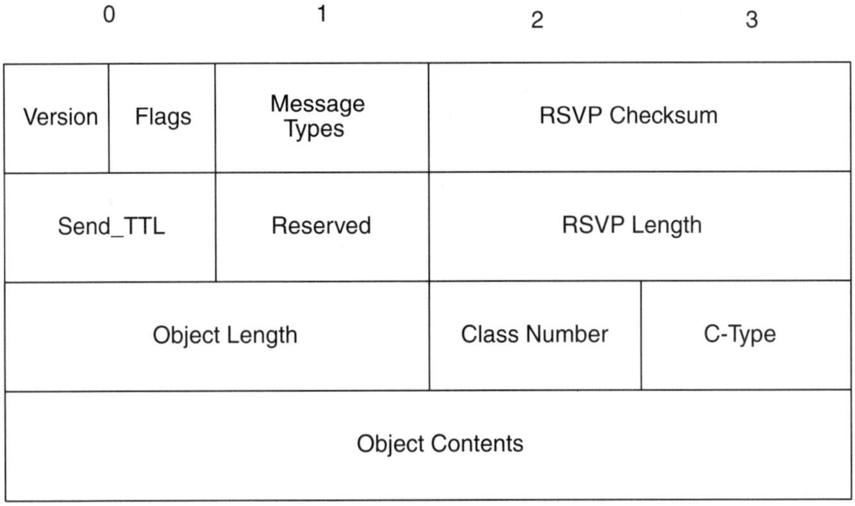

0	1	2	3

Version	Flags	Message Types	RSVP Checksum	
Send_TTL		Reserved	RSVP Length	
Object Length			Class Number	C-Type
Object Contents				

Version – specifies the protocol number
Flags – undefined
Message Type – RSVP Signal Type
    1 – PATH
    2 – Resv
    3 – Path Error
    4 – Resv Error
    5 – Path Tear
    6 – Resv Tear
    7 – Resv Confirmation
Checksum – calculated over entire message
Send_TTL – corresponds to the IP TTL
Object Length – indicates length of the individual object variable
Class Number – specifies the object class
C-Type – represents the object's class type

Figure 14.2   RSVP Packet Header fields.

PATH messages contain the following fields:

- Session ID
- Previous hop address of the upstream RSVP neighbor
- Sender descriptor (filter + TSpec)
- Options (integrity object, policy data, ADspec)

The PATH messages are sent at a quasi-periodic rate to protect the systems from changes in state. If a network failure causes the route the PATH messages took to change, then the next PATH will reserve resources on the next cycle. If there are interconnecting devices along the old path unable to be reached, their stored state will time-out when they do not receive the quasi-periodic PATH message. The PATH message contains the previous hop address of the upstream RSVP neighbor. The previous hop IP address is used to determine the path along which subsequent RESV messages will be forwarded. Finally, the PATH message contains a SENDER_TEMPLATE which describes data traffic originated by the sender.

If the receiver elects to communicate with the sender, it then sends a reservation message upstream along the same route the PATH message used. If the RESV message fails at one of the intermediate routers, an error message is generated and transmitted to the requester. In order to improve network efficiency, if two or more RESV messages for the same source pass through a common router or switch, the device can attempt to merge the reservation. The merged reservation is then forwarded as an aggregate request to the next upstream node. The RESV messages are addressed to the upstream node with the source address becoming the receiver. The RESV contains a TSpec corresponding to the session's source.

RESV messages contain the following fields:

- Session ID
- Previous hop address (downstream RSVP neighbor)
- Reservation style
- Flow descriptor (different combinations of flow and Flowspec are used based on reservation style)
- Option (integrity, policy data)

If the request is admitted, then in addition to forwarding the RESV messages upstream, the host or router will install packet filtering in its forwarding database. The forwarding database is queried when the device has a packet to be transmitted and is used to segregate traffic into different classes. The flow parameters established for this QoS-enabled traffic will also be passed to the packet scheduler. The scheduler forwards packets at a rate compliant with the flow's description using the signalled parameters.

If the interconnecting network contains routers that do not understand the RSVP protocol, the PATH/RESV messages are forwarded through the non-RSVP cloud because they are just regular IP packets. As shown in Figure 14.3, routers at the edge of an RSVP system communicate with their neighbors as if they were side by side. The protocol will operate in this environment; however, the quality of the reservations will be mitigated by the fact that the network now contains spots providing best-effort performance. The performance across these spots must be estimated and communicated to the receivers in ADSPEC messages.

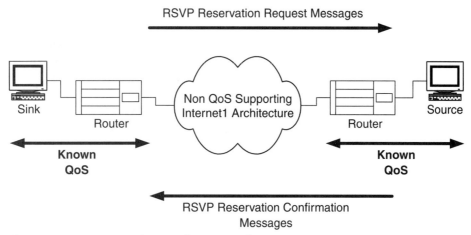

Figure 14.3   Non-RSVP intermediate networks.

The above messages perform the heart of the RSVP protocol. The following miscellaneous message types add features not critical for operation. In fact, because RSVP is soft state, the protocol could function without these additional messages.

TEARDOWN Message

An additional message in the specification is called the TEARDOWN. It is issued when either side of a session wishes to terminate communications. In this event, the device generates a TEARDOWN message that propagates across the network and releases the reservation, thus freeing resources for other users.

There are two types of TEARDOWN messages, PathTear and ResvTear. If the source issues the termination request, then a PathTear is generated. In the case of multicast, all resources associated with the session will be deleted as the message propagates down the multicast tree toward the receivers. This message will remove the source's state, in addition to all reservations made for the source's data flow. When a receiver initiates a termination, it does so by sending a ResvTear message. This message travels upstream and differs from the PathTear because it removes only the Reservation State of the receiver.

The TEARDOWN is optional with RSVP because the protocol is soft state; all reservations will automatically expire if they are not manually refreshed. The only drawback to reliance on the time-outs for reclaiming resources occurs when the time is set high. In this case, the resources will be waiting for their timer to expire, and even though they are no longer used the resources will be locked out from other sources.

ResvConf Message

RSVP allows a receiver to query the network to determine what state has been reserved for its session. The explicit RESV_CONFIRM object is required in a RESV message because the protocol's "single pass" model (Shenker 1995) does not provide the receiver with any information about the success of its request. A RESV message with a RESV_CONFIRM object that contains the IP address of the receiver is passed upstream toward the source and, at each router, the Flowspec associated with the reservation is compared to reserved reservations from the downstream router. If the reservation in the current router is equal to, or larger than, the receiver's, the RESV_CONFIRM forwarding stops, and the receiver is returned a ResvConf message with Flowspec values from the current router.

Two obvious problems are associated with this approach. First, the messages are transmitted unreliably and may be lost. All RSVP messages use IP or UDP/IP, however, so the user should accept that fact. The second problem occurs with cases involving multicast merging. Before the messages reach the source, they may encounter a router with a reserved state from a previous RESV of another receiver; consequently the merged RESV fails at some point farther upstream. In this case, the router sends a ResvConf downstream signifying that the RESV has been successful when, in fact, it has failed.

RSVP Operation

An application wishing to make use of RSVP signaling communicates with the protocol through an application program interface (API). Before receivers can make reservations, the network must have a clear understanding of the source's characteristics. This information is communicated across the API when the hosts register themselves. The RSVP code in the host then generates a SENDER_TSPEC object, which contains the details on the resources required and what the packet headers will look like. The source also constructs the initial ADSPEC containing generic parameters. Both of these objects are then transmitted in the PATH message (Minoli 1999).

As the PATH message travels from the source to the receivers, routers along the physical connection will modify the ADSPEC to reflect their current state. The traffic control module in the router will check the services requested in the original ADSPEC and the parameters associated with those services. If the values cannot be supported, the ADSPEC will be modified, or if the service is unavailable, a flag will be set in the ADSPEC to notify the receiver. By flagging exceptions, the ADSPEC will notify the receiver (a) if there are non-RSVP routers along the path, (b) if there are routers along the path that do not support one of the service categories, and (c) finally if a value for one of the service categories is different from the SENDER_TSPEC.

At the receiver, the ADSPEC and SENDER_TSPEC are removed from the PATH message and delivered to the receiving application. The receiver then uses the ADSPEC/SENDER_TSPEC combination to determine what resources it needs to receive the contents from the network. Because the receiver has the best understanding of how it interacts with the source application, it can accurately determine the packet headers and traffic parameter values for both directions of the session from the ADSPEC and SENDER_TSPEC. Finally, the receiver's Maximum Transfer Unit must be calculated because both Guaranteed and Controlled-Load QoS control services place an upper bound on packet size. Each source places the desired MTU in the SENDER_TSPEC, and routers may optionally modify the ADSPEC's MTU field on a per-class-of-service basis.

Once the receiver has identified the parameters required for the reservation, it will pass those values to the network via its RSVP API. The parameters from the TSpec and RSpec objects are used to form the Flowspec, which is placed in a RESV message and transmitted upstream using the default route. When an internetwork device receives it, the RESV message and its corresponding PATH message are used to select the correct resources to be reserved for the session (Minoli 1999).

An Introduction to Differentiated Services

As described above, another model for providing quality of service, called Differentiated Services (DiffServ), was developed shortly after the completion of the Integrated Services work. Differentiated service is an attempt to further simplify bandwidth allocation. The DiffServ model proposes that only a few types of premium service are necessary. It also proposes that bandwidth can be controlled by a central authority in an administrative domain and that authority can establish and disseminate policy to routers. This model could be relatively simple because its operation involves applications, or people, setting policy at an access control server or bandwidth broker and then the broker controls bandwidth-sharing on the routers. Currently, various models of bandwidth brokers (a concept discussed in a later section) are being developed by researchers. Communication between the application and the access control uses RSVP and communication between the access control and the routers can use any proprietary protocol. It is important to note that the access control server is not an active element in the forwarding path of the packets. It is strictly there as a policy-enforcement agent on the RSVP messages. Similarly, the routers can also perform admission control based on the signaling.

The routers in a differentiated service network perform several functions. Their primary function, of course, is to forward packets, but they also are responsible for marking packets according to policy. They can also be used for reidentification of the end user on the network. For example, if the edge router is within the domain of the campus network, it may be useful to identify specific end users and locations.

In differentiated services, application software contains a generic QoS system interface that allows socket-based (Comer 1995) applications to establish quality-of-service requests. The endsystem can signal QoS utilizing RSVP. It is also possible to have implicit signaling (per packet identification). The access control server processes the signaling messages, and its policy model is fairly straightforward because it is based on either per-user or per-subnetwork types. Both types can be regulated by human intervention.

Bandwidth control over individual application types may be very fine and could require tremendous overhead introduced by the access servers processing bandwidth requests. For example, in the case of large multinational corporations, there may be tens of thousands of workstations that wish to utilize differentiated services. If each machine generated thousands of QoS requests in a short period, it could overload the bandwidth managers. In order to cope with large systems, one needs to construct a hierarchy of bandwidth brokers or give the job of aggregation to the edge routers. In the second model, the edge router in essence becomes a proxy device for the workstations connected to the subnetworks that it services.

The DiffServ model has evolved over the last few years based on a desire to simplify the previous efforts and build a scalable quality-of-service system that could provide end-to-end services crossing administrative domains. One of the primary concerns about the integrated service model's scalability had to do with the amount of states contained in individual routers. To reduce that per-flow state contained in routers, the DiffServ model aggregates traffic flows into a small number of differentiated service classes.

DiffServ places the burden of flow identification on the edge routers and frees the core routers to focus on high-speed forwarding. Each traffic flow is identified and tagged at an edge router according to a service contract, and the flow can subsequently be policed with a token bucket. Downstream networks use the packet tagging to determine how to correctly queue packets for the correct end-to-end service. This division of labor is critical for scalability.

Building Differentiated Services-Enabled Networks

The differentiated service architecture (shown in Figure 14.4) contains three main components:

Edge routers. Responsible for traffic identification and marking of packets based on their priority. Edge routers communicate with access servers to establish priority policy and authentication. Packet tagging is accomplished by modifying the IP header TOS bits (Comer 1995).

Access servers. Responsible for administrative policy control and enforcement. These devices have knowledge of a campus's bandwidth supply and allocate bandwidth in response to changes in demand by authenticated users. This information is communicated to the edge routers for appropriate tagging of packets.

Traffic classification. Responsible for defining behavior of individual traffic aggregates or types of service so that applications know what to expect from the network. These parameters are also used to define the behavior of individual routers as they process packet flows.

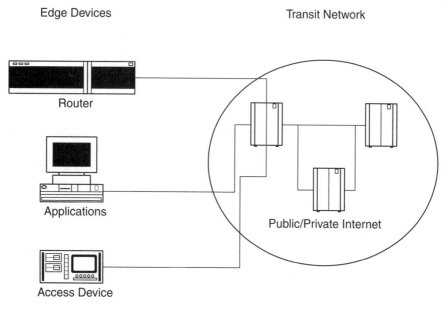

Edge Devices   Transit Network

Router

Applications

Public/Private Internet

Access Device

Responsible for classifying and   Network elements process packets
marking TOS bits in packet   based on TOS bits in header
header based service policy

Figure 14.4   Differentiated services model.

As data enters a router, the packets are classified by what is called the per-hop behavior (PHB). The PHB determines how traffic should flow through the network, and the flows are policed according to the profile. Traffic that is compliant with the PHB profile is forwarded, and noncompliant flows may be discarded or placed into a different PHB category.

Admission and policy control are the responsibilities of the access server. Before QoS-enabled communication can take place, applications must signal to their bandwidth broker. After authentication, the bandwidth broker notifies the IP routers of the flow's traits and what PHB should be associated. Communication between the application and the bandwidth broker can take many forms. The bandwidth broker could use a globally well-known address, or conversely it could be accessed through the default router. For simplicity, most implementations allow applications to forward their bandwidth requests to their default router, and the router is responsible for forwarding the request to the bandwidth broker.

In the DiffServ model, end-to-end service categories are used to define flow characteristics. These categories are somewhat similar to those defined by the integrated service working group. They are as follows:

Premium. Used to emulate the behavior of a private-line dedicated circuit. The end-to-end behavior provides low queuing delay, low packet loss, and low jitter.

Assured. Provides the same class of service as a lightly loaded network which is similar to Integrated Services' controlled load.

Default. Best-effort service.

Of the three classes of end-to-end service, it is likely that the Premium service will be implemented first. This service offers a simple definition that can be used by applications requiring high QoS. When using the Premium service, flows are defined only by their peak rate. Packets in the flow are tagged at the edge router and egress shaped to conform to the rate requirements of the end-to-end service. This end-to-end service may be the easiest to implement initially because the allocation is done for the peak rate. Therefore, if the bandwidth broker allocates Premium service to multiple hosts, then the allocations are summed to determine the total amount of bandwidth needed.

Typically, the mechanism implemented within routers to realize differentiated services is called weighted RED. This algorithm expects tagged packets of either low or high priority to arrive. Then the router, as a way to control who receives better service when the network is congested, drops packets based on the implemented system of preferences. When there is no congestion, then no packets are dropped. In addition, the algorithm has a smoothing or averaging behavior. This is important because it is possible to create a greater range of profiles that can realize a wide range of control algorithms.

Differentiated services are policed when a router establishes a token bucket for the traffic class. That is the extent of the negotiation; there is no real-time negotiation; there is no setup at connection establishment. Users are allocated resources that they can use with their bandwidth broker to set up the token bucket, whose size is based purely on committed resources. The token bucket marks the priority traffic. Any user that wishes to transmit traffic at a higher priority sets the TOS bits to some value specified by the network administrator. When tagged traffic passes through the token bucket, it is placed in a priority queue. Therefore, the IP routers are configured to do priority queuing or pseudo-priority queuing. Service providers configured their routers to do weighted round-robin, giving weighted share to the premium traffic. If the remainder of the traffic is not given a priority share, it is given a lower weight in the round-robin queue.

Internet service providers that want to provide premium transport products can do so by configuring their routers to support DiffServ's priority queuing. Then, they configure the border routers to police inbound traffic, and then core routers focus only on forwarding traffic. By segregating and policing at the border routers, the remainder of traffic management work is accomplished by the client generating the traffic. Traffic that is to be tagged (for example, a researcher exchanging traffic across a premium network) will be processed at the client by communicating with its local site policy manager (bandwidth broker). The bandwidth broker may also implement policy based on where the request originated. In this case, policy can be based on financial contribution to the network or who has been deemed a more justified user of the limited priority service.

Bandwidth Brokers

The bandwidth broker is a central repository where information is stored on how much resource has been allocated and how future resource should be allocated. (See Figure 14.5.) When the user wants a service that is better than best effort, it sends a request to the bandwidth broker or policy agent and that then notifies the routers that the user has been authorized for a higher priority of service. The proposed technique for communicating this information to the routers is to pass a flow specification that uniquely identifies a traffic flow. For example, the RSVP flow specification can identify source and destination IP addresses or the dependent IP header bits.

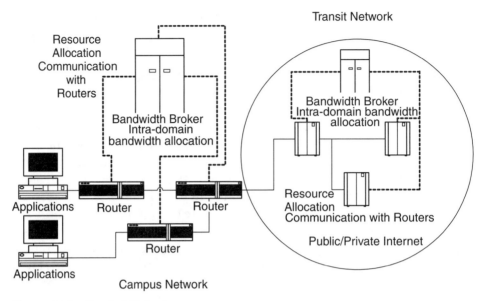

Figure 14.5 Bandwidth broker.

As a simple example of how the service operates, consider two computers wishing to utilize a premium service for leased-line emulation. The originating client sends a message using a signaling protocol, RSVP. The default router forwards the message to the bandwidth broker. The message contains (a) the traffic signature, (b) the service category of a certain amount of Mbps, (c) the duration in time for the transmission (seconds, minutes, or hours), and (d) a public-key certificate authenticating this type of request. If the bandwidth broker approves the request (that is, the client is authorized to make the request and the resource being requested is available) then the bandwidth broker will notify the ingress routers associated with the source. Any traffic above the bit rate of the requested premium service will receive best-effort treatment by the ingress router.

One of the key benefits of the differentiated services model is that when different traffic flows are aggregated in the network because of the way bandwidth brokers meter the leased line service, multiple traffic flows will be able to realize the premium service. If 100 percent of the aggregation is shared by 1,000 users, then they will all receive equal shares of the leased-line service. The aggregation property of differentiated services is a critical point when attempting to scale the service to suit a network the size of the Internet's. It is not clear that other resource allocation schemes, such as ATM's, possess this ability.

From the perspective of the application program interface, the implementation of differentiated services is quite different (see Figure 14.6). The components in the endsystem include a quality-of-service provider that exposes the new application program interface in the system based on Winsock 2. This role allows application developers to write programs that utilize differentiated services available at the Network layer. The operating system can access utilities such as a packet scheduler that allows the user to establish individual flows of traffic into the network interface adapter (Ethernet). The system can also access a packet classifier that allows the user to state which flows are to receive a priority service and mark the flows based on either Data Link layer or Network layer information. The scheduler also has the ability to do shaping.

Prototype Differentiated QoS Systems

The previously described systems have recently been extensively prototyped in the next-generation Internet community. Typically, each site will contain wide area ATM circuits, at either OC3c or OC12c speed, and the access in the wide area network is made via an edge router. On the campus networks, there is a mixture of 10, 100, or gigabit Ethernet. The test hosts are connected to be Ethernet segments. A comparable configuration is reproduced at each participating site.

Configuration is accomplished by modifying the edge router to rate limit incoming traffic that has the precedent bits set. The router examines only prece-

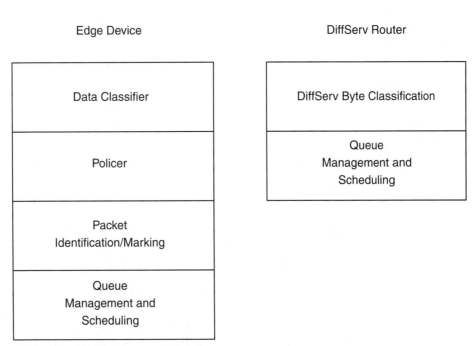

Figure 14.6 DiffServ protocol stack.

dent bits of a certain value, and the rest of the unidentified fields are treated as best effort. All of the policing procedures are based on IP precedent bit checks at leaf routers. A bandwidth broker running at each site communicates with the border router and informs the router to create access control lists.

In these prototype systems, the leaf routers have two jobs: First, the router must shape traffic with a higher priority and attempt to transmit the premium traffic first; second, the router must process and police traffic. In the initial systems, most of the traffic that is transmitted into the network is audio and video streams. An interesting phenomenon that has been noticed on these high-speed test beds is that the TCP streams are not being shaped by their access technologies. For example, TCP streams generated on 56K modems get "stretched out" to 56KB/second. Because the prototype systems are utilizing OC3c, there is no shaping from the transport media, and early implementers must use intrinsic shaping of the media and place hosts on 10 Mb Ethernet. In this configuration only one host on the Ethernet is allowed to utilize the premium service. This configuration is only temporary, and higher-speed access technology will be used as traffic shaping is adopted into the leaf routers.

Traffic shaping is also needed in the border routers because they aggregate multiple streams, and sometimes diversity in the aggregate can generate a large degree of bursting in the post-aggregate stream. For example, multiple bursty input streams can get in phase, producing a severely bursty load. Ideally, the border router would shape these multiple traffic streams and allow traffic that requires higher priority to have higher priority services, such as latency intolerant traffic which often currently utilizes only best-effort services.

Conclusion

This chapter has presented an introduction to the integrated service model and its associated protocols, RTP, RTSP, and RSVP. These protocols have received a great deal of attention and promise to be a valuable tool for real-time applications. Wide-scale deployment has yet to be realized; however, if RSVP proves successful, it may be attributed to design criteria requiring robustness and scalability. While developing the protocols, a great deal of emphasis was placed on experiences gained with multicast protocols on the Internet. That experience may yield techniques that scale well and keep pace with the Internet's continued explosive growth.

This chapter has also provided an introduction to the concepts and terminology behind QoS and its measurement. RTP has been developed with flexibility and scalability in mind and is being used as the transport protocol for real-time applications. It provides service for data with a notion of time. This optimized protocol includes only enough information to provide real-time support: a source identifier, sequence number, timestamp, and payload type. The RTCP provides basic session and monitoring features and integrates application-specific control information. With RTCP, application developers and end users have access to a query/response mechanism that will allow them to determine, in real-time, what QoS the network is actually delivering. RTSP performs the key functions of content-requesting and data-stream control. With RTSP, developers have a consistent interface to multimedia and other real-time content. RTSP clients generate messages directed to multimedia content servers, and the server uses the messages to control access to the content.

The foundation-building signaling protocol, RSVP, will play a critical role in next-generation networks. The protocol's designers did a good job of creating a means for finding the path that the data will use and then ensuring that the signaling information can be used to communicate QoS requests directly to the devices on the path. In addition, they built a protocol that is extensible because the RSVP protocol is generic enough to make bandwidth signaling requests for an entire scope of application types with a single reservation.

End Note

[1]Portions of this section are based on a treatment in *Internet Architectures*, by Dan Minoli and Andrew Schmidt (1999, John Wiley & Sons).

References

ATM Forum Technical Committee. 1996a. *ATM User-Network Interface Version 4.0*. Mountain View, CA: ATM Forum. ftp.atmforum.com/pub.

ATM Forum Technical Committee. 1996b. *Traffic Management Specification Version 4.0* (af-tm-0056.000). Mountain View, CA: ATM Forum. ftp.atmforum.com/pub.

Braden, R., D. Clark, S. Shenker. 1994. "Integrated Service in the Internet Architecture: An Overview." *RFC1633* (June). USC/Information Science Institute.

Comer, D. 1995. *Internetworking with TCP/IP*. Upper Saddle River, NJ: Prentice-Hall.

RFC 1633. 1994. *Integrated Service in the Internet Architecture: An Overview*. ftp://ftp.isi.edu/in-notes/rfc1633.txt

RFC 1771. 1995. Y. Rekhter and T. Li. *A Border Gateway Protocol 4 (BGP-4)*. ftp://ftp.isi.edu/in-notes/rfc1771txt. (draft standard).

Shenker, S. and L. Breslau. 1995. "Two Issues in Reservation Establishment." *Proc. ACM SIGCOMM '95*. Cambridge, MA.

Shenker S. and J. Wroclawski. 1996a. "Network Element QoS Control Service Specification Template," Internet Draft. (July). ftp://mercury.lcs.mit.edu/pub/intserv/drafts/draft-ietf-intserv-svc-template-03.txt.

Shenker, S., C. Partridge, and R. Guerin. 1996b. "Specification of Guaranteed Quality of Service," Internet Draft. (July). ftp://mercury.lcs.mit.edu/pub/intserv/drafts/draft-ietf-intserv-guaranteed-svc-06.txt

CHAPTER 15

Optical Networking and MPLS

Introduction

The technologies that make up the Internet continue to evolve at many levels. Previous chapters describe a number of related technologies and initiatives that are part of current efforts to advance networking in response to continuing demand for enhanced capabilities. This chapter presents two technologies that are particularly significant to the future development of the Internet, optical networking and an emerging technique for traffic management. It also briefly discusses next-generation routing technologies.

This chapter begins with a discussion of optical networking, which allows for the development of new types of core infrastructure. This topic is followed by an overview of a model for traffic management and related functions called Multiprotocol Label Switching (MPLS). Finally, several routing architectures and protocols used for high-performance networks are presented. This information is important because it indicates the general direction of these particular technologies and how they may be deployed to enhance current network capabilities. To help illustrate these particular advances, each section presents a context for the technology, comparisons among current technologies, and their relative advantages.

Dense Wave Division Multiplexing

Two of the most crucial issues in the networking industry today are the explosion of demand for capacity expansion and the explosion of demand for increasing amounts of bandwidth, both of which are driven by ongoing growth in data traffic volume. These requirements are driving designs of innovative new types of network infrastructure because significant improvements are needed to accommodate these major increases in demand for capacity. One important response to the need for large amounts of additional capacity is the development of dense wave division multiplexing (DWDM), which allows for significantly more data to be communicated through optical fiber than the technologies generally used currently. DWDM allows for optimal use of the light transmitted through fiber. DWDM is being deployed not only in response to today's demands but also to establish a basic infrastructure that will keep pace with both exponential growth in demand and expansion over the long term.

Several key, advantageous features of DWDM technology (either individually or in combination) provide compelling reasons for communications providers to deploy it. One such reason is basic economics. DWDM allows for the design and development of networks that provide significantly more capacity while lowering the cost per bit, including the cost of individual components. For example, the per-bit costs of high-capacity router interfaces are much lower than those of low bit-rate interfaces.

Another reason for the increased popularity of optical networks as a solution to scaling and capacity issues is that they provide for a much faster growth of bit-rate capacity than traditional systems. SONET and other time-division multiplexing systems tend to quadruple in capacity every four years. On the other hand, DWDM network manufacturers produce a new product almost every year. Initial versions of OC3 (155 Mbps) interfaces were introduced in 1996, and an evolution before the year 2000 to OC192 (2.4 Gbps) interfaces has been announced. This trend has demonstrated that routers on an optical network can grow at a quicker pace than those on traditional SONET networks. Consequently, many forecasters have argued that in 2000 SONET systems will no longer provide a viable platform for interconnecting high-performance routers. For example, currently a single router pair can utilize the entire capacity of a traditional SONET ring. On the other hand, performance growth of DWDM networks has kept pace with the enhanced capabilities of routers.

Also contributing to the popularity of optical networks is that they allow for significantly reduced complexity through the elimination of systems composed of multiple layers, each with separate components and management systems. As noted in earlier chapters, IP networks have often been built on top of several layers; for example, many are ATM/SONET/DWDM.

Designing IP over optical networks using DWDM ("IP over lightwave") to eliminate some of these layers has many advantages. Reducing the number of these layers is motivated by basic economics in that it reduces many operating costs. For example, it eliminates equipment cost because the overlay components are no longer required. It also substantially reduces management complexity and engineering resource requirements because far fewer protocols and management systems are required. These savings can be a significant portion of current large-scale IP networking costs. Finally, because there are fewer layers in IP over lightwave networks, they have the potential for freeing resources that can be devoted to the development of specialized services and for the rapid deployment of new services.

The following sections provide an overview of the basics of DWDM, as well as contextual information related to its development and deployment. DWDM was originally developed as part of a capability for long-haul networks. More recently, communications providers began migrating these technologies to metropolitan areas. Increasingly, new strategies are being devised to specify requirements for deploying applications utilizing metropolitan, regional, national, and international optical networks. If the usual technology deployment pattern holds, DWDM will migrate to large organizational networks.

Wave Division Multiplexing Basics

Wave division multiplexing (WDM) systems are optical transmission systems in which a single fiber carries multiple optical signals in parallel. The term "dense wave division multiplexing" was coined to describe the increase in capability of WDM technology as its potential rapidly evolved.

A WDM system is composed of a number of optical amplifiers that can be placed approximately 100 km apart. WDM systems utilize optical amplifiers optimized for specific wavelengths, currently 1550 nm. A wavelength of 1550 nm is usually selected because, when it is utilized with state-of-the-art fiber-optic systems, it operates with low attenuation and limited dispersion.

As shown in Figure 15.1, the transmitter typically contains inputs from a local device. In Figure 15.1, these are shown as optical inputs in the 1310 nm range, which could be the product of SONET multiplexers. The input signal is translated into a precise wavelength corresponding to one of the wavelengths used on the WDM system. The conversion to the output wavelength is usually accomplished through an external modulator. This method provides for a stable wavelength, utilizing a constant laser at the correct frequency and then modulating the light to produce the correct output wavelength.

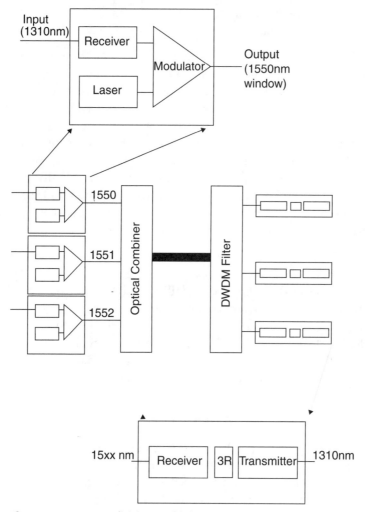

Figure 15.1 Wave division multiplexing.

At the receiver, an optical filter is used to segregate the optical signal into the various channels. These individual channels are then routed to optical receivers that can convert the light into electrical signals. The next step in the WDM receiver is to pass through a "3R" system, that is, a system that reamplifies, reshapes, and retimes the signal. Subsequently, the electrical signal can be reconverted into an optical signal (in the case of Figure 15.1, 1310 nm) and can then be delivered to a SONET node.

Evolution of Wave Division Multiplexing

When wave division multiplexing was first introduced in the late 1980s, it supported only two wavelengths. First-generation long-haul optical systems used 1310 nm lasers. When 1510 nm lasers became viable for production systems, they were quickly introduced into early WDM deployments, utilizing 1310 nm and 1550 nm optics running on the same light guide. This type of system, although functional, introduced two different types of dispersion as well as two different types of attenuation on a fiber span; consequently, it was difficult to use in production.

Second-generation WDM was introduced in the early 1990s. These WDM systems standardized on 1550 nm, but the spacing between channels was wide and implementations supported only a few concurrent channels. The spacing on these systems was typically 400+ GHz, which yielded 2 to 4 channels in the 1550 nm window. Later, when a higher level was achieved, of approximately 16 channels, WDM was renamed DWDM. The basic WDM technology remained the same. From 1993 to 1994 the International Telecommunications Union (ITU) began to focus on standardizing WDM, which was soon accomplished for the 100 to 200 GHz spacing around the 1550 nm window.

DWDM has experienced a constant growth in capacity, similar to high-performance IP routers. To continue this ongoing improvement, developers are creating increasingly larger systems by employing two basic techniques. First, next-generation DWDM provides for increased capacity by implementing narrower spacing between the individual channels. For example, many systems now support 50 GHz spacing, and soon the spacing may be as low as 10 GHz. This high degree of segregation allows the optical fibers to support an ever-increasing capacity on the same infrastructure. Second, next-generation DWDM provides for increased capacity by improving on the amplifier's ability to transmit an ever-increasing band of channels. In other words, developers create components that allow the DWDM channel counts to be wider; that is, to allow for more channels to run concurrently on a single fiber. The state of the art today is 160 channels, each capable of carrying 10 Gbps.

The Impetus for Wave Division Multiplexing

Beyond technology capabilities and advantages, several significant industry macro-dynamics are driving the introduction of DWDM technology into next-generation Internet. Traditionally the communications industry has been driven from the demand side, building only exactly what was anticipated as a need and only when there were identified customers who were committed to paying for the resources that were to be built. This approach derives from the concept of considering a communications system a scarce resource that must be carefully allocated.

Recently, a new approach has been introduced to the industry; that is, building networks based on a supply-side model. A number of communications companies today are rapidly developing networks, not in response to known customer demand, but rather in the anticipation that the demand will emerge when the capacity is created. Tens of thousands of miles of fiber are being rapidly deployed worldwide. This supply-side approach is complementary to, and drives, DWDM deployment. DWDM optimizes the use of that fiber by significantly increasing its capacity.

DWDM provides for significantly more capacity than time-division multiplexing (TDM). TDM provides for a fairly consistent potential for capacity growth. On the other hand, unlike WDM, it supports only a single stream of data. TDM systems expand capacity primarily by increasing the speed of a single optical carrier, such as migrating from OC3 to OC12. Dense wave division multiplexing (DWDM) offers the ability to expand capacity along two dimensions. DWDM is similar to computerized parallel processing in which application requirements are distributed across multiple dynamically allocated resources and additional overall capacity can be added by increasing the number of central processing units. Similarly, DWDM allows for expanded capacity along two dimensions by utilizing additional optical channels. DWDM provides for both increased "pipe size" and increases in the number of parallel channels or wavelengths being driven into a particular fiber.

By multiplexing several wavelengths in parallel, it is possible to build optical systems with far greater capacity than with TDM. Clearly, the opportunity for DWDM to be the infrastructure for long-term capacity expansion is due to its ability to increase capacity much more rapidly into much higher levels than what is possible with time-division multiplexing. The potential for DWDM capacity expansion also allows for a significant economic advantage over time-division multiplexing. DWDM allows for a major reduction in cost per bit because of its substantial capacity potential, which is a core requirement of next-generation networks.

DWDM also provides for another major advantage—format independence, enabling a single facility to carry multiple types of Data Link and Network layer protocols simultaneously. DWDM systems operate independently of the higher layer protocols and, in essence, act as point-to-point bit pipes. Some systems are intentionally built to support different interface types and need to know only the physical parameters of the input to establish correct clocking. From that point on, they carry the input to the destination where it is returned to the matching Physical layer of the input.

The potential of optical networking to serve as a unifying technology not only in long-haul networks but also in regional and metropolitan networks is critical to its current evolution and deployment. DWDM systems can simultaneously carry a very wide variety of different protocols. For example, because DWDM systems carry different channels of light in parallel on a single fiber, it is possible for each light channel to carry a unique protocol. This allows the network infrastructure to seamlessly support any combination of SONET, ATM, and IP traffic at the same time and in parallel. This potential is important for large-scale communications systems because it allows service providers to support a broad range of services, including those integrated with legacy systems, customized systems, new services, and even experimental services.

A major benefit to service providers using DWDM is that new services can be provided at a far faster rate than with traditional systems. As the Internet evolves, new services and protocols are continually being created, and supporting them is increasingly crucial. The traditional length of time for network services development and deployment cannot be sustained in an age increasingly influenced by Internet time. Also, because protocols evolve and change rapidly, a generic transport medium is an important attribute. In the past, this rapid change has forced traditional transport systems to develop new multiplexing and mapping schemes every time a new protocol did not conform to the existing mappings.

Optical networking presents an opportunity to take advantage of the flexible data rates and format independence of DWDM to consolidate and unify various protocols on a single transport infrastructure. Ideally, this deployment will eliminate the barriers and time-to-market restrictions related to transport methods that currently hinder the introduction of new communication services. New services can be transported on new wavelengths, utilizing DWDM bit-rate performance and format independence.

In conclusion, DWDM provides multiple benefits. It allows for significant capacity expansion so that service providers can install fiber-optic cable and then utilize that facility to carry multiple logical channels as if the carrier were using multiple fibers. Currently, optical systems support several dozen concurrent optical channels. Future systems (currently being tested) will support several hundred channels.

Optical Networking Applications

Currently driven by economics and capacity capabilities, the predominant dense wave division multiplexing (DWDM) application is long-haul transport. Long-haul transport of data takes advantage of inline optical amplifiers to simultaneously amplify all channels over long distances much more economically than traditional TDM multiplexing. A rapidly emerging trend is the migration of DWDM from long-haul applications into regional and metro transport and to corporate WANs. Access is provided through the optimization of architectures based on optical transport in metropolitan applications. Several factors are driving the widespread deployment of DWDM and establishing a set of requirements that enable this migration. One of the keys in the metropolitan environment is an analysis of the broad set of requirements that can support the migration of this technology.

In a long-haul network, the need to prevent capacity exhaustion is an important motivation for the deployment of DWDM. Similarly, DWDM can also improve the transport efficiency within the metropolitan environment. A typical example where an improvement can be realized is a SONET ring (because of the close relationship between its backbone operation and TDM networking). On a SONET ring each node on the TDM ring needs to operate at the maximum line rate, that is, if the ring supports OC12 then all nodes must be able to operate at 622 Mbps, even if endpoints need to support that capacity for only a single subscriber.

Using DWDM, it is possible to assign only the appropriate amount of bandwidth required and the interface technology to each node within the single shared network infrastructure. For example, a carrier could build a multi-wavelength system so that wavelength No.1 would be OC12 ATM, wavelength No. 2 would be OC3 voice, and wavelength No. 3 would be Gigabit Ethernet. By designing networks in which individual wavelengths are associated with individual high-capacity applications, DWDM systems are more focused and flexible, and they allow engineers to meet the particular needs of each node more exactly.

Another strength of DWDM networks is its support for the direct transport of data. DWDM infrastructure can be used to eliminate intermediary multiplexing and mapping stages within the transport network. For example, an ATM signal coming from an ATM switch can be transported directly as a wavelength on an optical networking infrastructure without traversing intermediate SONET multiplexers. Of course, this implementation means that the DWDM systems will require additional functionality in order to retain some of the reliability currently provided when transporting services over traditional protection switched networks, such as those depending on the "self-healing" properties of SONET. For some the solution to this issue is MPLS, discussed in subsequent sections.

Finally, another opportunity for next-generation DWDM systems is the ability of carriers to segregate their network and to lease high-capacity channels to other carriers or customers. This fairly new type of service creates additional requirements for equipment designers, for example, ensuring that the ingress and egress communication is limited to a certain bandwidth and a specific quality of service over that particular interface.

When DWDM is implemented in metropolitan areas, fiber deployments and bandwidth can be optimized, new services can be deployed more rapidly, and new applications, such as bandwidth leasing, can be created.

Dense Wave Division Multiplexing Architectures

Like many networking technologies, DWDM is evolving and new architectures are being developed. Many of the decisions and driving factors for next-generation DWDM systems come from an analysis of current traffic patterns and traffic distributions. Observations from distribution models have shown that the actual demand is similar to a full mesh between interoffice nodes. In actuality, in an optical network infrastructure, a physical ring is logically created on an optical mesh. This is sometimes referred to as a *ring-based lambda mesh*. The ring-based lambda mesh architecture imposes criteria on the network design and, in particular, imposes a significant need for add/drop multiplexer functionality to support the traffic distribution. That is, the ability to add and drop wavelengths at nodes around the ring becomes very important in order to allow flexibility in the distribution of traffic.

Another interesting attribute involving carrier ring-based lambda distribution is the wavelength count that must be supported on each node. If one looks at the particular ring-based network application of a service provider's network and considers the distribution of traffic between the nodes on the ring, it is notable that the channel count on an individual span is equal to $((n*n)-n)/2$. In other words, the total is calculated by the number of nodes squared, minus the number of nodes, divided by 2. This channel count is the limit of the number of wavelengths required to support a fully interconnected wavelength mesh across the ring network and is also, therefore, the minimum for a flexible regional distribution system. The network will need additional channel count ability if the number of services carried between customers is greater than 1.

As an example of a channel count on a metropolitan system, consider a 16-node ring, which is typical in traditional SONET deployment. If one wavelength needs to be distributed from each node to every other node on the ring, the system will require 120 wavelengths to fully support the ring-based lambda mesh. Over time, the wavelength requirements of DWDM systems will be driven by ring-based architectures and will require optical systems that support significantly higher channel counts.

Additionally, the often-overlooked advantage for dense wave division architectures is the actual fiber infrastructure interconnecting the DWDM nodes. Fiber is supporting ever-growing channel counts over time and establishing a future-proof infrastructure that accommodates current or long-term channel growth. Clearly, installing subterranean fiber-optic cable is a long-term investment; therefore, the network service providers need to consider the long-term potential of such a facility. It must be able to support channel count growth. Currently implemented advanced fiber-optic systems have a potential channel count of approximately 240 wavelengths, whereas newer fiber has been optimized for ring-based lambda mesh architectures that may achieve 400 or more unique channels. Fiber will play a key role in facilitating long-term capacity expansion potential and in establishing an infrastructure that keeps pace with the needs of ring-based lambda mesh architectures.

Dense Wave Division Multiplexing Conclusions

As a conclusion to the discussion of dense wave division multiplexing (DWDM), this section will review principal features the technology offers. First and foremost is that high-capacity optical networking solutions are needed to keep pace with the phenomenon of supply-driven growth that the Internet has created. Much of the first-generation deployment of DWDM systems has been in wide area networking. For the Internet's bandwidth growth to continue, metropolitan DWDM networks are also being established. Optical metropolitan, or "last mile," networks, therefore, become an important element in enabling the long-term growth of next-generation systems because they become extensions of the long-distance, high-capacity backbones.

Optical networking is economically advantageous because it allows for network simplification. A key goal for a number of next-generation Internet projects is the implementation of networks that provide for IP to be carried directly over WDM. This architecture can yield reduced cost and complexity because the hardware and other resources required for operating ATM and SONET are eliminated.

Optical networking provides a unifying technology to allow a wide diversity of services and protocols to be carried on a single high-capacity infrastructure. It eliminates the need for multiple physical overlay networks. Optical networking also offers the advantage of providing multiple virtual overlay networks, each of a potentially different network or data link technology on a single network.

Finally, optimized DWDM systems and fiber-optic cable will enable the continuation of the communications evolution. Clear requirements must be met on DWDM systems and fiber-optic cable for long-term capacity evolution. The combination of those two elements is important for long-term scalability and capacity management. DWDM can ensure a networking infrastructure capable of keeping pace with long-term growth. On the other hand, time-division multiplexing (TDM) supports only a single dimension of capacity expansion. DWDM supports a two-dimensional expansion model of both speed and parallel wavelengths, yielding the kind of capacity growth that will be needed long-term in the Internet.

Multiprotocol Label Switching

In the last several years, many new technologies have promised to change the way data is moved on the Internet. One of the most promising is Multiprotocol Label Switching (MPLS) (Davie 1998). MPLS is a technique for forwarding data that is very similar to related functions of ATM switches. MPLS, unlike

ATM, however, was designed to work closely with IP and other Internet protocol design philosophies. By combining the best of several individual approaches, the MPLS protocol has been able to create a data-forwarding scheme that provides speed and simplicity, along with IP's scalability and flexibility. Currently, MPLS architecture is being developed by the IETF, and several MPLS drafts have been submitted, including "A Framework for Multiprotocol Label Switching," "Multiprotocol Label Switching Architecture," and "Use of Label Switching with RSVP." The Framework document states that "the primary goal of the MPLS working group is to standardize a base technology that integrates the label swapping forwarding paradigm with network layer routing." The benefits are "to improve the price/performance of the network layer routing, improve scalability of the network layer, and provide greater flexibility in the delivery of (new) routing services (by allowing new routing services to be added without a change to the forwarding paradigm)."

From the perspective of a high level of abstraction, MPLS creates a set of protocols that enables traffic management. It does this by creating an association between a packet's destination and a *label*. When a set of labels has been created to designate different endpoints on the Internet, the labels can subsequently be used to quickly forward IP packets without consulting IP routing algorithms/protocols.

In MPLS, a label is a short, fixed-length identifier that is used to forward packets. Like ATM virtual circuit identifiers, label values are normally local to a single link and typically have no end-to-end significance. An MPLS device will use the labels to make forwarding decisions on packets and will usually replace the label in a packet with some new value before forwarding it on to the next hop. For this reason, the MPLS devices are sometimes called "label swapping" or Label Switching Routers (LSR).

MPLS devices run standard IP routing protocols to determine how to establish their label forwarding table, in the same way they would create routing tables. In fact, MPLS devices blur the lines between traditional routers and switches. IP routers can support MPLS just as MPLS allows unmodified ATM hardware to implement the protocols.

MPLS History

Like many of the developments addressed in this chapter, MPLS was created to further evolve the routing functionality of the Internet and IP networks. In addition, because the MPLS forwarding algorithm is very similar to core functions of ATM switches, it was believed that MPLS would result in significant performance increases for IP routers. Another advantage to MPLS is that the forwarding algorithm is fixed, but the control algorithm (used to create the forwarding tables) could be changed. Therefore, the protocol allowed for future growth in routing yet helped maintain the baseline hardware platform.

The work on MPLS tied together several different efforts underway in the ATM Forum, the IETF, and the ITU. The standardization within the IETF was started when they chartered a working group in early 1997. The name MPLS was chosen because it was a vendor-neutral term at a time when names like IP Switching and Tag Switching were already associated with vendors such as Ipsilon and Cisco, respectively.

Several reasons are cited as motivating factors for the development of MPLS. The following lists and explains those reasons and illustrates how the protocol has evolved to meet user requirements (Callon 1999).

- One of the primary reasons for MPLS is the design goal of integrated functionality—through the development of a protocol that will allow equipment manufacturers to build devices that combine, in a low-cost package, all of the functionality of routers and switches. Once accomplished, the product will have the price/performance characteristics of a switch and will also support the sophisticated algorithms of a router.

- A second factor driving the development of MPLS is the goal of designing a product yielding a tight integration of ATM and IP. Previous attempts at integrating ATM and IP are difficult to implement primarily because of the problems posed in combining ATM's connection-oriented methodology with IP's connectionless approach. Original ATM protocol work focused on utilizing ATM as a networking panacea; however, they later realized that the main application for ATM is forwarding IP datagrams. MPLS seeks to control an ATM switch in such a way that it naturally forwards IP packets without the help of servers mapping between IP and ATM. MPLS reduces the complexity created separately by the ATM Forum and IETF. Instead of working with two different addressing, routing, and resource allocation schemes, MPLS runs directly on the ATM hardware. The ATM switches still forward data according to virtual circuit value swapping. The translation tables are built using IP control protocols, thus eliminating the need to map between IP and ATM control models.

- MPLS also enables functionality beyond what can be provided with traditional IP routing techniques. The most common example is traffic management and the ability of network engineers to determine data flows based on policy and not just on topology. In addition, MPLS allows any field in the packet to determine the packet's destination. This differs from traditional routers that make forwarding decisions based on the destination IP address.

MPLS Operation

The operation of an MPLS device can be subdivided into two components: control and forwarding (Rosen 1999). The control component concerns global routing and policy enforcement, while the forwarding process concerns movement of data within a device or between adjacent devices. Forwarding decisions are made based on the forwarding table within the LSR and the label carried in the incoming packet.

The forwarding table in an LSR is made up of a series of entries where each entry consists of an ingress label and an egress label. The forwarding table is indexed by the ingress label. The egress label is made up of the output port number and the label value that should be placed on the packet before it is sent to the next router. In addition, the table may contain information on the resources (for example, those related to QoS) that the packet may use.

Again, those familiar with ATM can see the close parallels to VPI/VCI lookups in the switch translation table. Thus, simplicity of the forwarding algorithm facilitates inexpensive implementations in hardware. In most cases, the ingress table lookup can be done in just one memory access, which in turn enables faster forwarding performance without requiring expensive hardware.

The control component of conventional routers and LSRs is intentionally similar. In fact, MPLS utilizes protocols such as BGP and OSPF. The control component of an MPLS device is responsible for the following:

- Distributing routing updates between MPLS devices
- Converting routing updates into forwarding tables

In MPLS, each device implementing the protocol participates in unicast routing protocols. It uses the information provided by these protocols to construct its mapping between layer 3 addresses (or address prefixes) and their corresponding next hops. Once an MPLS device has determined a mapping between a Layer 3 address and the next hop, the LSR is ready to build an entry in its label-switching forwarding table. The information needed to construct the entry is provided from policy established by network management, routing protocol updates, and table entries that are received from other reliable LSRs.

When an LSR creates a forwarding table, it must inform its neighbors of the table entries so they can use the table values to forward packets received from that LSR. The forwarding information that an LSR distributes to other LSRs consists of a set of value <address prefix, label>. The address prefix identifies a particular layer 3 entry, and the label defines the value that the

LSR uses for its forwarding table associated with the IP address prefix. When the LSR completes its local forwarding table it must then determine the outgoing labels. The LSR determines the labels from the binding distributed from other LSRs.

MPLS Summary

Although this description of MPLS is brief, it does illustrate some key points of the protocol design and operation. The primary design criteria are to create a new protocol that provides improved price/performance, tight integration of IP/ATM, and flexibility of IP protocol deployment/development. MPLS allows equipment manufacturers to utilize unmodified ATM hardware to implement the protocols. In addition, this technology does not require the use of ATM or any other specific Layer 2 technology, and MPLS implementation can be built on Frame Relay or Ethernet instead.

At the time of this writing (July 1999) the final phases of the IETF's draft were being written, and early implementations are already coming to market. Some implementations are beginning to use MPLS to provide traffic management and other control functions within IP-over-lightwave networks as a means of replacing functionality lost with the elimination of other layers such as SONET. Others are attempting to use MPLS to provide certain types of QoS.

Next-Generation Routing Architectures

Next-generation routers and routing protocols are following many paths, and complete coverage is beyond the scope of this book. This section, though, will examine a subset of the work and, in particular, look at two problems of building cost-effective hardware and new algorithms for resource allocation. This discussion will be presented from both the router's perspective and the network perspective. In addition, it discusses some issues related to quality of service (QoS) on next-generation networks.

Hardware Perspective

IP routers have evolved from single-processor systems supporting only one or a few protocols to complex multiprocessor devices yielding very high performance. As technologies such as wave division multiplexing and QoS become established, they place additional demands on the routing infrastructure. If a router cannot keep pace with WDM or QoS requests, it becomes the weak link in the chain, and packets are discarded or queued at the router. This problem, referred to as a "head of line blocking," has been long studied on the Internet and is clearly something to be avoided.

The first issue to examine is the architectures of next-generation routers. Several router behaviors are important for next-generation products. They form the basis for establishing architectural requirements. The requirements that must be supported are these:

- Providing QoS, which would include the ability of the router to process a packet stream and apply policy based on individual packet characteristics.
- Treating packets differently based on their source or destination. This technique is a packet process based on subnetwork source and destination. This process is sometimes termed "policy-based routing."
- Addressing the problem of overload control, which takes effect when a forwarding path on a network fails.

The most-common higher-performance routing architectures today focus on multiprocessor systems. In a multiprocessor router, each port typically contains its own processor responsible for a central controller that manages forwarding packets and the port card. The central controller is usually responsible for maintaining routing tables and has a separate communication path to the port cards.

The interface cards are further subdivided to allow specific processors to be assigned to individual functions on the port. For example, unique processors can be assigned the RSVP tasks of packet classification, scheduling, and buffering. The result of segregating the router into discrete components is that a very high-performance device can be built from off-the-shelf components.

Network Perspective

From the network level, when a router is instrumented with QoS support, advanced flow identification, fair queuing, and policy enforcement, the most important issue becomes monitoring the network. The most common proposal for achieving manageable large-scale networks is to utilize MPLS. MPLS, in this case, provides a framework for management that can combine different services. For example, if a network designer wants to allocate bandwidth to a particular application between known source and destination computers, it is possible to accomplish this with MPLS by establishing Label Switched Paths. At the same time, however, a differentiated services paradigm can be overlapped on the routers to achieve general-purpose, ubiquitous QoS. From a services management perspective, the network can be viewed as always providing core *best effort* services that are augmented with differentiated services and, finally, guaranteed bandwidth.

Of interest currently is the problem of how to establish the path through the network and maximize the utilization of the network. The challenge of the network management system is twofold: first, maximizing the network utilization, and second, establishing the MPLS paths to provide the requested service classes.

From a management application-development perspective, the easiest implementation is a centralized server, much like a bandwidth broker, used to oversee path creation. This server determines the topological relationships on the network via routing protocols like OSPF. In addition, the server is manually configured with policy via a command-line or WWW interface. Once it is established with policy and topological information, it will disseminate the network policy to the routers in the domain and maximize network utilization. The edge routers can then establish parameters, such as MPLS, explicit routes, and access lists, to satisfy the network policy. Once the system is running, the central manager can keep abreast of the topological change via OSPF updates and make any necessary path changes.

In the case of a single server, providing policy on a network with a single path from source to destination, the implementation can be straightforward. However, if multiple paths exist between the source and destination, then both path selection and maintaining high path utilization become difficult problems.

The common approach to these problems is to use a least-cost routing algorithm. In this case, if the central server needs to reserve bandwidth between two points on the network, it will analyze a graph of the network from several perspectives. First, the server will eliminate all paths that do not contain adequate bandwidth for the request. Next, the problem of path selection is addressed. If the server uses the shortest path at all times, then it can be shown that bandwidth allocation would not maximize network utilization, in the case where multiple paths exist.

This situation is illustrated in Figure 15.2. When multiple paths exist, for example, from nodes 1 to 9 and from nodes 6 to 9, the bottleneck exists on the link from nodes 7 to 9. If the reservation request for bandwidth between computers A and C arrives first, then the short-path algorithm will route the request across the bottom links because the path along 1-2-3-4-5-7-8-9 is longer than that along 1-6-7-8-9. If a subsequent request for bandwidth arrives from computers B and C then it will be rejected. It can be seen that if the initial request is routed along the top path, then both requests could be accepted; that is, if the bandwidth allocation server accepts the initial request over the longer path, then it can accept additional requests.

To address this problem, work on path selection has developed the Least Interference Algorithm (Radia 1992). In order to optimize the bandwidth allocation, the server needs to find a path that interferes least with future

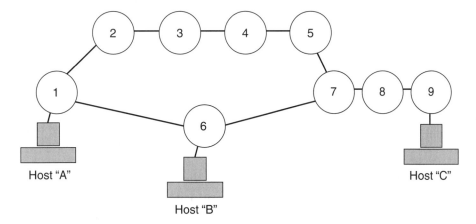

Figure 15.2 Least interference example.

requests. This is being done by analyzing heuristics and the potential traffic flows between source/destination pairs. The Least Interference Algorithm operates by first determining common traffic paths on the network. Next, it associates *weight* on each link in proportion to the number of bandwidth requests at the ingress and egress points that may traverse the link. Once the weights are established, a Weighted Minimum Shortest Path algorithm can be run by the server. It can be shown that this scheme provides substantial performance improvement in terms of the number of bandwidth requests that can be accepted by the network.

Routing Summary

A great effort is being focused on next-generation routing. Two key areas include developing expensive hardware architectures that scale in both speed and the number of ports supported. Several "myths versus realities" are being uncovered as work on next-generation routers progresses:

Problem 1. Many people argue that packet classification is too difficult; however, recent hardware developments have proven this incorrect. One of the developments to help address the problem of packet classification is a device called the Ternary CAM. This device is a content addressable memory in which each bit can be a zero, a one, or don't care. The result is that inexpensive router filters can be built with these devices that contain thousands of rules for processing packets.

Problem 2. Another myth is that as routing tables continue to grow, the process of looking up the forwarding path from the IP address table (that is, finding the destination from a table) will become too taxing for the routers to be accomplished expeditiously. This problem is also being addressed with Ternary CAMs, which allow the process to be completed quickly even when faced with the larger table sizes, as previously discussed.

Problem 3. Packet classification is too difficult for real-world application. This observation is somewhat true; however, there are several different applications of packet classification, and not all lead to performance degradation. For example, if the router is used to identify flows and to perform accounting on individual flows, then network failures can cause severe problems because the packets traverse slower paths. However, if packet classification were used only to map packets into a queue, then under extreme load the only difficulty would be packet discard at the queue. Even in the worst case, packets would still be forwarded.

As noted in this section, these efforts are progressing, and those who use the Internet should assume that these technologies will make their way into products and services in the near future. In addition, sophisticated bandwidth management algorithms and traffic management provided through MPLS are also very reliable, and independently or combined, bandwidth management algorithms and traffic management can be used to build networks that provide differentiated services, including reliable QoS.

Conclusion

The technologies that make up the Internet are driving a worldwide digital communications revolution—a revolution that has barely begun. Although this book provides only an overview of those technologies, perhaps it sufficiently conveys their importance to the development of a new model for communications that provides for increasingly powerful, innovative global communications services, systems, and infrastructure fabrics. The next-generation Internet is already beginning to support integrated digital voice, video, data, specialized services, innovative new services, and sophisticated applications—all with a high degree of interoperability. Increasingly, these capabilities are fundamentally changing almost every sector of society, and these changes, in turn, are stimulating demand for ever more dynamic technical invention.

References

Callon, R., et al. 1999. "A Framework for Multiprotocol Label Switching." ID: draft-ietf-mpls-framework-03.txt

Davie, Bruce S., P. Doolan, and Y. Rekhter. 1998. *Switching in IP Networks: IP Switching, Tag Switching, and Related Technologies*. The Morgan Kaufmann Series in Networking. New York: Academic Press.

Davie, Bruce, et al. 1998. "Use of Label Switching with RSVP."
ID: draft-ietf-mpls-rsvp-00.txt

Radia, Perlman. 1992. *Interconnections: Bridges and Routers*. Reading, MA: Addison-Wesley.

Rosen, Eric, et al. 1999. "Multiprotocol Label Switching Architecture."
ID: draft-ietf-mpls-arch-05.txt

Stern, Thomas E. and K. Bala. 1999. *Multiwavelength Optical Networks: A Layered Approach*. Reading, MA: Addison-Wesley.